AFRICAN

African Fabbers Atlas
Manual of Synthetic Vernacular Architecture
Published by
Actar Publishers, New York, Barcelona
www.actar.com
Author
Paolo Cascone
Edited by
Paolo Cascone and Maddalena Laddaga
Graphic Design
Mauro Bubbico
With contributions by
Chirstian Benimana, MASS (Architect/Rwanda)
Cheick Diallo (Designer/Mali)
Ron Eglash (Professor of Information/ University of Michigan/USA)
Ugo La Pietra (Designer/Italy)
Hanif Kara, AKT II (Professor in practice of technology/GSD Harvard/USA)
Vincent Kitio (UN–Habitat/Kenya)
Giancarlo Mazzanti, El Equipo Mazzanti (Architect/Colombia)
Ronald Rael, Rael San Fratello (Professor of Architecture/University of California Berkeley/USA)
AbdouMaliq Simone (Senior Professional Fellow at the Urban Institute/University of Sheffield/UK)
Françoise N'Thépé, FNT (Architect/ France–Cameroon).
Copy editing and proofreading
Angela Kay Bunning
Printing and binding
Arlequin & Pierrot, Barcelona

Distribution
Actar D, Inc. New York, Barcelona.
New York
440 Park Avenue South, 17th Floor
New York, NY 10016, USA
T +1 2129662207
salesnewyork@actar-d.com
Barcelona
Roca i Batlle 2
08023 Barcelona, Spain
T +34 933 282 183
eurosales@actar-d.com
Indexing
English ISBN: 9781948765626
Library of Congress Control Number: 2024936961
Printed in Spain, Europe
Publication date: September 2024
Cover image: Mauro Bubbico

FABBERS ATLAS

MANUAL OF SYNTHETIC VERNACULAR ARCHITECTURE

PAOLO CASCONE

CONTENTS

INTRODUCTION p.7

1. TOWARDS SYNTHETIC VERNACULAR ARCHITECTURE p.9
1.1 Climate change and its consequences in Africa p.11
1.2 The origins of the African Fabbers project p.16

2. CONVERSATIONS p.27
Premise p.29
2.1 Christian Benimana p.30
2.2 Cheick Diallo p.34
2.3 Ron Eglash p.37
2.4 Ugo La Pietra p.42
2.5 Hanif Kara p.45
2.6 Vincent Kitio p.48
2.7 Giancarlo Mazzanti p.51
2.8 Ronald Rael p.55
2.9 AbduMaliq Simone p.57
2.10 Françoise N'Thépé p.62

3. AFRICAN FABBERS TAXONOMIES
CONNECTING HIGH AND LOW-TECH CULTURES p.67
Intro p.68
3.1 From generative components to living infrastructures p.70
Cultural centre (Mali) p.71
Smart shell world urban forum (UN Habitat) p.86
3.2 The self-construction of relational spaces p.94
Earth play the ground (Burkina Faso) p.95
Khaima Urban Tent (Morocco) p.105
3.3 On cities as factories and local industries p.115
Marrakech Lab (Morocco) p.117
Open Air Lab (Senegal) p.127

4. THE DOUALA CULTURAL PLATFORM p.141
4.1 Educational models for independent schools p.142
4.2 The African Fabbers School Sessions in Douala p.153
Cultural Hub (Cameroon) p.179

5. AFRICAN OFF-GRID HOUSING p.195
5.1 On precarious Habitat in Sub Saharan Africa p.196
5.2 The African Off-grid Housing research project p.200

BIOGRAPHY p.210
ACKNOWLEDGMENTS p.212
ILLUSTRATION CREDITS p.214

INTRODUCTION

The African Fabbers Atlas is a compendium of essays, conversations and projects conceived as an adaptive platform on synthetic-vernacular architecture in Africa and its potential role as cultural driver for global scenarios. Based on almost 15 years of applied research in Africa carried out by Paolo Cascone and his CODESIGNLAB practice, the book investigates the potential role of indigenous and spontaneous architecture in the contemporary debate on sustainability in architectural design.

How do we respond to climatic changes reconciling nature with techné? What is the social role of technology? How can architects reconsider their practices supporting community-oriented projects? These questions are discussed through a number of paradigmatic projects and conversations between the author and a panel of experts from different backgrounds in order to shape an interdisciplinary approach that bridges different fields of knowledge.

The theoretical underpinnings of this investigation are based on the observation of cause-effect relations between different urban and architectural configurations and their performance (social, environmental, structural, etc.) in both pre-colonial and informal cultures around Africa. Following many years of post-colonial studies, the diachronic approach intends to generate an operative agenda of possible strategies in keeping with different contextual conditions – namely anthropological and climatic. This agenda responds to a global cultural need for an ecological shift in contemporary design and manufacturing processes, which should bridge high-and low-tech cultures. In that sense, the book is also conceived as a sort of manual that is articulated around emergent principles inspired by traditional and informal African practices and architectures: self-similarity and diversified typologies, material optimisation and the circular economy, self-sufficiency and responsive dwellings.

Each principle is also contrasted with the work of pioneers such as Hassan Fathy and Fabrizio Carola, among others, with the aim of sharing and evolving this tremendous heritage by introducing the case studies realised in the context of the African Fabbers [AF] project over the last decade. The [AF] project was developed as a research platform and a traveling school offering training programmes and community-oriented initiatives that combine digital and traditional manufacturing for sustainable living. This approach responds to the lack of architecture schools in the region,which persists the economic growth of these countries and their need for social housing and basic infrastructures. This book aims to distil these on-site experiences and their theoretical background into a decolonised approach to architectural education, and it points to the conclusion that we should start seriously considering African solutions for global problems.

I

TOWARDS SYNTHETIC VERNACULAR ARCHITECTURE

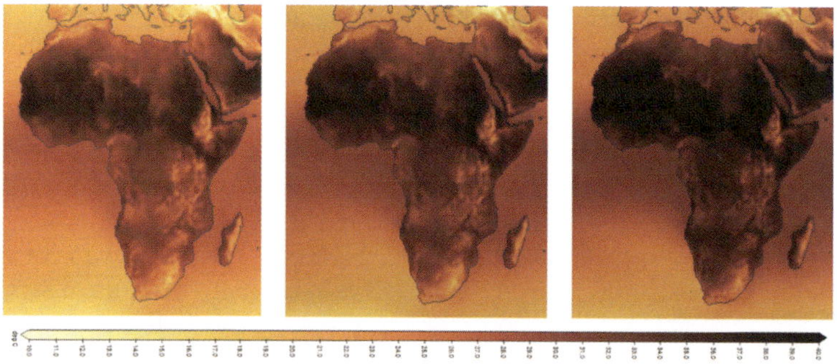

Maximum Temperature (TX) – (deg C). Long Term (2081 – 2100) (RCP8.5). CORDEX Africa - Annual (31 models).
Figure generated using the AR6 WGI Interactive Atlas

Flooding in Ahoada, Rivers state Nigeria

1.1 Climate Change and Its Consequences in Africa

The African Fabbers [AF] agenda responds to the urgent need to reconsider and expand precolonial knowledge to inform performative architecture in Africa that can respond to the global and local challenges derived from climate change in the region and beyond. Under this premise, this book intends to reconsider the question of developing a climate sensitive design approach that can bridge traditional and advanced construction technologies. This agenda is informed by the interrelations between a critical understanding of how climatic and social dynamics are affecting African architecture and an evolutionary approach to studying African vernacular precedents.

The AF agenda has been gradually developed through a series of masterclass, workshops and community-oriented projects realized in different African climatic regions. The methodological apparatus related to such live projects intends to contribute to the cultural debate on architectural education and sustainable design practices along with ecological manufacturing for local communities in the Global South. For the above-mentioned reasons, this research proposes a set of evidence-based considerations to inform a climate sensitive design approach. Although Africa has produced only around 4 percent of global total greenhouse gas (GHG) emissions, the lowest of any region, its ecosystems have already suffered disproportionately from the effects of a changing climate.

In 2022, the mean temperature across the African continent was 0.16 degrees Celsius above the long-term average for the period of 1991-2020 as reported by World Meteorological Organization -WMO[1] at the Africa Climate Summit in September 2023 (ACS2023).

On average, Africa's near-surface temperature increased by about 0.3°C every 10 years between 1991 and 2022, as compared to about 0.2°C per decade or 10 years between 1961 and 1990, according to the findings. All six African sub-regions – North Africa, West Africa, Central Africa, East Africa, Southern Africa, and the Indian Ocean Island countries – have experienced an increase in the temperature trend over the past 60 years compared to the period before 1960. Furthermore, the year 2023 marked Africa's 31st consecutive year with temperatures above average.

Intense rain and associated flash flooding pose a major hazard for African societies, particularly in urban areas. This trend is consistent with an increasing temperature gradient across the Sahel, with the Sahara warming more rapidly than most tropical Africa due to increasing greenhouse gas concentrations. However, the UN – Intergovernmental Panel on Climate Change (IPCC), the world's foremost authority for the science of climate change, still considers the possibility of limiting the global temperature rise to 1.5°C – if, and only if, there are "rapid and far-reaching transitions in land, energy, industry, buildings, transport, and cities"[2].

An increase of the world's warming by more than 1.5°C may affect dramatically Sub-Saharan Africa. In fact, regions in Africa within 15 degrees from the equator are projected to have an increase in hot nights as well as longer and more frequent heat waves as they have experienced more frequent and more intense climate extremes over the past decades.

Recognising the increasing threat of climate change, the UN Climate Change Conference (COP21) in Paris marked the beginning of a shift towards a net-zero emissions world and the limitation of climate change to well below 2°C and drafted a durable framework to guide the global effort for decades to come. The

Land of the Dogons vernacular architecture in Mali

Djenné local market Mali

Maker workshop in Douala, Cameroon

agreement has formally entered into force in November 2016 and was signed by 184 countries, including almost all African countries. But even at that time it was recognised that the commitments on the table would not be enough, especially for developing countries.

More recently the COP28 (Dubai, December 2023), which had the objective of taking stock of the progress made by the parties on the implementation of the Paris Agreement and to chart a course of action to dramatically reduce greenhouse gas emissions and protect lives and livelihood. It eventually concluded with an unprecedented call on governments to "transition away" from fossil fuels as part of a broader agenda to keep 1.5°C within reach.

This call is a positive stand in response to dramatic projections made by the IPCC, which predicts for the western Sahel region and Central Africa an increase in the maximum length of dry spells, a decrease in the length of wet spells and a slight increase in heavy rainfall.

Climate change will be likely to lessen crop yields and production, with resulting impacts on food security. At the same time the IPCC predicted that the western part of Southern Africa will become drier toward the end of the 21st century, heat waves and drought frequency will dramatically increase. According to projections, Western and Central Africa are set to experience an increase in the number of hot days, global temperatures rise by either 1.5°C or 2°C, while the Sahel, largely dependent on rain-fed agriculture, is already being hit regularly by droughts and floods, with enormous consequences to people's food security. Climate-related crises have also had a stark impact. One example is the recent case of Cyclone Idai (March 2019) which has mainly affected the Mozambique 's Sofala province. In this case the UN estimated that the related flooding destroyed more than 100,00 homes as well as major infrastructures and institutional buildings.

More generally, some of the side effects related to this climatic scenario are creeping into other aspects of the African societies.

The World Bank's flagship report "Groundswell – Preparing for Internal Climate Migration"[3] underscores that internal climate migration is becoming a reality and that, by 2050, without concrete climate and development action, more than 85 million people may be forced to move out of sub-Saharan Africa as a consequence of climate change.

Meanwhile there is a strong correlation between malaria, cholera, meningitis, and climatic elements, which can affect negatively. Furthermore, climate change leads to contamination in the water supply, which in turn can increase the prevalence of certain diseases. Climate change is expected to aggravate the incidence and intensity of impending disease outbreaks, ACRC 2019[4]. These factors all mean that any kind of housing policy in Africa will need to take into account this critical climatic scenario in defining ecological protocols for the construction process and environmental performative criteria for architectural configurations.

In addition to the above-mentioned statistics it is important to highlight some paradoxes and potentialities that could eventually help the African society to deal with such extreme climatic condition. Africa is home to approximately 30% of the Earth's remaining mineral resources, as recently reported by Al Jazeera[5]. The African continent is home to five of the world's top oil-producing countries, with an estimated 57% of Africa's export earnings coming from hydrocarbons (nearly $2 trillion). In addition to oil and gas, Africa is rich in precious minerals and forests, among other resources:

trans african highways

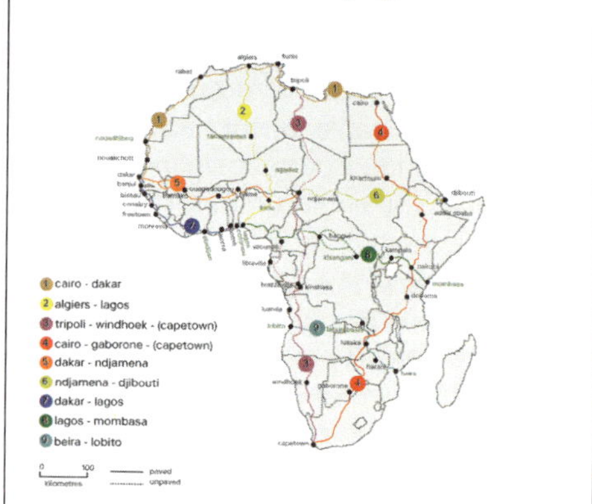

source: wikipedia

areas most at risk from climate change in africa

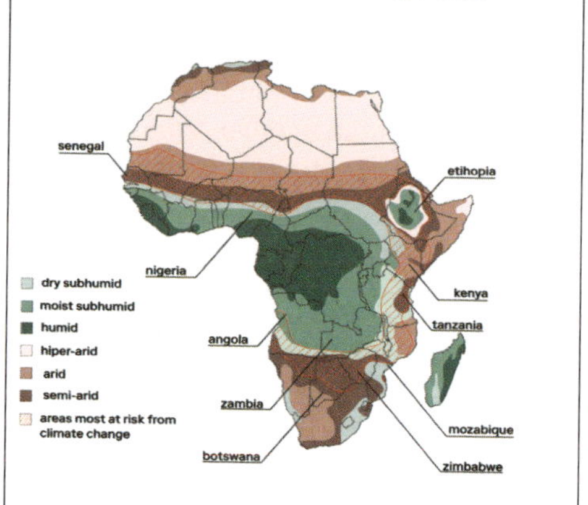

source: grid-arendal, columbia university

food insecurity and climate change

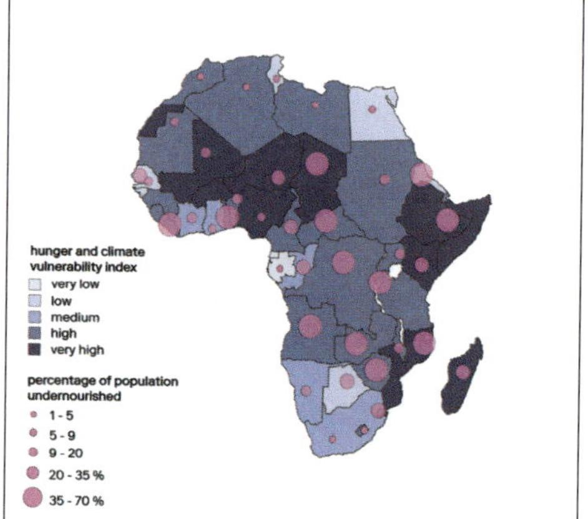

source: wfp.org

"...mobile phones are more common than access to electricity"

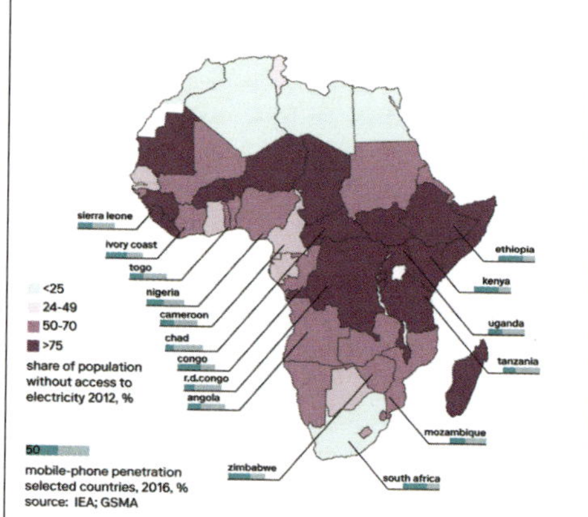

source: economist.com

school of architecture in africa

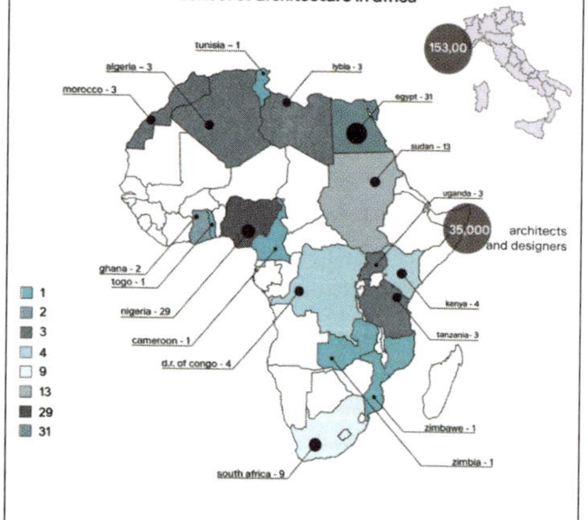

source: wikipedia "list of architecture schools"

african fab lab

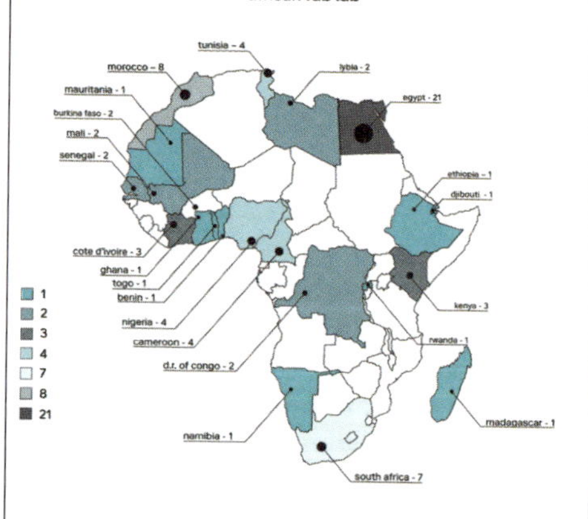

source: fablab.io

diamonds: Angola, Botswana, Central African Republic, Democratic Republic of Congo; gold: Benin, Burkina Faso, Djibouti, Mali, South Africa, Tanzania, nickel and uranium: Burundi; pozzolana: Cape Verde; fish: Comoros, Guinea-Bissau, Mauritius, Sao Tome and Principe, Senegal, Seychelles; timber: Liberia, titanium: Gambia, graphite: Madagascar, tobacco: Malawi, iron ore: Mauritania; phosphates: Western Sahara, Morocco, aluminium and gas: Guinea, Mozambique; copper: Uganda, Zambia.

Despite this huge number of resources and the largest workforce of young people in the world the job market is still undeveloped and the GDP per capita is very low. The prevalence of working poverty in Africa is still overwhelming.

In 2016 up to 70% of African workers were "working poor", the highest rate globally as reported by the International Labour Organisation (ILO). The organisation added that "the number of poor working youth has increased by as much as 80% for the past 25 years"[6]. ILO has also estimated in 2018 that it still represents 56% of world's working poor; conversely Africa represents only 14% of world's employment. Comparative studies made more recently by ILO do not show any reduction on the rate of working poor in Africa instead show that countries with highest working poor rate are also those with highest informal employment rate, which drives to the conclusions of lack also in social protection and job security. Such contradictions, are based on the fact that Africa's export structure is biased towards natural-resource-based commodities rather than labour-intensive manufacturing exports.

As a matter of fact, one of the main reasons why the export revenues are not equally distributed across society, generating precarious jobs, is because of the lack of local industries able to transform raw materials in finished products. Likewise, Africa has plentiful renewable energy resources, and the projected power consumption of the continent is smaller than its economic potential growth, as recently reported by the International Energy Agency (IEA)[7].

In reality, Africa is home to many of the minerals essential to the energy industry: for example, DR Congo accounts for almost two-thirds of global cobalt production (a vital element in batteries), and South Africa produces 70% of the world's platinum, which is used in hydrogen fuel cells.

The continent also produces a large share of key minerals such as platinum (cars and fuel cells), chromium (wind turbines) and manganese (batteries), which will play a major role in powering the global energy transition. Despite the fact that Africa has the richest solar resources on the planet, so far only 5 gigawatt of solar photovoltaic (PV) have been installed, less than 1% of global capacity[7]. With a fifth of the world's population, Africa accounts for only 6% of the global energy demand while average energy consumption per capita in most African countries is well below the world average and largely comparable to that of India. Bioenergy is the largest source of energy in Africa today, meeting 45% of primary energy demand and over half of final energy consumption.

Even if there are still 595 million of people without electricity in Africa, since year 2013 some slowly progress has been led especially by Kenya, Ethiopia and Tanzania, which account for more than 50% of those gaining access. However, the situation in Sub Saharan Africa remains critical according to most recent information on its electrification rate of 45%.

Given such scenario, to achieve the UN–SDG 7 goals African counties would need to learn from developing Asia, where since 2010 more than 1 billion people have gained access to electricity (IEA), introducing easier access to financing and more concerted policies.

Especially in the case of informal settlements, slums or shanty towns where there is an irregular electricity supply, with frequent blackouts, and quantity and quality problems associated with the electrical grid, inhabitants often resort to informal or illegal connections. At the same time, UN estimates that the demand of global water will probably increase by some 55% due to growing consumption rates from manufacturing (+400%), thermal electricity generation (+140%) and domestic use (+130%).

1.2 The origins of the African Fabbers project

Beyond the statistics on socio-economic and environmental dynamics, the problems of African societies are often depicted by Western media as just an object for humanitarian aid. However, reputed international analysts and agencies agree on the fact that three powerful positive trends are likely to support Africa's growth in the near future, as mentioned by UNDP. Africa has a young population with a growing labour force, representing a valuable asset in an ageing world. In fact, analysts have predicted that in 2034, Africa will have a working-age population of 1.1 billion, presumably the largest in the world.

Therefore, an innovative education system is needed in order to respond to the lack of universities in the region and to create new stable and qualified jobs. African countries are still in the process of urbanisation, which should generate an economic benefit for the near future as the productivity in cities is estimated to be three times higher than in rural areas. Over the next decade, an additional 187 million Africans are also expected to move into cities, and this urban expansion should contribute to rapid growth in consumption among households and businesses. At the same time, urbanisation can generate social and environmental problems. In response, a new model of circular economy must be researched within an interdisciplinary approach in order to forge a more sustainable relationship between urban and rural development.

African economies are also well positioned to benefit from rapid technological changes that can unlock growth and overcome the limitations and costs of physical infrastructures in important areas of the economy. This aspect could be crucial in developing local 4.0 industries, which will able to transform and repurpose local materials within an ecological approach to reconcile nature with tekhné, thus minimising greenhouse gas emissions. Some crucial questions arise regarding the aforementioned factors:

What kind of cultural and ecological shift would be needed to support the recent economic growth, and how might this transform the post-colonial vision of African industrialisation?

How, eventually, could the development of post-colonial cities be generated by new paradigms reconciling pre-colonial culture with the colonial urban organisation? Last, but not least, what can Western and Chinese societies learn from this African ecological development to address their own crises?

Some of these questions were answered by Wole Soyinka, the Nigerian winner of the Nobel Prize for Literature, in an open letter co-signed by over 100 intellectuals from the African continent and addressed to their governments during the COVID-19 crisis:

THE TIME TO ACT IS NOW

Letter Addressed to African Leaders Concerning the COVID-19 Crisis[8]

The threats that are hanging over the African continent with regards to the spread of COVID-19 demand our individual and collective attention. The situation is critical. Yet this is not about mitigating another 'African' humanitarian crisis but to diffuse the potentially damaging effects of a virus that has shaken the global order and put under question the bases of our living-together. The coronavirus pandemic lays bare that which well-to-do middle classes in African cities have thus far refused to confront. In the past 10 years, various media, intellectuals, politicians and international financial institutions have clung to an idea of an Africa on the move, of Africa as the new frontier of capitalist expansion; an Africa on the path to 'emerging' with growth rates that are the envy of northern countries. Such a representation, repeated at will to the point of becoming a received truth, has been torn apart by a crisis that has not entirely revealed the extent of its destructive potential. At the same time, any prospect of an inclusive multilateralism – ostensibly kept alive by years of treaty-making – is forbidding. The global order is disintegrating before our very eyes, giving way to a vicious geopolitical tussle. The new context of economic war of all against all leaves out countries of the Global South so to speak stranded. Once again we are reminded of their perennial status in the world order in-the-making: that of docile spectators.

Like a tectonic storm, the COVID-19 pandemic threatens to shatter the foundations of states and institutions whose profound failings have been ignored for too long. It is impossible to list these, suffice it to mention chronic under-investment in public health and fundamental research, limited achievements in food self-sufficiency, the mismanagement of public finances, the prioritization of road and airport infrastructures at the expense of human well-being. All of this has in fact been the object of an abundant specialized research, except that it seems to have escaped attention in spheres of governance on the continent. The management of the ongoing crisis constitutes most glaring evidence of this gap.

https://www.aljazeera.com/features/2020/4/17/open-letter-from-african-intellectuals-to-leaders-over-covid-19

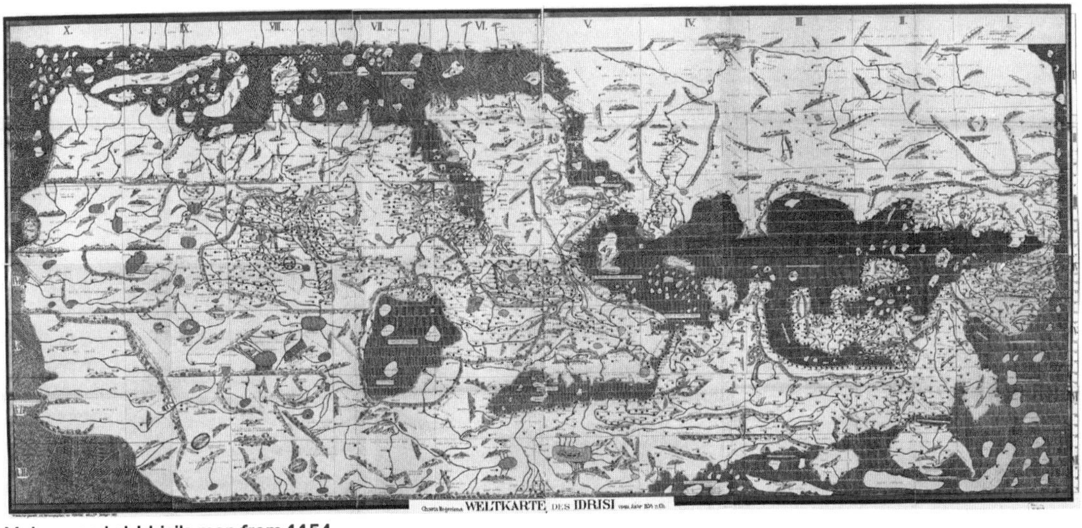

Muhammad al-Idrisi's map from 1154

In response to Western media and the WHO's 'Afro-catastrophism', Soyinka believes that Africa has to reawaken and regain control over its own destiny, in the light of the enormous material and human resources it contains. The various forms of resilience and creativity activated by many young scientists and researchers during the pandemic prove the continent's enormous potential. Felwine Sarr describes this potential very well in his book *Afrotopia*, inspired by the work of Aimé Césaire and Frantz Fanon. The Senegalese philosopher highlights the value of precolonial concepts such as *mihigo, tawfekh, noflay* and ubuntu as possible social and cultural drivers for Africa's own "metaphors for the future." These concepts, based on a balanced relation between individual and community well-being, are considered in opposition to the imitation of Western models. Sarr's approach, rather than closing the door to hybridising cultures, claims the freedom for Africans to eventually choose solutions that have worked well elsewhere.

It is clear that, to get out of this systemic planetary crisis, we will have to learn from that approach and pay closer attention to "African solutions to solve global problems," moving away from the paternalistic culture of emergency design towards the culture of emergent design. This shift in perspective was anticipated by the Moroccan geographer Al-Idrisi in his *Tabula Rogeriana*, an atlas of maps commissioned by the Norman King Roger II in 1138, in which the maps are oriented with north at the bottom and south at the top.

With this non-humanitarian premise, the African Fabbers project has gradually developed its own research agenda as an independent platform investigating the relation between climate dynamics, manufacturing processes, and community-oriented design. The project looks at the role of manufacturing and craftsmanship in contemporary African society as a key aspect of the sustainable development of the continent and its influential role in Western and Chinese economies. In this vein, the word "fabbers" highlights a unique tradition and takes inspiration from the Latin definition of the homo faber, first used by Appius Claudius Caecus in his *Sententiæ* to describe "the ability of man to control his destiny and what surrounds him by self-producing his own tools and objects". This philosophical concept was picked up by intellectuals such as Hannah Arendt and Max Scheler in the 20th century and reinterpreted by Henri Bergson in his *Creative Evolution*. Bergson's definition of intelligence also emphasises the "faculty to create artificial objects, in particular tools to make tools, and to indefinitely variate its makings." As explained more recently by Richard Sennet in his book *The Craftsman*, reconnecting thinking with making could generate an added value in our contemporary society, enriching our lives and avoiding the dynamics of pure competition.

While Western societies, with their industrial and digital revolutions, have gradually lost touch with the notion of *homo faber* and its manufacturing culture, the potential of the African economy is mainly based on the diffuse network of makers and their technical knowledge. Given this strong propensity for manufacturing, which has generated a fairly widespread familiarity with technology, it is not surprising that the second fab lab in the world, after the one at MIT in Boston, was opened in Sekondi in Ghana. In this context, the AF project was born from the need to investigate the lack of an African industrial culture from another perspective, and in relation to the attitude of the new inhabitants of the growing sub-Saharan metropolises who make up for that lack using hybrid and low-tech production processes. This approach makes artisanal manufacturing the driving force of their contemporary economies.

In consequence, the field of investigation was mainly related to those neighbourhoods that arise spontaneously as real artisan districts. They are understood as "urban fabrication laboratories", centres for storing and transforming recycled materials that are re-purposed for the most disparate uses. At the same time, the relationship between the development of these informal makers' districts and the exponential growth of African cities is a relatively recent topic, and the scientific literature is currently rather lacking in studies of the phenomenon. This deficiency depends on many factors, not least the difficulty in finding reliable data on the informal economy, which represents well over 40% of the gross domestic product in the sub-Saharan region today (as indicated by the International Labour Organisation in its recent report).

Another difficulty comes from continuing to apply categories and indicators that are poorly suited to the African context, which is transitioning from the first Industrial Revolution to the fourth in a matter of just decades and practically without intermediate steps. While this process has been interpreted as an enormous gap to cover, it is also clear that due to the current situation, Africa has a tremendous opportunity to become a laboratory for an alternative economic model, especially considering the environmental impact of industrialisation on climate change. Thus, in order to study and facilitate this process, an analytical and diachronic method needs to be intertwined with an empirical one. This approach will also be useful in understanding, on the one hand, the side effects of Western industrialisation in African cities (which, in the best of cases, have acted as logistical platforms for the export of raw materials to Europe and China) and, on the other hand, the contradictions of China's systematic commercial penetration in the continent. In the midst of this controversial and constantly changing geopolitical scenario, as is well documented in the issue of the magazine *Limes* called "Africa contro Occidente"[9], the ability of African cities to self-organise from an urban and productive point of view emerges in the absence of institutional top-down policies.

This bottom-up ability to organise themselves into communities of "fabbers" capable of self-production and resource optimisation has generated circular economies aimed at reusing and recycling. This mechanism is fundamental to understanding the complexity of urban spaces, conceived as places of production and socialisation at the same time. This extreme fragmentation of the productive fabric, spread out across the city, generates a series of spatial scenarios and social mixity, which contrasts with the standards of industrialised cities, often divided into siloed compartments. While these predominantly self-regulated dynamics pose a series of health and infrastructural issues, they also offer a winning economic model due to their density and promiscuity.

Based on this hypothesis, the AF research agenda aims to learn innovative strategies from these informal dynamics to enhance the quality of the production processes of these communities by using the bottom-up regeneration of the spontaneous fabric without distorting the social and economic logics.

For this reason, the AF project looks at the African continent not as a land of conquest but of learning, with the aim of developing a critical understanding of the challenges facing Western society. Therefore, the cultural drivers of the investigation process are very transversal and range from the craftsmen in the Douala slum to the African and non-African pioneers who, over time, have experimented with new forms of ecological living. In this sense, the choice to set up AF's project "by dealing with what was there before" is consistent with this premise, starting from the vernacular culture of production to better understand how it has been transformed. For this reason, an interdisciplinary approach capable of associating anthropological and environmental issues with economic and urban dynamics in a correlated manner was appropriate. The AF project is, therefore, based on a theory by practice apparatus, built over time by alternating on-site experiments and the study of very different contributions. This approach was fed by a mix of professional as well as personal experiences, since for family reasons, I spent a lot of time in Africa during my school years.

At that time, non-linear cultural paths were more uncommon, and I still remember the scepticism of some of my teachers at my junior high school in Italy when I decided, after returning from a long period in Africa, to write my final dissertation on Patrice Lumumba, Leopold Senghor, and other African cultural and political leaders from the 1960s. A few years later, I experienced a similar reaction when I decided to develop my first research thesis at the School of Architecture of Naples on Caribbean indigenous dwellings. That multicultural approach has also influenced the AF's vision of the history of architecture as a more comprehensive and generative tool able to recognise and analyse the performative principles behind pre-colonial taxonomies. Beyond the traditional way of classifying vernacular dwellings proposed by Bernard Rudofsky *Architecture without Architects* and, more recently, Paul Oliver *Dwellings*, we have started to focus on the related evolutionary aspects analysed by anthropologists and scientists.

This interdisciplinary approach to the behavioural logics behind patterns and material organisations emerging in spontaneous architecture has gradually informed our alternative bibliography and shortlist of some unknown precedents. One of the pillars of this decolonised pantheon of cultural references is the book *African Fractals*, on modern computing and indigenous design, by the ethno-mathematician Ron Eglash. In his book, Eglash explains that whereas Cartesian coordinate systems characterised Euro-American culture as a 'state society' with a top-down organisation, fractals and complex geometry are more characteristic of pre-colonial cultures, as decentralised social groups with a bottom-up organisation. In this case, the geometry becomes a cultural, social, and generative medium for non-linear forms and climate-sensitive architectural configurations. The geometric and vernacular designs are then analysed according to the use of recursive construction processes that can generate differentiated and self-organised systems in response to microclimatic conditions and social constraints. That common interest was the reason why Ron first invited me to the Rensselaer Polytechnic Institute to start a conversation and share knowledge with his students and colleagues.

The result of this dialogue was based not on the naive image with which Western culture has associated African production for centuries, but rather on a computational understanding of the range of similar but extremely diversified formal solutions, to paraphrase the concepts from Gilles Deleuze's *Difference and Repetition*. These "implicit" algorithms generate "emergent" systems (which persist over time by evolving) as described in *The Architecture of Emergence* by Mike Weinstock. It is worth remembering that many of these themes were understood by members of the Bauhaus, including Paul Klee and Anni Albers, among others, as well as by Aldo van Eyck, who studied the pre-colonial architecture of the Dogon of northern Mali. Only under this premise, without any ideological prejudice, can the effects of colonial culture be analysed in the self-construction of a new African society, starting from the creation of its institutions and its cities. Even the most enlightened experiences, such as the creation of modern African universities after independence, have struggled to develop in relation to the demands of the context, which is why many of these efforts have failed miserably. The potential of this approach in the field of architectural design is well explained in the work of Peter Trummer on synthetic-vernacular and associative design, engendering intuitive, generative processes as explicit trans-scalar models for ecological architecture as living infrastructures.

Over the years, the AF project has developed its own research-based identity analysing different post-colonial experiments undertaken from the Department of Tropical Architecture, co-founded in the 1950s by a group of African students at the AA. From that controversial experience, many interesting schools of architecture were born on the continent such as the school in Zaria, where Demas Nwoko (Golden Lion for Lifetime Achievement at the Venice Biennale of Architecture 2023) was trained. While the debate on the development of these schools and their failures is still open, it is clear that a hybrid educational system surpassing the black/white dichotomy is now needed.

On this delicate topic, more recently I discovered a very interesting conversation on Western education systems between the Italian director and writer Pier Paolo Pasolini and a group of African students who appeared in the documentary *Notes Towards an African Orestes* (1970). I have to say that some of the comments on how to connect the two cultures from the group of African students at the Sapienza University of Rome are still very relevant. At the same time, they appear to be vaguely amused by Pasolini's implication that social progress in Africa via the adoption of Western education systems should be distrusted in favour of his romanticised ideals of communal tribal systems and the dignity of labour. It is also worth pointing out that, even in the case of the most visionary projects linked to the construction industry – such as that of the Tropical House (1949-52), by Jean Prouvé, who, with an important French company, attempted the path of prefabrication for the African context – this modernist approach turns out to be a failure. Even though the project responded to a pressing demand for housing in many African countries, and despite the high quality of the construction and the bioclimatic logic, the project was never applied on a large scale beyond a few 1-to-1 scale prototypes. The reason for this failure lies in the colonial production process: all the materials, partly coming from Africa, were processed and imported from Europe, increasing costs and limiting the impact on the local economy to a minimum.

In this regard, the contributions of the architect and Aga Khan winner Fabrizio Carola, who spent his life in working sub-Saharan Africa, are essential. Carola, with his profound knowledge of African society, understood how important it was to transform construction into an opportunity to redistribute wealth more equally through a community (such as a village or a town district). His idea of conceiving the building site as a factory (for bricks, above all) and a knowledge exchange platform became a strategic element for a sustainable approach that kept the dependency on imported materials to a minimum. Above all, his idea of focusing on the self-construction of tools, evolving Hassan Fathy's compass (the grandfather of the robotic arm) to create building shells (such as domes and vaults) entirely using local materials, is one example of his anticipatory approach.

In this sense, it is crucial to test that approach in a more urban dimension in relation to the local development of real factory neighbourhoods. The urban dynamics of such neighbourhoods are explained very well by Rem Koolhaas in his research *Project on the City* developed with Kunle Adeyemi and his Harvard GSD students in Lagos (2001-2004). Many topics for a critical reflection on this urban issue arise from reading essays by Saskia Sassen in the A+U issue entitled "Diversified Solutions"[10] and Mohsen Mostafavi's *Ecological Urbanism* (2010), which offers a possible model for the productive city aimed at contextualising and integrating new production and technological processes in emerging urban contexts such as those in Africa. In this sense, the pre-colonial culture of optimisation and that of survival in the post-colonial city have some points of contact, which are interesting to analyse. In fact, it is clear that in the African case, it is not a question of rethinking de-industrialised places that are the result of an industrialisation that never really happened. Rather, it is a question of analysing and possibly strengthening these new hybrid fabrics, which we could call "fab cities". One interesting scenario to consider, widely anticipated by African cities, and which is explained by Chris Anderson in his book *Makers* (2012), would be a global economy based on the concept of product customisation through a dense network of "personal factories" made up of advanced craftsmen. Cities understood as urban fabrication laboratories are increasingly global, in which the boundaries between public space, production space, and housing are extremely permeable.

These new, dynamic and flexible scenarios are the field of study that AF began to investigate many years ago involving people from very different backgrounds. African Fabbers are understood as drivers of their micro-communities and capable of regenerating small pieces of the city from the bottom up, setting in motion new innovative processes. Therefore, the Atlas intends to restore the collective dimension of these processes and an experimental approach in the practice and teaching, which inspires a few clear principles contained in the statement below.

Notes for responsible architecture:

When, almost 15 years ago, we started to design the itinerant school of self-construction, we could never think that one day we would contribute to the creation of a cultural hub in Africa or to participate in the Venice Architecture Biennale. However, we had clear in mind that the role of the architect had to be radically revised in his approach to the client and to the climatic aspects of our planet. The reason why we decided to start from Africa is not accidental, but it is linked to a combination of human/personal and cultural factors. As students first, and then as architects and researchers, we soon understood that the origins of ecological architecture, in osmosis with the context, reside in the so-called Global South and especially in sub-Saharan Africa. In these years, during which we have accumulated many experiences, we have had little time to write, but a lot to experiment and concretely reflect on some focal points concerning the different way of doing and teaching architecture between Europe and Africa. And it is probably also thanks to the pandemic that, in setting up the work for the Biennale and for the book African Fabbers Atlas, we have begun to systematize some fundamental principles that are the basis of our work.

Client / sharing / authorship

The architects of our generation have never had a client in the traditional sense of the term. At the same time, there are more and more people and communities around the world who need to live and work in adequate spaces, possibly created in a responsible way. Starting from this assumption, we politically chose to seek our reference customers in the relationship with more or less organized groups of citizens and/or associations: a very fragmented and complex scenario in which, in many cases, we are involved from the zero-phase of the project in the search for funds. At the same time, beyond any rhetoric on participatory processes, we have never considered it necessary to renounce our authorship to be credible in the eyes of our interlocutors. The aspects of trying to synthesize, mediate, facilitate in complex social contexts and with often quite non-existent budgets are part of our creative process. These dynamics often require us to take responsibility towards the communities we collaborate with, in some cases bordering on unpopularity. These are the risks of what we call shared authorship; after all, those who work in this dimension can only go beyond the stereotypes of a profession that no longer exists. In this sense, we have put aside any anxiety about starting a studio. Our studio, our classroom, have almost always been the public space and the workshops of the artisans with whom we have had the good fortune to collaborate.

Production / Technology / self-sufficiency

These years of experimentation in Europe and Africa led us to believe that we need a decolonization of the cultural and production processes in order to redistribute wealth and redefine the relationship between nature and tekne. We think that decolonization is a collective process in which everyone must question themselves and do their part, without exception. As white/European people, we feel the distrust of those who, from their offices and professorships in London, New York... think they have the exclusivity on these issues, yet being careful not to develop them. This distrust actually led us to directly deal with the informal dynamics of the contemporary city, using the production as a medium to overturn some logic imposed by the dominant cultures, in Western countries as well in the Global South. This implies a shift of paradigm on the social role of technology, generating local responses to global problems. For this reason, many of our projects result from the creation of self-production workshops for and with the local communities. Working with an evolutionary approach to the traditional techniques and designing work tools to transform materials on site is a central theme for us. Beyond any autarchic drift, today those who deal with the relationship between architecture and ecology must deal with this issue, which conditions the final result of the architect's work.

Experimentation / Teaching / Construction

Reviewing the outcomes of the workshops developed over time with the students of the African Fabbers School, we realized that the quality

– originality, concreteness... – of what has been produced is often more interesting than what developed by our students at traditional universities. If we then think about the starting conditions of the students and of the infrastructures, the question becomes clear. In fact, the experience of AFS constantly leads us to question our teaching methods, adapting them to the local context and rethinking the relationship between theory and practice in a learning by doing logic. These are some of the transversal themes that are the guiding thread of the various building sites – school developed over time: diversity: artisans, art and engineering students work together in our laboratories... of different ages and backgrounds. The exchange of knowledge between students becomes the added value.

Responsibility: no participant gets a grade, but from the very beginning the students interact collectively directly with the local community. This generates self-esteem, empowerment and self-organization. experimentation: the theme is the result of a dialogue with the local community, but, despite the realization of concrete outputs, we leave the students free to investigate the controversial relationship between informal and digital culture. They learn by building, they accept failure. What we have learned so far with our students and local partners systematically updates our research agenda and is certainly part of a process of decolonization of the way architecture is taught that we believe is necessary to spread in Europe as well.

Architecture/device/open work

In this intertwining of professional practice, teaching and research we have developed over time the interest in architecture understood as a device, open to subsequent spatial and functional variations. The experience of the years spent in Cameroon for the CAMon! project summarizes some of the above themes, precisely because of the methodological sequence in which the work was developed. With the COE ngo and other local partners, we have won an AICS call to implement a cultural hub in Douala. The first step was to create a first self-production workshop – digital and traditional manufacturing – for architecture and design on the site of the future Hub. The multifunctional building is an urban infrastructure that includes digital manufacturing laboratories, exhibition spaces, coworking, study rooms, guest spaces. Now, despite the pandemic, the Hub and its laboratories are operational and many of our students have finished their training path. The project was exhibited at the Venice Biennale, inside the Italian Pavilion. Despite the many difficulties, a sense of great satisfaction mixed with uncertainty prevails in us. We hope that this cultural centre, the only one of its kind in Africa, will continue to proceed autonomously in constant dialogue with the local community.

Notes

1 “State of the Climate in Africa 2022”, World Meteorological Organization, WMO nº1330. 2023. https://library.wmo.int/viewer/67761/download?file=1330_State-of-the-Climate-in-Africa-2022_en.pdf&type=pdf&navigator=1#:~:text=In%202022%2C%20the%20African%20mean,decade%20between%201961%20and%201990

2 “Summary for Policymakers of IPCC Special Report on Global Warming of 1.5ºC approved by governments”, IPCC, Accessed December 1, 2023 , https://www.ipcc.ch/2018/10/08/summary-for-policymakers-of-ipcc-special-report-on-global-warming-of-1-5c-approved-by-governments/.

3 Kanta Kumari Rigaud, et al “Groundswell: Preparing for Internal Climate Migration”, The World Bank. Washington, DC (2018), Accessed December 1, 2023 , https://www.worldbank.org/en/news/infographic/2018/03/19/groundswell---preparing-for-internal-climate-migration

4 “Summary report African Climate Risks Conference (ACRC) 2019”,IISD Earth Negotiations Bulletin, International Institute for Sustainable Development, Accessed December 4, 2023, https://enb.iisd.org/events/african-climate-risks-conference-acrc-2019/summary-report-7-9-october-2019

5 “Mapping Africa’s natural resources”, Al Jazeera Staff, Al Jazeera, last modified February 15, 2022, https://www.aljazeera.com/news/2018/2/20/mapping-africas-natural-resources

6 “Africa’s jobless youth cast a shadow over economic growth”, Kingsley Ighobo, Africa Renewal: Special Edition on Youth 2017, accessed December 6, 2023. https://www.un.org/africarenewal/magazine/special-edition-youth-2017/africas-jobless-youth-cast-shadow-over-economic-growth#:~:text=The%20organization%20added%20that%20%E2%80%9Cthe,youth%2C%20talent%20and%20creativity.%E2%80%9D

7 “Africa Energy Outlook 2022”, IEA, revised version, May 2023, https://www.iea.org/reports/africa-energy-outlook-2022

8 “Open letter from African intellectuals to leaders over COVID-19”, Aljazeera , last modified April 17, 2020, https://www.aljazeera.com/features/2020/4/17/open-letter-from-african-intellectuals-to-leaders-over-covid-19

9 “Africa contro occidente /Africa against the West” Limes 8/2023, Rome: 2023.

10 Saskia Sassen ,“Urbanizing Technologies”, a+u 2011:02 Diversified Solutions – A New Beginning in Architecture (2011): 90-91.

Bibliography

Anderson, Chris. *Makers: The New Industrial Revolution*. UK: Random House, 2012.

Al jazeera. “Open letter from African intellectuals to leaders over COVID-19.” Last modified April 17, 2020. https://www.aljazeera.com/features/2020/4/17/open-letter-from-african-intellectuals-to-leaders-over-covid-19

Al Jazeera. “Mapping Africa’s natural resources.” Al Jazeera. last modified February 15, 2022. https://www.aljazeera.com/news/2018/2/20/mapping-africas-natural-resources

Bergson, Henri. *Creative Evolution*. USA: University Press of America, 1984.

Chung, Chuihua Judy, Jeffrey Inaba, Rem Koolhaas, Sze Tsung Leong, Tae-wook Cha, Harvard University Graduate School of Design, and Harvard Project on the City. *Harvard Design School Guide to Shopping.* Köln: Taschen, 2001.

IISD Earth Negotiations Bulletin “Summary report African Climate Risks Conference (ACRC) 2019.” International Institute for Sustainable Development. Accessed December 4, 2024. https://enb.iisd.org/events/african-climate-risks-conference-acrc-2019/summary-report-7-9-october-2019

Cascone, Paolo. “From emergency to emergent design.” Interni web. Last modified July, 20, 2020. https://www.internimagazine.com/features/opinions/paolo-cascone-africa/

Eglash, Ron. *African fractals : modern computing and indigenous design*. UK: Rutgers University Press, 1999. IEA International Energy Agency. “Africa Energy Outlook 2022.” Revised version May, 2023. https://www.iea.org/reports/africa-energy-outlook-2022

Ighobo, Kingsley. “Africa’s jobless youth cast a shadow over economic growth.” Africa Renewal: Special Edition on Youth 2017. Accessed December 6, 2023.

Kumari Rigaud, Kanta, Alex de Sherbinin, Bryan Jones, Jonas Bergmann, Viviane Clement, Kayly Ober, Jacob Schewe, Susana Adamo, Brent McCusker, Silke Heuser, and Amelia Midgley. 2018. “Groundswell: Preparing for Internal Climate Migration.” The World Bank. Washington, DC (2018) https://www.worldbank.org/en/news/infographic/2018/03/19/groundswell---preparing-for-internal-climate-migration

Limes, “Africa against the West” Limes 8/2023. Rome:2023.

Mostafavi, Mohsen, Gareth Doherty, and Harvard University. Graduate School of Design. *Ecological Urbanism*. Baden, Switzerland: Lars Müller, 2010.

Oliver, Paul. *Dwellings: The Vernacular House World Wide*. Germany: Phaidon Press, 2007.

Sarr, Felwine. *Afrotopia.* USA: University of Minnesota Press, 2020.

Pasolini, Paolo dir. Appunti per un’orestiade Africana. (Rome: 1973). Edizioni Cineteca di Bologna, Bologna 2008

Weinstock, Michael. *The Architecture of Emergence: The Evolution of Form in Nature and Civilisation.* UK: Wiley, 2010.

World Meteorological Organization. “State of the Climate in Africa 2022.” WMO nº 1330. 2023. https://library.wmo.int/viewer/67761/download?file=1330_State-of-the-Climate-in-Africa-2022_en.pdf&type=pdf&navigator=1#:~:text=In%202022%2C%20the%20African%20mean,decade%20between%201961%20and%201990.

Rudofsky, Bernard. *Architecture without architects*. UK: University of New Mexico Press, 1987.

Borderwall architecture project by Rael San Fratello

II
Conversations

Christian Benimana
Cheick Diallo
Ron Eglash
Ugo La Pietra
Hanif Kara
Vincent Kitio
Giancarlo Mazzanti
Ronald Rael
AbdouMaliq Simone
Françoise N'Thépé

PREMISE

The AF project is the result of many collaborations but also intellectual exchanges and dialogues that, over time, have shaped and stimulated our way of thinking and acting in relation to different contexts. These dialogues were developed in very different and informal ways, with the aim of learning about different multi-cultural personal and educational experiences in both Western countries and the Global South. For this reason, we were interested to hear from people from different backgrounds about how these paths impacted their careers as well as their critical understanding of the role of African informal culture and indigenous technologies in contemporary society. Therefore, we had conversations with people from a wide variety of disciplines: from ethnomathematics to manufacturing and digital fabrication, from sociology to architectural design and structural engineering, etc. Our aim was not just to understand the different practices and discuss critical dynamics, but also to investigate a possible common ground based on integrating alternative approaches. At the same time, beyond any attempt at political correctness, it is no coincidence that the people involved in these conversations also represented a mix of generations and origins: African, African diaspora, and non-African.

While Ron Eglash highlighted the complexity and contextual algorithms that exist in pre-colonial culture from a scientific standpoint, AbdouMaliq Simone explained his African experiences as a sociologist and urban activist, introducing the notion of “black urbanism” and the social relevance of self-organisation in informal and spontaneous settlements. In parallel, Ugo La Pietra explained the role of radical pedagogies from the Global Tools experience of the 1970s, in particular, how they might be integrated with the African vernacular culture of optimisation towards new paradigmatic educational models. On the same topic, Christian Benimana introduced us, more recently, to the African Design Centre project in Kigali, conceived to support a new generation of Rwandan architects. This question of the role of the new generation of designers in Africa was also mentioned by Françoise N’Thépé, who talked about her experience as a female architect working between Paris and the sub-Saharan region. With the Colombian architect Giancarlo Mazzanti, we tried to understand how to learn from his community-oriented, tropical architecture in terms of social and environmental performance to respond to similar climatic conditions. The conversation with Cheick Diallo investigated the circular economy and manufacturing, looking at the role of “designers as producers” through the model of his atelier in Bamako conceived as a sort of “local industry”. We discussed the question of digital manufacturing and sustainable construction with Ronald Rael, based on his experiments with natural materials and 3D printing. The relation between climate, materiality, and tectonics came up with Hanif Kara, including the opportunity of recycling waste to boost African economies through the construction industry. The conversations with Vincent Kitio dealt with renewable energy and housing policies in Africa, focusing on the UN-Habitat collaborations with African governments. Thanks to these generous contributions, we were able to share knowledge with our local partners and shape some of the main principles behind the AF project.

Christian Benimana

Christian Benimana
is co-founder of the African Design Centre, a field-based apprenticeship that is set to be the BAUHAUS of Africa with the mission to empower the leaders who will design
a more equitable, just, and sustainable world. Benimana graduated from Tongji University's College of Architecture and Urban Planning in Shanghai with a bachelor of science in architecture. After graduating he joined LongiLat Architecture before becoming a global health corps design fellow at MASS Design Group in 2010, where he is currently principal and managing director.

PC you are originally from Rwanda, you have studied architecture in China and now you work with an American firm. Could you tell me about your path, how your education and personal life have affected your interests in the field of architecture?

CB My education and personal life didn't contribute to my interest in Architecture. The only early influence I can trace my ambitions to become an architect to is my parents telling me that because I loved drawing houses, I would enjoy being an architect. Beyond that, Architecture and what Architects do were foreign concepts to me.

PC How did you decide to study in China and how was your experience as a young African student in Shanghai?

CB When I finished High School I was awarded a scholarship to study in China. The decision was very much to study abroad and study in the field of studies needed in the country at the time and schools in the country didn't have the programs for. The experience in China was very eye-opening to me. At that time I didn't fully appreciate the cultural shock and the influence it will have on how broaden my view and take on life will be. But now I cherish it. The Architecture education was simple and well structured, but disconnected to the reality of my country of origin. It was more tied to global ideals we hold for developed societies and less about the opportunities to create a healthy diversity of this definition for the millions communities less represented in the field of Architecture.

PC What did you learn from your Chinese experience and from studying at the Tongji University?

CB Modernity and development are not simple concepts, globalization is not necessarily a good thing and the human experience must shape outcomes of underlying political, social-Economic and Environmental systems that our collective survival of society depends on. That Architecture is a powerful force in shaping these outcomes and therefore a critical tool to deploy rightly to impact positively these systems.

PC **It looks like a new generation of African architects with a very international background is the more and more involved in the future of the continent. How do you explain this phenomenon?**

CB There are many reasons for that, but I think the major one is that Afri-ca is obviously seen as the future. The increase in population and the econom-ic growth associated is a natural attraction to all architects, and not just African Architects. But beyond that, there is also a movement of young professionals that have had an opportunity to travel and experience the world around us, and have realized that what Africa needs is a whole new set of approaches to plan-ning the future of the continent.

PC **how your international background is affecting your understanding of informal dynamics and traditional African architecture?**

CB My understanding of informal dynamics and traditional African Architecture is mostly influenced by my place as a citizen of a country that embraces both intentionally to create home grown solutions that are not short of international standards. My international experience only helps me understand where these stand in the frame of global perspectives.

PC **How could this mix of knowledge generate a new approach to sustainability in architecture?**

CB When we stop thinking of traditional African Architecture of anything short of modern, sustainable and award winning worthy of architecture, then we stand a chance of embracing the many ways traditional African architecture was truly the architecture meant for the places it was created for, fully embedded in the lifestyle of the residents, enshrined in the cultural customs and traditions, socio-economic activity of the communities it was meant to serve and most importantly the protection of the environment that gave it birth and sustained it.

PC **The work at MASS is informed by an idea of social justice and human dignity. How do you decline these concepts in your work with them in Rwanda?**

CB The progress of every society is mainly shaped by moments of restorative justice and progressive justice. Rwanda as a country that has a very difficult history, understands that we can be a role model of how a community torn apart by the worst events in history could emerge from it and become a beacon of hope. The foundation of the quest is deploying all efforts to fight for and uphold human dignity. We understand that in this country, and because of that our work has been driven by this national ambition. This is something that has in return also shaped MASS as an organization.

PC **Beyond any humanitarian rhetoric, what is the social role of architects in Africa?**

CB Architects shouldn't engage in humanitarian rhetoric. We all bring contributions to our communities when humanitarian efforts are needed, but we should do some because we are humans but not because we are architects. Therefore the social role of architects in Africa should be the same as the social role of architects elsewhere in the world. There is no need to be different because the practice is in Africa. What needs to be questioned instead is if the profession of architects is producing professionals and solutions that are socially conscious, not just in Africa, but everywhere on the planet. I argue that it doesn't. For a long time we in the profession of architecture have engaged in a practice that treats these responsibilities as an addition to the needs of the clients - defined by who pays us and what they set to be the boundaries of what they are willing to accept as worthy of the financial value they are providing in the form of budgets.

PC How is this role perceived by the local community?

CB When done superficially, it is received with cynicism and oftentimes ignored. In our case, we have observed that when we truly engage with these issues and embed ourselves in the communities we work with, the transformation that happens as a result of this process is what makes the role we played received with enthusiasm and accepted as meaningful.

PC Who are your main clients?

CB They range from multinationals, foundations, government agencies and ministries.

PC The work that you develop in Kigali has a lot to do with materiality and low-tech construction. How do you think traditional manufacturing could affect contemporary architecture in Africa?

CB All truly good architecture should demonstrate how it has leveraged the available means of productions of the place it is meant to. If traditional manufacturing doesn't affect contemporary architecture in Africa it means the contemporary architecture created is not for Africa. It should be a norm, and not an option.

Let's not forget that the traditional manufacturing mentioned is a product of centuries of knowledge and adaptation to the available materials, skills, tools, quality assurance processes and supply chain embedded in the structure of these communities. Leveraging these already established means of productions is the most sensible thing to do when developing contemporary architecture on the continent.

PC What could be the key aspects to develop for generating a circular economy approach in such context?

CB Mandatory minimum requirements for re-use of spaces and materials in the case of developing brown fields.

Minimum compliance for sourcing materials and labor locally or regionally. Clear embodied CO2 emissions in addition to the environmental performance targets for passive systems for the operation of the buildings and other architectural solutions.

PC How do you involve the local community in the construction of your buildings?

CB In all projects we seek to establish which parts of the works could be intentionally designed to benefit from available skills in the local communities. In addition we yearn to innovate in a way that there could be architecture systems that can also benefit from creating new teachable skills to the same people in these communities as well.

PC You are involved in educational projects with the African Design Centre in Kigali. How do you see the situation of African school of architecture?

CB The Architecture schools in Africa are dealing with two major problems at the same time. Creating programs that can meet the demand and make the programs relevant to the current trends as well as local contexts the graduates are meant to serve when they graduate from these institutions and programs. The schools are caught in the middle of this tension between seizing the opportunity to be able to create programs that are groundbreaking in their way of en-gaging core issues affecting the different communities on the continent, and creating programs that can be accepted and adopted by the academic com-munity that seems to continue to embrace and reward the rigid format of 16th century models of education. All this of course with an added complexity of be-ing resources strapped. This creates an environment in which people that are motivated to help imagine what these programs could be are disincentivized to put their efforts and time towards this goal. As a result of this, it falls on the graduates to find support systems that give them opportunities to supplement the knowledge they finish school with, in order to create work relevant to these challenging conditions they are faced with when entering the work market.

PC **What are the key courses that you are developing in the Centre?**

CB At the African Design Centre Fellowship, modules cycle between field-based learning, classroom and workshop education, and independent workshops. In addition to the design-build focus, the curriculum includes topics that helped build technical skills in software, design, construction, and professional practice, as well as explore humanities workshops focused on storytelling, history, social justice, international development, and leadership. Training on these diverse and critical skills is delivered by practitioners, academics, and visiting thought-leaders. They also lead academic support for fellows to pursue research on pressing issues including urbanization, climate change, and social equity.

PC **What kind of students do you involve?**

CB The goal of interviews is to evaluate the applicant's desire to learn, ability to contribute to the program, understanding of the challenge, and drive and potential to become a thought leader. The participants need to demonstrate excellence in their:

1. Understanding of design impact. This would most likely be exhibited in their essay answers and their past work.
2. Drive in using design for impact. Role of design in their life (now and future), described through their essay answers. Will this applicant will be an advocate for impact-driven design in their career beyond the ADC?
3. Communication skills both verbally and in writing. The former is to be exhibited during interviews and the later communication skills exhibited in essays
4. Visual communicate their work through portfolios in various mediums.
5. Potential. Our assessment of their potential to become a design and thought leader

PC **How would you imagine a decolonised approach to architectural education?**

CB This can only be answered with Buckminster R. Fuller's quote below: "In order to change an existing paradigm you do not struggle to change the problematic model. You create a new model and make the old one obsolete."
Buckminster R. Fuller

Cheick Diallo

Cheick Diallo
was born in Bamako, Mali in 1960. He began his education in the French school of Bamako. He was then sent to continue his education in a small family village in the rural Sahelian region of Senegal. After his graduation from secondary school he was admitted to the School of Architecture of Rouen in France, where he obtained a Master's degree in architectural design.
He began his career commuting for almost 35 years between France and Mali. He is well known worldwide for his work in giving new life to the poor materials he finds in his native country – scrap metal, plastic, wrapping paper, fabric, wood, earth – to make furniture and contemporary functional and decorative objects. His pieces, which he produces himself, are made onsite, by hand by local artisans. He is a designer and an entrepreneur who contributes to the country's economy, and his design is inseparable from a civic commitment.

PC **Can you please tell us about your educational path spanning Mali, Senegal, and France? What was your experience like in France and with the European educational system, the lifestyle in France?**

CD The experience in rural Senegal certainly marked me. For instance, I have seen people building their houses with their own hands. In contrast, the school of architecture of Rouen meant the discovery of a multidisciplinary approach. I felt the need to learn about all forms of architecture – as opposed to my father's approach, which was just promoting Sahelian/Sudanese architecture. I was a sponge, ready to absorb any different forms of architecture and new proposals. I started to grasp the need to understand one's own environment and, at the same time, apply new proposals. But in the meantime, it was very difficult to affirm a Sahelian identity in Normandy. Furthermore, I was the only African in my course. I started to develop a consciousness of being African there. As a matter of fact, it was that contact, life in Europe, that made feel more like an African. In a way, I was forced to develop my African identity.

I was sent to France by my family with the aim of modernising myself, but once in Normandy I began to appreciate the differences in our cultures. The identity-based approach forced me to orient my thoughts and my research towards the development of a modern African design, and I started to set myself the goal of affirming a "global" architecture with African roots. I was hungry for knowledge, and I think that my studies at the design school really opened my mind, and Europe influenced me in becoming African. I wanted an African modernity that would be able to hold its own worldwide. I started to go back to Mali as a "commuter". Europe has been always the place where I draw and set up the showcase, whereas I started and developed the production in Mali.

PC So you started production in Africa. This seems like a paradox, the opposite of the common dynamic based on exporting products to Africa. How do you see the use of new technologies within this process?

CD I look at new technologies as tools that can be used toward our main goal: to develop a better production, a quality production in Africa. We don't necessarily need to produce more, although it is crucial to insure a local production of good quality as our resources are not unlimited.

The image of African production today is still archaic, and we need to substantially change that. Designers can play a crucial role in this process as vectors for African concepts with universal values. African production should be considered of universal value. We need to be proud of our production and reject the idea that anything coming from overseas is better.

A lower cost production with better quality is feasible if we pay attention to the transition from traditional manual craftsmanship toward a modern, locally based production cycle with innovative technologies and ideas, while respecting our traditional culture. We are also starting to transform raw materials here in Africa. By merging these principles and criteria, we can overcome the cost of a limited manual production (craftsmanship).

Education and training are the keys for advancing in this process. As a matter of fact, craftsmen don't receive proper education/training, especially in the sense of integrating and adding value to manual work through the introduction of new technologies.

New technologies can help in educating and developing an awareness of crucial values: for instance, protecting and not wasting wood, consuming smartly, storing food properly, and eventually recycling whatever can be re-used. In this regard, design can play an important role as both a facilitator and an indicator of good communication. However, design today is still too elitist, and we must transform it into a cultural vector and economic tool.

PC What are your views on the possibility of transforming craftsmanship into a small-scale industry by using new technologies, while preventing a loss of identity?

CD It is possible. We mainly have to look at examples coming from Asia (the Philippines, India, Thailand), but also Mexico, where they have developed the use of new technologies without losing their identities. We must look at our rural areas and find the opportunities to adapt new technologies to our environment while preventing that modernisation from rejecting tradition. Instead, traditional values should represent a benchmark. Africa should not cut itself off from the world. It should communicate its identity to others, and design can play an important role in that.

It's a question of attitude. For instance, it has been important for me to change our perspective on the objects of daily life and shift how we look at them. A dining table, traditionally, has a different layout in Europe and in Africa. We are traditionally used to eating on the ground; therefore, we use small and low tables, and sometimes we sit on short stools tabourés. I have decided to maintain these customs while focusing on a modern layout, employing traditional or recycled materials, and using new technologies to implement this approach. A similar example is the production of short chairs that stick to a traditional layout but are produced using recycled materials from old cars. My focus while I am designing is on basic functions – eating, sitting, and sleeping – with the aim of producing furniture that is comfortable, while occupying space and functioning in a traditional way. Ultimately, a large-scale production and its commercialisation can only be achieved with a strong communication that focuses on the concept of adaptation: adaptation to functions, and adaptation of modernity to tradition.

PC How did you manage to set up your production in Bamako? How did you train your collaborators?

CD There are about 10 people who work permanently in my main workshop (factory) in Bamako. I design all the models, and I manage the preparation of a prototype on a 1-to-1 scale in collaboration with my employees. The process of transferring the design of the model into a prototype involves everyone. Participation is the key issue as my workers do not have a formal education, but they have specific skills born from their working experience. Eventually, the construction of the first prototype entails participation from everyone and serves as the basis of the training for the production. In the end, the entire team feels ownership over the prototype and the entire process; each one of them knows their role during the production phase. Education and training are not academic, but very practical. It is a learning-by-doing process. The method that I apply in Bamako is different from that of a technical school in Europe. It also gives meaning to the objects that we are producing, within our process of putting modernity in the service of tradition.

PC Have you ever taught in Europe, and what are the challenges that need to be overcome there?

CD Yes, but only in workshops. I teach a vision of things, of objects, a creative approach and a process. For instance, they might ask me about conceiving a chair, a piece of furniture, using a digital tool. I approach the issue as a designer, not as an African, with a focus on functions, services, coherence, evidence. Subsequently, we analyse the constraints given by the local availability of materials. For instance, I may give the example of chairs made from a car that has crossed Africa. The metal becomes a pretext to give value to the action of recycling and the communication of additional (i.e., traditional) values.

Ron Eglash

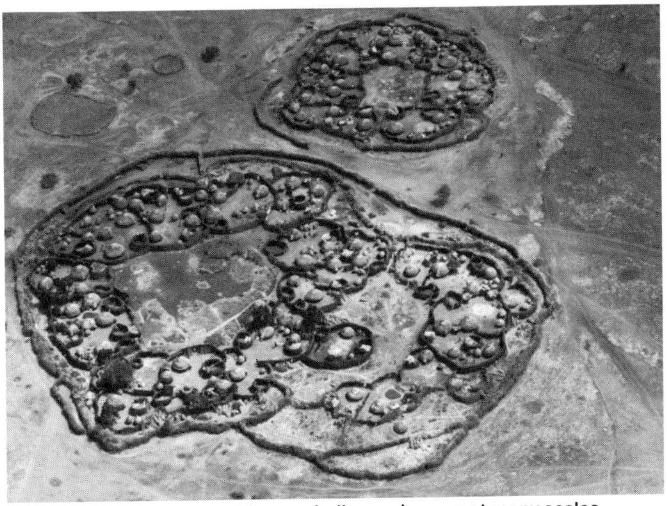

Organically growing fractal forms-similar enclosures at many scales-in a Karamojong community in Uganda. Image courtesy Luanne Cadd

Ron Eglash
is a Professor in the School of Information at the University of Michigan. He received his B.S. in Cybernetics, his M.S. in Systems Engineering, and his PhD in History of Consciousness, all from the University of California. He is best known as the author of African Fractals: modern computing and Indigenous design. His work includes the Culturally Situated Design Tools app suite (csdt.org), which offers decolonial computing for K-12 STEM education; and the generative justice framework (generativejustice.org), which develops AI, digital fabrication and other emerging technologies for empowering low-income communities.

PC It was a freezing February of 2011 when you invited me to join a seminar with your students on ethnomathematics at the Rensselaer Polytechnic Institute in Troy. I was coming back from a very intensive experience in the Dogon region in Mali and your book African Fractals was giving me the opportunity as a designer to really understand the question of contextual algorithms in spontaneous settlements. How would you explain ethnomathematics as a discipline? Why and how you have started to be interested in African culture? What was the starting point of your investigations?

RE I noticed the fractal patterns of African settlements in aerial photos. At first I thought of them as embodiment of bottom-up. Later I realized that calling them "spontaneous" or "emergent" was only partially the reason for those patterns. The other part is the construction algorithm: the set of rules, practices, and frameworks for how one goes about making those forms. To use an analogy from nature, both termite mounds and bee hives are emergent, bottom-up structures. But the reason termite mounds look nothing like bee hives is that they have different construction algorithms. For insects that knowledge is in their DNA. For African architects that knowledge is in their culture. It's a combination of geometric understandings, algorithm-like sequences, relations with local types of soil and plants, and so on. To call that "African mathematics" is not entirely accurate, since it blends across the categories (geometry, art, architecture, agriculture, etc.) that Europeans deliberately separated. But colonists used that as an excuse to say they have no math understanding, which is equally inaccurate. Thus to say we are studying "ethnomathematics" understandings of the formal properties of shape, number, time and other abstractions as they were created in different cultures – is a reasonable compromise.

PC In your book you have started to underline the relation between recursive geometry and social organisation in Africa. Could you explain the relation between African fractals and the political economy related to such culture? How this question of difference of repetition affects the organisation African traditional society? Do you think that these aspects are evolving in their contemporary communities? What Euro-American societies could learn from this evolution if any?

RE Fractals are the result of some recursive process: repeating similar arrangements of line segments at different scales on a computer screen, repeating similar cellulose structures at different scales in the case of branching plants, and so on. Today we often hear that a sustainable economy would be better for people and the planet. So asking what was learned about the circulations in societies that prototyped this kind of system for the last few millennia might be useful! Traditional African architecture is adaptive and emergent; it can respond to changing conditions, accommodate increased needs with increased structure, and harmlessly return to the ecosystem when no longer in use. Those are all characteristics that a modern, high tech generative economy would require. Architects and scientists are always talking about what they learned from nature-there are fields such as biomorphic architecture, biodesign, and so on. But Indigenous cultures are rarely treated as potential sources of guidance and insight in the same way. That is partly from fear of saying something wrong-scholars do not want to be branded racially insensitive. And partly due to IP rights: if you steal from nature no one accuses you of theft (whereas pharmaceutical companies learned the hard way that Indigenous cultures will fight back). But it is mostly due to the stereotypes of "primitive society" that we need to overcome. When Black culture is dismissed as intellectually inferior, we all lose. Supremacist movements today are also behind the destruction of the Amazon in Brazil; destruction of civil rights in India, and so on. What holds us back from a generative economy is not insufficient data on global warming. It is a set of forces empowered by racial politics. It comes as much from China's authoritarian communism as it does from US capitalism. It is the ideology of extractive economies.

PC In the last decade you have been more and more involved in this debate on Open Source culture and your work has inspired a lot of architects and designers. Could you explain why African settlements can be considered as one of the best examples of Open Architecture? How are these models dealing with material optimisation and environmental issues? How a digital tool could help local communities to evolve and improve such implicit models?

RE The opposite of an extractive economy is a generative economy; one that typified Indigenous traditions. Here value is not extracted, but flows back to those who generated it, in unalienated forms. But it's not a simple circle: the flows are happening as reciprocal relations between humans and nature; a foundational concept for African traditions. You asked how that works in terms of "material optimization", but that phrase is already framing it in a very western way of thinking. Consider, for example, this quote from Karl Pearson, a founder of statistics: "My view – and I think it may be called the scientific view of a nation – is that of an organized whole, kept up to a high pitch of internal efficiency by insuring that its numbers are substantially recruited from the better stocks, and kept up to a high pitch of external efficiency by contest, chiefly by way of war with inferior races." I am sure that when you were getting your degree (it was in parametric design, no?) words like efficiency and optimization came up a lot, and perhaps you used Pearson's coefficient to perform those calculations. It was the same for me getting my master's in systems engineering.

Even those of us born from "lesser stocks" can appropriate such statistical tools for less racist purposes than Pearson intended. But perhaps there are other conceptual tools, other ways of approaching mathematical modeling. Consider this symbol in the Asante temples of Ghana. It shows two stools, the symbol of Ghanaian authority. One stool represents humans, the other the forest spirits. Erupting out of the stool are flows of value, which become the structure of the other stool. The image as a whole is isomorphic to the famous Escher print "drawing hands". Now if I ask computer scientists about the mathematical meaning of Escher's drawing, they will wax philosophic about bootstrapping, recursive programming, and human-machine collaboration.[1] But the Ghanaian stools created this concept long before Escher, and in many ways those knowledge systems underlie even more profound forms of recursion: mutualism between human and nonhuman agencies that circulate value in unalienated forms; thus the maintenance of health, creativity, ecological sustainability, egalitarian labor and other phenomena that can emerge in Indigenous lifeways. The term we use in my network to describe this circulation of unalienated value is "generative justice".[2] To the extent that tools like digital technologies or statistics can empower these generative forms, we should embrace them. But we also need to be wary of how tools can bring a certain "habitus" (as Bourdieu called it) with them. Mark Twain said the same thing without any fancy latin phrases: "when your only tool is a hammer, all problems look like nails".

Many of my colleagues use statistical tools to seek out racial bias in algorithms. That's great, but eliminating bias in bank loans or housing rentals does nothing to address the incredible injustice in the power wielded by banks and property ownership regimes in the first place. Rather than focus exclusively on bias in the various commercial platforms that exist (facebook, Amazon, Uber, etc.), we need to create platforms that are owned by the users themselves. In the US the name for that is "platform cooperativism".[3] The African versions predate that by a few milennia (when I say ubuntu I don't mean the linux distribution). So they have advantages in their pre-integration with African ecosystems, forms of justice, etc. But for that very reason there are challenges in creating hybrids with modern tools; especially if we want that hybrid to embody the habitus of ubuntu rather than Uber.

PC Your NSF-funded research in USA on "generative STEM" investigates on new approaches to putting science and innovation at the service of under-served populations. What is going to be the social role of innovation technology in African countries? What would be the best way of bridging digital fabrication and indigenous material technologies in African economies? What would be the environmental impact?

RE As I implied above, central to many African cultures are a cluster of concepts around power of self-generation: how a plant produces a seedling; a human produces a baby; a culture gives birth to its arts, language, music and so on. We have unfortunately been inundated with the Disney version, "the great cycle of life". But circles are actually pretty boring dynamics. Misrepresenting African cultural dynamics as circles, the "timeless ancient culture" trope was invented to help colonizers create the illusion of primitive people stuck in the past. Actual Indigenous cultures include hybrids, mutations, innovations: the great evolution of cultural life.

So while I sometimes use the term "circular economy" in order to communicate with a wider audience, I am not very happy with that phrase. Usually advocates of the circular economy really mean 100% recycled industry, not any change in wealth ownership or democratization of power. We might look towards African generative models as a better alternative: not just unalienated ecological value, but also unalienated labor value (working as artisans) and unalienated social value (prior to colonialism the "acephalous" African Indigenous cultures enjoyed included more liberated forms of sexual expression; spiritual diversity; autonomy and so on). Contemporary innovations have been most successful at creating hybrids between these Indigenous traditions and contemporary technology at the small scale. Could we create a fractal economy; one in which similar integrations of justice and sustainability can happen at every scale?

Some of our experiments towards that end involve stitching together small projects into larger networks. For example the adinkra textile dye in Ghana is made from tree bark, harvested such that it does not kill the tree. The harvesters are an active force against deforestation, so that technologies to enhance production actually protect more forests. The solar production of dye to replace wood fires makes the process carbon free, reduces the cost, and eliminates the health hazard of smoke. Another component of that network included adinkra in education. We found that the logarithmic spiral is often featured in adinkra symbols that modeled organic forms in nature. Children using simulations of adinkra[4] learned the math and computing lessons more effectively, and showed more computing career interest, in controlled studies.[5] Learning about adinkra use in an HIV campaign led to the development of a DIY condom vending machine.[6] In the most recent twist, we had folks who embroidered adinkra on clothing producing symbols on the computer, cutting the fabric with a laser cutter, and incorporating a matching face mask for virus protection.[7] As these become networked together (as in this diagram) we can imagine how innovations in AI, GIS and other information technologies might aid in developing networks of networks (for more about that see our article "automation for the artisanal economy").[9]

PC You are also involved in education at the Stamps School of Art & Design of the University of Michigan. What is the kind of teaching agenda of an ethno-mathematician teaching in a school of art and design? In which way are you sharing your African knowledge with your American students? How would you shape your teaching agenda if you were asked to teach in a school of art and design in Africa? How would you imagine a decolonised approach to architectural education?

RE I start my students with our Culturally Situated Design Tools[10] (CSDTs) so they can try out the fractals in African design themselves, and creatively think with African algorithms from day 1. In one outreach project we teamed up our undergrads with Detroit African American high school students. They did some great work using the CSDTs to simulate everything from local graffiti to african textiles. The high school students tended towards local interests, so that pushed the teams towards local design examples. One surprising result of that was the prevalence of scaling designs in the buildings created by Black architects, such as the nonlinear circles in the roof of the AME church designed by Nathan Johnson, or in the African art museum designed by Howard Sims. Both had traveled to Africa, and you can see echoes of Indigenous scaling geometries in their work.

Of course my students also end up reading about African culture as well. Last semester I had them train a bit in basic systems science concepts, running feedback simulations and such from our website.[11] Then I gave them a stack of African culture readings – Indigenous use of fire in savannah maintenance; restorative justice in traditional culture; the role of play in hunter-gatherer societies; and so on-and asked them to create system flow charts showing where value was generated and how it circulated back. The work by the Stamps school undergrads was amazing!

The most recent teaching experiments started in Kumasi, Ghana with Creativity Group, who hosted our CSDT workshop in August 2019. Those students, mostly from Kwame Nkrumah University of Science and Technology, took a radial algorithm we had used to simulate Native American quilts from the Anishinaabe tradition (radial because they are based on the medicine wheel). They applied adinkra symbols, creating a sort of cross-Indigenous mashup. No one said ethnocomputing has to create ethnic silos! Then in the spring our Stamps students took those designs into a collaboration with the MBAD African Bead Museum in Detroit. We started with using the CSDTs to create other variations on traditional African algorithms, laser cutting them into wood and then applying plant-based dyes in a collaboration with Olayami Dabls, the director. Taking that a step further, we received a grant from the UM Poverty Solutions program to create what we are calling an African Futurist Greenhouse. The plans include both some innovative geometric forms as well as digital technologies like soil sensors and AI. The idea is to grow the plants that get turned into beads, such as the Job's Tears seed used by the Zulu, as well as food, dye plants for coloring craftwork, and so on. So it will give our grad students in the Stamps MDES program a chance to put generative justice to work as a set of design principles, and reconnect growing, making and living in accordance with African tradition, but empowered by contemporary technologies.

1 Babbitt, William, Michael Lachney, Enoch Bulley, and Ron Eglash. "Adinkra mathematics: A study of ethnocomputing in Ghana." Multidiscipli nary Journal of Educational Research 5, nº 2 (2015): 110–135.
2 https://generativejustice.org/diy-condom-vending-machine/
3 https://generativejustice.org/artisanal-cyborgs/
4 Eglash, R. (2018). A Generative Perspective on Engineering: Why the Destructive Force of Artifacts Is Immune to Politics. In Engineering a Better Future (pp. 75–88). Springer, Cham.
5 Babbitt, William, Michael Lachney, Enoch Bulley, and Ron Eglash. "Adinkra mathematics: A study of ethnocomputing in Ghana." Multidisciplinary Journal of Educational Research 5, nº 2 (2015): 110–135.
6 https://generativejustice.org/diy-condom-vending-machine/
7 https://generativejustice.org/artisanal-cyborgs/
8 Eglash, R. (2018). A Generative Perspective on Engineering: Why the Destructive Force of Artifacts Is Immune to Politics. In Engineering a Better Future (pp. 75–88). Springer, Cham.
9 https://www.researchgate.net/publication/335058237_Automation_for_the_Artisanal_Economy_Enhancing_the_Economic_and_Environmental_Sustainability_of_Crafting_Professions_with_Human-Machine_Collaboration.
10 https://csdt.org/
11 https://csdt.org/culture/systemsscience/index.html
12 https://generativejustice.org/afg/

Ugo La Pietra

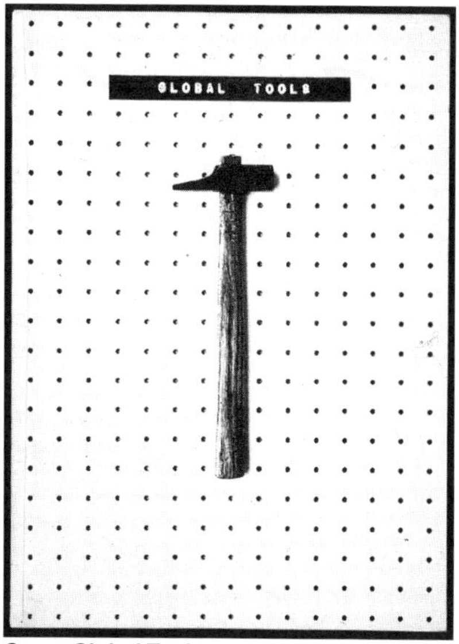

Cover Global Tools

Ugo La Pietra
born in 1938, he studied at the Polytechnic in Milan and in 1964 he got a degree in Architecture; at the same time he made researches on visual arts and music. Architect, artist, designer and researcher in the big area of the systems of communication, he communicates his researches through works and exhibitions; he has been the Director of many magazines, he has worked as a teacher in Universities and Art Schools. His works are part of the most important international Museums' collections.

PC Since decades, "traditional" educational models in the field of design and architecture have been in crisis. For this reason, in an attempt to develop valid and independent alternatives that can generate and share the knowledge, the experience of Global Tools seems crucial. How would you describe that experience today? On what principles was it based?

ULP Yes, since the 60s and 70s there have been attempts, sometimes aborted, sometimes partially successful, to start courses or forms of educational structures capable of starting from the definition of the culture of doing, from the transformation of the material and from self-production (as it was defined that which was already defined in the 60s and 70s). Something that could be the creation of works or objects, something capable of being transformed and transforming a material, which does not always is a raw material though sometimes it is a recycled material. That recycled material, which can be defined as the resources of the territory. This ambition to develop such teaching was tested several times in the 70s, the most recognized and recognizable one was the Global Tools which was an aggregation of radical artists and architects; but then there have been other occasions in which an attempt has been made to start such a path.

PC How did you then apply the Global Tools experience in your path?

ULP From a point of view of what is the desire of creating innovative schools capable of entering a contemporary dimension, the true invention or the real possible method to be developed is what I have identified during my last educational engagement, which was at the academy of fine arts Brera in Milan. In this occasion I founded a department inside the academy based on an artistic design starting from the resources of the territory. A project could not start if it does not look deeply at resources, which are not only physical and material. In fact, I also refer to the resources of a more submerged reality, those stratifications of things and habits and behaviours, in short, of the history that a territory has. This path was a demanding challenge for the globalization to come. The assumption is working in the opposite direction, working to try to enhance the identity of a place against the path of globalization that goes in the opposite direction.

PC **How to subvert the aspects of globalization through teaching?**

ULP Sometimes I am asked what is the way of teaching or the type of teaching that I would like to do. I must say that within a teaching structure, my model is to be able to create models capable of starting from resources, indeed going to discover these resources which is more my attitude as an anthropologist. This could be found in all my researches that I have done in the urban space, a job that even if it has been translated into works, objects, paintings, films, installations. Inside, or better, first of all there is my exploratory capacity of the territory. An anthropologist attitude, the preliminary phase of the design aspect that I had already introduced in my department, which has been identified in a subject called 'Resources of the territory'. The role of the professor was to accompany the students in the territory and make them discover these realities, reveal these values.

PC **How do you see the use of local resources as a cultural approach to teaching compared to a school that takes place in a very young continent like the African one with great unexpressed potential?**

ULP In a small way it is what we had to discover here in Italy, in a period of high globalization: that of being able to give our territories tools to reveal their identity. Why this? Because even in Africa, even if I don't know and attend, the problem is the same. Today in Africa a process of strong globalization of markets is also underway; we all know what the invasion of the Chinese economy is within the African reality. And we all know how this leads to the concealment of all those resources that soon will no longer be seen and it will take the diviner, or rather the diviner anthropologist who goes to these territories and goes to rediscover these values. As a matter of facts also the African society the more and more is discovering today how the economy and the global markets is profoundly changing its organisation. Finally, also the Africans will have a salary soon or later, something they have never really experienced before and this will throw them into a consumer society affecting the transformation of their city. Because even the very low salary, provided by the Chinese and the globalised economy through the exploitation of low-cost labour, could be considered a sort of revolution. This situation is very similar to what happens to our peasant society in 1940s and 1950s when we moved to a pseudo-industrial society where workers with salary and guarantees started to become consumers asking for loans in order to buy cars, TV, fridge etc. This type of dynamic that is being triggered now in Africa will bring them very soon to the values of a globalised consumer society. We in Europe didn't take long, in the 60s we were in this way of compulsive consumption Already Pasolini in the 70s condemned our western society for what we were doing. Africans will probably take less, less than 10 years. So here comes our role, the role of dowsers who go to rediscover and rediscover the add value of these aspects based on the respect of local territories and their resources. This path will be probably done by people like you and by a generation that will operate in the nearly future following this direction. The key question is related to the resources of the territory and the role of designers in dealing (aesthetically and operatively) with a reality in continuous evolution and deep transformation.

PC Which laboratory would you propose to the African Fabbers School students, what would be the title and the activities that you would propose to the students?

ULP Talking about a laboratory is always very difficult. For example, in our faculties of architecture professors talk about the laboratory. Then you go and see that there is nothing as a laboratory, at least like I always thought of it, which is: an informal place where you experiment, where what you do not have to lead necessary to something specific. To me, laboratory means trying, trying and trying. So, having an attitude for experimentation, without particular objectives, without proposing specific objectives. For example, if we say we organize a laboratory to make many baskets, this is a relative laboratory. The real laboratory should be the one that transversally looks through the world of the making and use of things. The laboratory is a place of pure research, in the experimental sense of the word. I believe that the laboratory is an informal place capable of informing and manipulating materials.

PC What is the role of those who teach in a laboratory?

ULP It is clear that an important role is played by the professor, who is the one who looks, stimulates, develops paths and through these paths and can perceive the what I call moments of precipitation. Exactly what I always explained to my students: to understand something and to invent something you have to have a unique experience in the world, which is to observe how the materials are transformed. If I start from materials and I arrive at an object, the path is almost never seen. But if I immerse myself in this process, I will get a tremendous number of information, which will enable me to make an invention. The professor is the one who leaves the students in a manipulation stage and in an open process in order to really let them understand the contribution of experimentation in the creative process.

Hanif Kara

AKT II project-Qasr Al Muwaiji

Hanif Kara
has taught Design Internationally and is currently Professor in practice of technology at the Graduate School of Design Harvard.
He has published widely about design and the interdisciplinarity between Art architecture and technology.
He is a co-founder of AKTII a design led engineering studio in London that has won many design awards including the engineering of 5 RIBA Stirling prize buildings. Hanif was awarded an OBE in 2022 for his services to Architecture, Education and Engineering and awarded the 2022 Fazlur khan Lifetime achievement award for tall buildings and urban habitat. He is the first Engineer in 2023 to be awarded the London Design medal. He is a fellow of the royal academy of engineering, fellow of the institutions of Structural and civil engineers and Honorary fellow of the royal institute of British architects.
He became the first engineer to be appointed to serve on the steering committee and master jury of the Aga khan award for Architecture and first engineer to be appointed in the UK Commission for Architecture and Built Environment and currently serves as a London Mayors Advocate.

PC **Despite the economic growth and the need of basic infrastructures in Africa there is still a lack of African engineers and architects. Can you please tell us about your cultural path since you born in Uganda from an Indian family and educated in UK? How your African origins have influenced your life? how was the life in Bombo in the 70'? what was the impact with European educational system and the lifestyle in UK?**

HK I am of Indian ethnicity, but my grandparents and parents were born in south and east Africa as was I hence I feel close to the continent. My cultural compass and values therefore benefit from this duality add to that I have been in UK four decades and I feel so lucky to have such a rich mixture in life. Life in the small town I was born in was happy and at the edge of rural we were born at home in formal tin shacks brought up on fresh produce and had to fetch our own fresh water; what we often see on videos of kids making toys fetching water etc was a reality form. School was not free but as it was a former British colony we work to the Cambridge syllabus and in the whole town only our headmaster and a doctor at the hospital were of European origin. These formative years made me realise as I grew up the value of infrastructure both literally in terms of land but also systematically and I learnt early they civil engineering offers so much to quality of life; wellness but also the stability of communities and ultimately the state. It is that which gave fuel to my interest in construction.

PC Looking at statistics, despite the climate change the African cities and economies are growing faster than expected. In 1996 you have established AKT II in London, one of the most successful and cutting-edge engineering firms worldwide. Have you ever realized a project in Africa during these years? If yes what were the most interesting/problematic aspects that you were experiencing from the environmental and construction points of view? If not, why this didn't happen yet and what is your relation with African architecture? In any cases, how the new generation of African engineers and architects could face this rapid urban growth within a climate sensitive approach? Could you propose 3 key concepts of such agenda?

HK Yes we have realised a number of pro-bono projects such as schools in east and west Africa over 25 years but in terms of major public projects we are jut about to open the 1800 seat Grand Theatre de Rabat Morocco; it was a design competition we won some 9 years ago and has taken lot of time as we stuck to the winning design; a distinctive Zaha Hadid approach that was inspired by the Bouregreg river between Rabat and Sale. As we didn't comprise on this a lot of capacity had to be built locally to deliver it despite the sound knowledge of Morocco in construction it pushed the industry hard. We are also on site working with Adjaye Architects to build the National cathedral of Ghana which was conceived as part of the 60th anniversary celebrations in Accra. Yes there is a lack of Architects and Practicing engineers on the continent; it's a bit sporadic in that the Maghreb has more capacity than the east or west whilst south Africa has a bigger advantage. This stems also from a lack of education systems on the continent that train disciplines and professions. We have done a lot to encourage and inspire the next generations where we can in places like Kenya; Rwanda; Ghana, and my latest contribution is to act as a Patron of the recently formed African Futures Institute (AFI-Accra). I am very optimistic that the next generations of Africans are going to leap-frog the continent into a very climate sensitive approach Fundamental to that will be the use of climate caring technologies that deal with the context in different parts of the continent including transfer of technology the most basic one being mobility and transportation (air; cars etc); by recognising the correlation of built environment to carbon footprint and learning lessons from mistakes in developed countries (eg materials; waste; flood preventions) and most of all trying had to reduce the gap in equity that exists in the continent.

PC As Design Director of AKT II you have developed a particular "led-design" inter-disciplinary approach connecting structural and environmental criteria towards sustainable constructions. How would you see the relation between an advanced approach and indigenous construction systems? How these would inspire contemporary architecture evolving the pre-colonial culture and translating the logic behind spontaneous tectonics into a more contemporary design agenda? How could we learn from these vernacular techniques and eventually apply these in Western contexts?

HK To be honest I get a little frustrated when we are always searching for the "new" or acting as "do Gooding tourist from the west" there is a lot to find in the indigenous construction especially when we view it with the most advance lens of technologies and tools. That is an approach that requires research on one hand but relies heavily on capacity building locally so that there is a social impact but also encouragement to not be frightened of modernisation. Better planning or Rural-Urban and Ruraban is a key to unlocking the approach going forward. Considering all the species is also part of that approach. I feel there is not enough data often when we are looking at projects in Africa and we end up reliant on Codes that were drafted long ago which builds in alien approaches and prevents innovations.

PC **You have recently published a book on "Waste ad Architecture" which seems to be one of the main issues to tackle in African cities in the near future. How would you deal with the question of accessible "waste to energy" solutions for Global South? How would you develop a local construction industry approach for architectural components within a circular economy approach in Africa? What would be the social role of technology and digital manufacturing in such process?**

HK This would need a long study and I would be very cautious plucking from the air answers from the lens you refer to as that work was pretty specific in encouraging a comparison between two developed parts of the world ;North America (where landfill is still prevalent) with Sweden and Scandinavia (almost zero landfill) where the waste is also used for making Energy which though not entirely clean better than land-filling. Africa has become a dumping ground for much waste from the west so the first thing that needs to happen is to stop that and it actually means interventions into policy that are continent wide as each country is so different in its attitude and economic challenges.

There are good examples of circular economy that have been around for centuries such as the Coptic communities in Cairo that recycle almost ever thing they collect in the city. I think digital technology can help at several scales from monitoring; tracing to even helping recycle and manufacture materials again a lot is going on in this field; I am aware of examples that are aimed at eliminating child labour for instance.

PC **You have born in Africa and like many others you had to study in UK and US where you have been also involved in teaching. How this mix of cultures influences your educational activities? How are you sharing your "African" knowledge with your students at the GS Harvard? How would you shape your teaching agenda if you were asked to teach structural engineering in Africa? How would you imagine a decolonised approach to architectural engineering education?**

HK These are extremely important; valid and big questions that require a much wider and deeper discussion which in this context is as you will recognise quite difficult to answer in short sound bites . I would off-course base all the answers around the use of technology and practical use of it through many precedents... I think design and build studios that have resource real exchange (students cross collaborating with universities in west rather that west just imposing a pedagogy) is something I would be interested in. I am also very keen on developing vocational training where crafts are taught locally to improve the built environment and at the other extreme engaging very young school children in the benefits of STEM education. We for example even worked on short term workshops in Addis Ababa on designing and making façades using local craft but combining that with advanced simulation and design tools the outcomes were incredible it showed there was not only an appetite but also a very capable potentiality. I have to say that knowledge is key where "African or European" and its transfer and use is blind to where you are as long as it delivers more contextual; relevant and sustainable outcome. What we cannot assume is that a universal approach would work everywhere in AFRICA, hence the answer to your question would depend very much on where exactly is Africa we were focusing on.

Vincent Kitio

Vincent Kitio
chief, Urban Energy Unit, Urban Basic Services Branch, UN-Habitat. Vincent Kitio is architect graduated from the Institute of Architecture of Venice and holds a PhD in Appropriate Energy Technologies (energy efficiency and renewable energy) for Developing Countries, from the University of Rome la "Sapienza", Italy. He heads the Urban Energy Unit of UN-HABITAT, a section that works on three focus areas: universal energy access for the urban poor; energy efficiency in the built environment and renewable energy technologies in urban areas. Vincent Kitio is overseeing the implementation of two regional programs in Africa: "Promoting Energy Efficiency in Buildings in East Africa".

PC You are a Cameroonian architect who graduated from the Institute of Architecture of Venice, and you earned a PhD in Appropriate Energy Technologies for Developing Countries from the University of Rome. With this background, you are now leading the Urban Energy Unit of UN-HABITAT in Nairobi, Kenya. How did your African background inform your interest in energy technologies for developing countries? What did you learn as an African student of architecture in Europe? How has this mix of cultural experiences affected your work at UN-Habitat?

VK I grew up in a secondary town in Cameroon with poor access to energy. In my rural village, where we used to spend most of the time during the holidays, there was no electricity at all. No energy means that all activities are done by hand, with limited productivity. As a student, I discovered that energy technologies were the main driver for development. As an African student of architecture living in Venice, I discovered that Venice was built when there was no electricity or fossil fuel, and therefore Africa should learn from ancient technologies that are human centred, considering that Africa has a huge human labour force and enormous untapped natural resources. Putting these resources to use will help Africa address its challenges.

The cultural mix helped me a lot in my daily work at UN-Habitat. First of all, talking about Africa, I'm aware of our daily challenges. I have relatives living in both poor and rich neighbourhoods, so I understand African problems. At the same time, my academic background gives me several technological solutions that might be borrowed to address some of today problems. I also have an ability to quickly analyse the appropriateness of the technology to the local social, cultural, economic, and environmental context.

PC Analysts report that Africa's population has nearly tripled from its estimated 478 million in 1980 to the current estimate of close to 1.3 billion, and it is projected to increase to 1.5 billion by 2025 and 2.4 billion by 2050. The number of people living in Africa's cities is expected to expand

by 600 million over the next two decades. At the same time, 60% of Africa's urban population is packed into slums – a far larger share than the average 34% seen in other developing countries. Only 16% of urban households in Africa have permanent roofs, and access is even lower in rural areas. How is UN-Habitat dealing with this complex scenario? Is the question of supporting policy makers and local governments having a real impact in African cities? Can you provide some concrete precedents that have been implemented? What might be an innovative paradigm to respond to the need for accessible and sustainable housing solutions for slums?

VK Rapid population growth and unplanned urbanisation are the top challenges of the 21st century. UN-Habitat is fully aware of that, and our work aims to assist both national and local governments to face the reality of unplanned urbanisation and the lack of adequate basic services with different tools, advisory services, policy reforms, etc. Yes, our work really impacts African cities. We have different projects around Africa, ranging from assisting government to develop their national urban development plans to helping them develop urban development strategies. Several blueprint documents have been developed in consultation with city stakeholders. SDG 11 on inclusive, safe, resilient cities and human settlements provides a road map on how to tackle cities' problems. We have developed a template to help countries and cities establish their housing profiles. We also help national governments to review their building codes by mainstreaming energy- and resource-efficiency measures. Addressing African urban challenges requires a structural response. We need systemic solutions, starting from an education system that addresses the basic needs of the population. We need government institutions that are well equipped to respond to these issues. Good governance needs to be put in place. Job creation should be the solution to African poverty. Africa should also add value to its raw materials. We need more technical and vocational training schools to form qualified experts; this will reduce dependency on external products.

PC **Today, 600 million people in Africa do not have access to electricity. At the same time, even if Africa has produced only around 2% of the world's energy-related CO2 emissions to date, its ecosystems have already suffered disproportionately from the effects of a changing climate. The year 2019 was among the top three warmest on record for Africa since 1950. Could you tell us how your Urban Energy Unit is facing with the issue of providing energy to informal housing? how do you see the question of energy self-sufficiency in this situation? How this could be integrated into new typological housing solutions generating micro-grid communities? Could you suggest 3 key concepts for this?**

VK UN-Habitat is the city agency, and 75% of all national energy is consumed in cities, producing 70% of greenhouse gas emissions. Therefore, UN-Habitat cannot ignore this issue, leaving energy in the hands of engineers alone. We advocate for the use of cleaner energy solutions for informal settlements. We have also worked with national government and power utility companies to develop alternative solutions for energy access in informal settlements. This has helped to remove barriers such as high connection fees and pre-payment systems. Energy independence or self-sufficiency are good options in remote areas and, in some cases, for urban and peri-urban areas where electricity is not reliable. The preference will be to use the national grid with some feed-in system or hybrid connection.

Where land is not an issue, solar rooftop installations can be a good solution. Micro-grid communities are gradually being considered in a move away from thermal power plants. UN-Habitat has been advocating for the mandatory use of solar hot water systems in tropical cities, as this could reduce the energy demand for households and release more energy for productive uses. The energy efficiency also needs to be adopted so that we can manage our demand. Passive building design could also reduce the need for energy for cooling, heating, lighting, etc. The following are three key measures: 1- proper design of buildings according to the local climate to minimise the use of energy; 2- energy demand management (energy efficiency measures) 3- off-grid energy generation (solar rooftop installations to generate additional energy).

PC **Africa holds the key to the global energy transition as it is the continent with the most important ingredients for producing critical technologies. For example, the Democratic Republic of the Congo accounts for two-thirds of the global production of cobalt (a vital element in batteries), and South Africa produces 70% of the world's platinum, which is used in hydrogen fuel cells. Why are renewable energy technologies still underdeveloped? What could accelerate the use of such technologies in architecture? How could this affect the development of local industries?**

VK Africa lacks qualified human resources to transform these potentials into useful wealth. We also need the political will and visionary leaders. Unless Africans develop their continent, no one will do it for them. The integration of these technologies into architecture will take a lot of time; the reason being that: Africa has a housing deficit of over 60 million social housing units and therefore the priority now be to build decent homes for 420 million African citizens who are living in informal settlements. To do this, we need to industrialise the construction industry. We need to put emphasis on mass production of houses.

PC **There is still a lack of architecture schools in Africa. The most reputed African architects (like you, Francis Keré, Mariam Kamara) and experts did not study architecture in Africa and are not involved in teaching on the continent. How do you explain this, and what is your opinions on the new generation of African architects? What would your focus if you were asked to teach energy technologies at a new school of architecture in Africa? How might it be possible to decolonise architectural education?**

VK I taught environmental building science for two years at the university of Nairobi. Therefore, I understand the issues. I mentioned before that the unplanned urbanisation in Africa is a structural problem. We have a very limited number of architecture schools. Following the independence of African nations, the priorities were to build governance institutions and administrations. Teaching science and technology was put in second or third place. Unfortunately, it has taken too long. I should also say that housing was not really the issue. People living in rural homes were, to some extent, living in decent homes. However, with rapid urbanisation due to rural-urban migration and the natural growth of the urban population, the need for building practitioners has become critical, and that is why more schools of architecture are now opening in Africa. Demand for architecture services is also growing now, which was not the case before. The market (supply and demand) will decolonise architectural education. As the need for the densification of urban areas increases, more and more architects will be needed. As decentralisation or devolution takes shape, local governments will need more experts, including architects and urban planners to issue building permits and plan new settlements.

Giancarlo Mazzanti

Prescolares de Atlantico

Giancarlo Mazzanti
born in Barranquilla, Giancarlo Mazzanti is an architect graduated from the Javeriana University in Colombia, with postgraduate studies in Florence, Italy.
He has academic experience as a visiting professor in Colombian universities, as well as in world-renowned universities such as Harvard, Columbia and Princeton; and is the first Colombian architect to have his works in the permanent collection of the Museum of Modern Art in New York (MoMa) and in the Center Pompidou, in Paris. Social values are at the center of Mazzanti's architecture, which seeks to realize projects that give value to social transformations and that build communities.
He has dedicated his professional life to improve the quality of life through the design of the environment and the idea of social equality.

PC **When we met for the first time, in Italy, in Senigallia, you were part of the jury for Housing the Human, and I was presenting the African Fabbers project. My submission wasn't selected, but at one o'clock in the morning you gave your talk about a series of social initiatives implemented in Colombia: schools, community spaces, etc. That lecture, and the conversations we had subsequently, inspired many of the decisions we made when developing the African Fabbers School. Beyond the rhetoric, what is the social role of architecture today? How does it interact with the community in the design process? How does it eventually involve the community in the construction/execution phase?**

GM Team Mazzanti is made up of three different groups: Mazzanti arquitectos, which is in charge of the architectural planning; jardín parlante, which is an exhibition and publishing platform; and the horizontal foundation, a foundation that explores the conceptualisation, implementation, and dissemination of collaborative design tools as a strategy for achieving social justice. We wanted to understand the clear balance and the large gap between how projects are designed, what the clients and the architects think, and the citizens' real desires. Our goal is to create more balanced, just, and sustainable environments. We want to bridge that gap through design strategies that are born from the context, articulate the actors involved, and recognise their wishes and needs.

1

❶ **Working horizontally:**
Transdisciplinary dialogues with experts that move beyond the limits of the problem, taking into account the agents in the context.

❷ **Co-creation:**
An active design and research process, based on play as a factor to generate trust, a testimonial, and social value.

❸ **Strategic design:**
Given that resources are limited, participatory contributions are transformed into design strategies that recognise unkept promises, modularity, and growth by phases as their main structure.

PC Without venturing into improbable comparisons between Colombia and some African contexts, it seems, nonetheless, that there are certain common themes in the relationship between architecture and informality when it comes to generating an idea of community and social resilience. At the same time, some concepts that you mention in your projects often reference the thought of the sociologist Bruno Latour, laid out in his book Reassembling the Social. How are those themes developed in your projects? How can informal culture improve certain aspects of contemporary architecture? Is there a way to translate some of the principles of pre-colonial and informal culture into contemporary architecture in these contexts? In what sense can that approach contribute to decolonising the design processes?

GM The way we approximate popular conditions has to do with participation and co-creation methods, in which we use game-based strategies. We look at the use of games and toys as a horizontal language of interaction and as a tool to produce new ways of interacting and, as a result, to foster new behaviours. Based on an understanding of the context and the interactions that take place there, we aim to create a bond of trust with the actors who are involved, to produce results that are oriented toward the common good.

In terms of co-creation, the aspects we work with include:

A **Map of Agents**
The sustainability of a project requires knowledge that is enriched by a variety of perspectives working simultaneously. Our projects attempt to generate maps of the actors present in the context, including: non-profit organisations, governments, educational institutions, companies, technology, and citizens in general, which provide an articulation with their knowledge, initiatives, and economic resources. This participatory tool recognises the economic and social realities of the context and lets us propose a range of complementary strategies, such as the progressive growth of infrastructures or public programs that focus on activating space and promoting its appropriation.

B **Living Laboratories**
Depending on the scale and the actors involved in a context, living laboratories are a qualitative tool for investigation that is always changing. Through interactive objects or events that influence the urban scale or public space, the idea is to produce environments for open innovation, focused on the user and often geared toward a strategy for intervention or to foster dialogue and awareness about specific problems. The end goal of the tool is, on the one hand, to integrate the processes of horizontal exploration, the space itself, and, on the other, to reach actors articulated through collaborations between the public and the private spheres.

C Events and Objects

We organise active co-creation processes in which we propose participatory urban interventions and activations for the purpose of understanding the context and promoting relationships and conversations with the community.

We create artifacts and apparatuses that activate architecture, making it into a dynamic element that is continually being transformed.

PC Your school designs foreground their role as cultural infrastructures on the scale of the neighbourhood and the city. In one of your recent talks, you defined these projects as "open works", in reference to Umberto Eco. How can schools be understood as cultural drivers in marginal neighbourhoods like the ones where you work in Colombia or where I work in Africa? In what sense can we understand schools as "open works" or open forms? What are the three key concepts when it comes to designing an innovative school in a multicultural tropical context, whether it is in Colombia or in Africa?

GM Any public building in a depressed area needs to be, by nature, a place capable of bringing the community together and offering multiple uses. So, we ask ourselves how a school can become a public market, a production centre, or a place to improve the economic conditions of those communities. In order for there to be citizen participation, and in this case community participation, the projects have to be open to change and participation; in that sense, the designs should be thought of as apparatuses. Above all, they have a strategic function: they foster specific actions, and in this case they are targeted at participation and social welfare. Spaces for education aren't just buildings, they are apparatuses that promote learning and exchange in a particular way. The space itself is a mechanism for learning.

"An apparatus is anything that has in some way the capacity to capture, orient, determine, intercept, model, control or secure the gestures, behaviours, opinions, or discourses of living beings." Giorgio Agamben.

PC What is striking about your projects is the spatial and formal richness that comes from the use of low-cost building components. At the same time, the construction systems manage to respond to extreme climate conditions, like the tropical conditions in Colombia. How do you define the strategy that shapes and articulates the interior and exterior spaces in your public projects? What role does digitalisation play in this process? How much of an impact do space and materials have on making your buildings "green" from an environmental point of view? What might be a new idea of "efficiency" in architecture?

GM Modern architecture is defined by maximum efficiency and productivity. That idea situates the factory as the foundation for all our architectural floor plans, which are essentially diagrams that express use connections, what we call function. Play leads to a crisis in that idea of function as the only way to define actions and connections in architecture. Play, anomaly, heterotopia help us to define different spatial situations and, ultimately, to construct new places and new ways of relating to one another in space.

For whom or for what are we designing in the Anthropocene age? Beyond human beings, architecture should explore practices that replace people as the only existing factor in its definition. Fostering accords between human and non-human actors allows for the construction of an inclusive and diversified post-humanist architecture within a global system made up of organic, inorganic, machinist, political, social, and environmental entities.

Rethinking architecture beyond humanity implies considering the notion of space. Rather than an abstract and infinite void, we understand space as a network of interrelations between different agents, human and otherwise. Space is a place for mediation between the different agents that define complex relationships of interaction to form assemblages of beings, living and dead.

PC **We conceived the project for the Cultural Hub in Douala, Cameroon (the current location of the African Fabbers School) as collective architecture, involving students from the outset of the process. The aim was to imagine the future of the space, understood as a place for exchange and production that would undergo continuous transformation. What do you think is the best way to handle the governance of these types of buildings once they are turned over to the community? How can architecture raise awareness in the community so they will maintain them over time? How can architecture "educate" in that sense? What would be the title of a course you would offer at the African Fabbers School, and which three books would you recommend to your students?**

GM When it comes to setting up a governance mechanism, the foundation of everything lies in trust. Without that, it's impossible to build agreements that help us learn to live together. The exchange of services and objects is clear between the parties involved in a project. True intermediation also has to be based on an exchange of ideas and a structure of support, always rooted in experimentation, always in the context of the laboratory. As I see it, there can be no governance or space for dialogue if it isn't supported by a structure (institutional, communication) that takes responsibility for facilitating meetings and generating settings for a dialogue that runs both ways. There are always imbalances, and we work to find other ways of doing things that respond to different levels of awareness, different levels of balance.

Reflecting on education is more like thinking about "learning" processes and not so much about "teaching". Working in the cultural sphere inevitably entails an ambiguous pedagogy, where meaning is neither inherent in the spectators/participants or imposed by an authority; rather, it comes to life in the moment of realisation. A school is a place for learning along multiple paths, which brings together a wide variety of human and non-human actors.

Ronald Rael

Mud Frontiers, Colorado

Ronald Rael (RRAEL), Designer (La Florida, Colorado – Oakland, California)
is a trained architect, activist, design technologist, multi-generational rancher, and traditional builder. His work blurs the borders between architecture, art, technology, land-based practices, and social justice. He writes books, forms startup companies, advocates for human rights at the U.S. – Mexico border, creates software, invents novel materials and new forms of construction, and designs buildings as an applied research enterprise. My work often combines indigenous and traditional materials and processes with contemporary technologies to speak to the contrasts, contradictions, and complexities of othered subjects, ranging from people to materials, and places, in contemporary society. His work can be found in the permanent collections of the Museum of Modern Art, The Cooper Hewitt Smithsonian Design Museum, The London Design Museum, LACMA, The San Francisco Museum of Modern Art, and the Renwick Smithsonian American Art Museum. He is the Chair of the Department of Art Practice and Eval Li Memorial Chair in Architecture at the University of California Berkeley.

PC The theme of natural materials is very prominent in your work, why are you interested in earth construction? How this approach could respond to both urban and rural contexts according to different climatic scenarios?

RR Earth construction is interesting, because the oldest construction material on the planet, and the oldest buildings on the planet are made of earth. It is also the most earth-friendly building material we as humanity have. Earth buildings exist of almost every typology, from airports, to factories, to government buildings, to agricultural structures. They also exist on every continent, except Antarctica, and in every climatic zone. Additionally, earth buildings make up the building stock in both urban and rural environments. More closely related to my own personal experience, my family has lived in earthen houses for the last several hundred, if not thousand, years. Therefore, I recognize how comfortable, beautiful and elegant earthen buildings are.

PC Looking at the work of Emerging Object the link between indigenous material technologies and digital fabrication is very important. How this could generate a new ecological deal in architecture? How do you see the balance between human labour and advanced technologies?

RR For many reasons indigenous knowledge is often quieted, destroyed, or ignored. This unfortunate circumstance has let to disastrous consequences for our planet's knowledge base. Language, food, medicine, agriculture, and the built environment have all been affected by rampant advances in what has been seen as 'progress', but which has set the planet back environmentally for several centuries. Often, advances in technology are available only to few, rather than many. The link Emerging Objects makes between technology and indigenous material practices is both a continuation of my own indigeneity, but also a way to broaden the conversation about who has access. Our goal has been to create software, hardware, and materials that are accessible to everyone, not only those who can afford it. Therefore, this is also a story about awareness, because our robots do cost money, but 3D printing has given earthen construction new attention, so even if 3D printing with earth is not possible for some (or yet), we can still share the story of the benefits of earthen construction.

PC You are are directly involved in the fabrication aspects of your projects, how manufacturing and prototyping is informing your creative process? Is this aspect strategically involving also the community you are dealing with?

RR I am directly involved in the fabrication aspects of all our projects as I have come from a tradition of building. The idea of access is also about sharing, so some of our projects have involved local community members, university students, and I also share the work with visitors who care to learn more about the traditions or advancements that the work encompasses.

PC In year 2019 you have installed three pink seesaws on the US-Mexico border to allow children on each side to play together. What should be the social/political role of architects? How architecture could deal with the question of migration and social equity?

RR I believe architects have a responsibility to improving the built environment, as well as respecting the non-built environment. What comes with this responsibility is recognizing who participates in the spaces one designs, and to that end, if there are spaces that are threatening to the public, I believe we have the skills to make corrections to those spaces. The definition of politic is to be sensible and judicious, and so therefore, it seems imperative for architects to understand the politics of their work. Your question about how architecture can deal with migration and social equity is not only for me to answer, but is really a question to all architects that is a call to action. There are so many ways that architects can contribute to this question, from designing the spaces and places that are inhabited by those who are under-represented to identifying new programs and building types that reflect a changing world. We should be designing anti-violent, anti-racist, and humanitarian spaces with optimism for the world to come.

PC You are also involved in education at the University of California Berkeley, how would you shape your teaching agenda if you were asked to teach in Africa? How would you imagine a decolonised approach to architectural education?

RR I have taught courses in the African context, envisioning projects for Africa, working with African students, and organizations from Africa. When doing so, I take the role of both teacher and student. The opportunity to teach in Africa is also an opportunity to learn. A decolonized approach to teaching begins first with listening and learning. I was fortunate as a student to have the opportunity to travel to Africa and have worked with groups in Senegal, Mali, Algeria, Morocco, Kenya, and Sudan. I count these experiences as a major part of my own education from the people (students, leaders, community members, and organizations) I count as my teachers. Recognizing the genius of those whose voices are less heard from is perhaps one way to envision a decolonised approach to architectural education.

Teetertotter, Slotted Through the U.S./Mexico Border Wall. Credit Ronald Real

AbdouMaliq Simone

Tanger suburb

AbdouMaliq Simone
is Senior Professorial Fellow at the Urban Institute, University of Sheffield, co-director of the Beyond Inhabitation Lab (Turin) and Visiting Professor of Urban Studies at the African Centre for Cities, University of Cape Town. Key publications include, For the City Yet to Come: Urban Change in Four African Cities, Duke University Press, 2004, and City Life from Jakarta to Dakar: Movements at the Crossroads: Routledge, 2009, Jakarta: Drawing the City Near: University of Minnesota Press, 2014, New Urban Worlds: Inhabiting Dissonant Times, Polity (with Edgar Pieterse, Polity 2017), Improvised Lives: Rhythms of Endurance for an Urban South (Polity 2018), and The Surrounds: Urban Life Within and Beyond Capture (Duke University Press 2022).

PC **Since 1977 you have been doing many jobs in different cities across Africa and Southeast Asia dealing with very diversified fields of investigation: community development, housing, social welfare etc. Could you tell about your path, how your education and personal life have affected your interests in African urban dynamics as an intellectual and activist? How your theory by practice approach has informed your research agenda?**

AMS Much of my early years was spent living just at the outskirts of one of those iconic long-established popular neighorhoods – Congo Town – in Sierra Leone's capital, and with annual summers spent in Detroit. These alternations, coming and going, inscribed a particular methodology of seeing and feeling the interstices and extensions of each urban context between and upon the other. Just living just on the other side of a set of multiple tracks, as a hinged door producing different angles on things; a livelihood based on circulation. In subsequent years as an adult a range of personal and professional circumstances would provide a formal platform for being somewhere but without sufficient substance in order to be sustainable, thus compelling the adoption of various practices and engagements in order to make ends meet – some of them developmental, others "far off the books." Within contexts where one is ultimately a stranger or denizen, the only option is often to parlay that status as a resource to someone, or to identify the slim threads of common belonging, such as being a Muslim, as a legitimacy to be present within emerging processes that could be steered in unusual ways. So the research agenda has always been informed by a series of tactical orientations to imposed situations, to turn different marginalia into a platform to both ambiguate the field but with a clear ethical imperative.

PC In most of your work, as an international development practitioners and urban theorist, there is a specific interest on analyzing informality issues related to the everyday life of African cities. What is the social role of informal economies in generating solidarity and distributing resources in African neighbors? How this is informing public and relational spaces? How these dynamics could inspire new ways of shaping and evolving the urban fabric of such neighbors?

AMS I must emphasize that my engagement with African cities has been limited over the past decade. Many things have changed quite radically, so any observations on my part must take this into consideration. First, the heterogeneity of urban formations and histories makes it difficult to generalize a useful overarching rubric of informality. While a long-rehearsed argument, African urban spaces were subject to many different modalities of systematic organization reflecting their positions within different circuits of trade, population flows, logics of sovereignties, religious and cultural expressions. Institutional formatting of space and economic activity could be quite definitive, and spatial arrangements would reflect formal deliberations among different associations and structures of power. Second, different stages of urban settlement and the macro-forces that impacted them have produced very different spatial products and patterns informed by their own internal logics of self-organization and external administration, and where the relationships among seeming discrete territories within a single urban setting require continuous mutating forms of articulation and coordination. Where rapid growth has exceeded the capacity of existing governance structures to effectively mandate adherence to specific laws, policies and procedures, the coherence of the city has been more or less attained through political technologies that may seem to be "informal" but rather are a panoply of negotiation, contestation, and autonomous regulation that are specific to the task of trying to suture together divergent historical, demographic and economic conditions. The enormous growth of many African metropolitan regions has necessitated the tacit strategic emphasis on attempting to convert the sheer fact of urbanization into a "market", whereby the exigencies of finding and substantiating a place in which to "settle" generates needs of all kind for which established systems of provisioning cannot adequately address, and so such provisioning becomes the locus of all kinds of more improvised, provisional arrangements, which require intricate choreographies among institutions of all kinds, of different actors being assembled in multiple ways to address those needs – often in ways that approximate our conventional notions of solidarity, but which also are not always contingent upon them.

PC The question of decolonising the contemporary cultural and economic models in Africa has a lot to do with the notion of self-sufficiency, reconsidering the add value of the "city as factory" African model. What is the role of indigenous material technology and local self-organised manufacturing activities in African society? What is the environmental impact of this self-organized model and how this spontaneous circular economy approach could be empowered and eventually declined also in other contexts?

AMS Processes of autoconstruction often prioritize the mobilization and repurposing of materials at hand in order to at least temporally establish some viable form of settlement. This is an aspect of what I have signalled above as the conversion of urbanization processes into new circuits of production and consumption "from below", if you will. Self-sufficiency also is not only a statement about autonomy but also a communication of the egalitarian, that in demonstrating that where and how one lives has been attained by one's own work there is a social calibration that mitigates the potential for envy, competition and conflict. Neighbors who all appear to live in modest, self-constructed dwellings may indeed vary greatly in their access to resources and income, but choose not to manifest this disparity within the built environment. This certainly is not the onky orientation as one can observe the opposite trend to building highly ostentatious structures, some of which will long remain nearly empty on the inside. Across the South, landscapes are replete with things that remain half-built – when residents have access to money they will build as much as they can, anticipating future needs; others simply run out of money, not able to realize the entirety of their plans; still others take advantage of various laws that peg property taxation to the completion of a structure. Here the symbolic values of concrete and other supposedly non-indigenous building materials far outweigh the salience of what might otherwise be considered more appropriate technologies and materials. That said, certainly highly elaborate circular economies do exist as easily witnessed in the voluminous markets of recycled materials of all kinds, many of which are indeed repurposed, but many of which end up going nowhere and rather exist of strange archives that signal a particular trader's prowess at accumulation. Local manufacturing has long been undermined by underinvestment, unviable commodity chains, and floods of cheap imports. But there is a long-established base of enduring production that has enabled cities to endure and expand, but requires more inventive and substantial mechanisms of integration into different trading regimes, as well as valorization by governments.

PC In your book "City Life from Jakarta to Dakar" you talk about "Inventive Methods for Engaging Urban Fields" in different Asian and African cities. Could you explain the key aspects of "black urbanism"? How these methods could generate new paradigms and evolutionary ways to define innovative approaches to shape community-oriented projects in Africa?

AMS There is presently a great deal of renewed attention to the notions of the "surrounds" of the urban – that which is simultaneously a part and apart. The surrounds is not simply a specific territory in relationship to cores, peripheries, suburbs or hinterlands, but also a social space, a space between clear trajectories of territorialization and deterritorialization. Additionally, the "surrounds" of urban space in the contemporary moment must now be extended to the sensing systems of planetary computation and control constitutive of the horizons for contemporary geopolitical and economic formulations, ones predicated on sustained and maintained inequities. Katherine McKittrick discusses the surrounds as the contexts that perpetuated plantation organization, geographies and life. As such the racial and spatial economy of the plantation contains within it the outlines of contemporary urbanism, especially in, but by no means limited to, the Global South. She argues that the extended concept of the plantation serves as "the shadow" for her "tracing of the geographic workings of dispossession, which intends to contextualize the plantation as a location that might also open up a discussion of black life within the context of contemporary global cities and futures". "The plantation" as site of self-contained economy, politics, law, built environment and surveillance "spatializes early conceptions of urban life within a racial economy," one that necessitated visual regimes of observation, tracking and control. The routinized violence of the plantation that haunts contemporary urban formations and built environments demands visual regimes of oversight, like that offered by satellites and other massive complex systems of surveillance and futural prediction. Here, the prevalent logic is maximum benefit with minimum responsibility. The concomitant risk is that, particularly in contemporary modalities of calculation, maximum benefits from specific and limited inputs will often deliver unanticipated results. Such is evident in all the ways in which urban populations are released from or "let go" of specific forms of anchorage to circulate across increasingly disjointed urban landscapes, consolidating basins of attraction here and there without aspirations for long term institutional emplacement.

McKittrick writes that "the city is the commercial expression of the plantation and its marginalized masses," with the plantation as "a persistent but ugly blueprint of our contemporary spatial troubles" – a blueprint reinscribed and intensified by large-scale teletechnological systems of calculation and remote control so that the urban of the black body happens "elsewhere" and not in the site from whence control ensues and to where benefits of said control accrue. But as with the plantation and slave uprisings, the belief in total control then and now is ill-founded and haunted by the specter of failure and fatality falling on another side of racial divides. Planetary computation understands this well although its narrative of self-justification rarely indicates it.

Additionally, the city existed as the locus through which certain of its inhabitants could reflect on their being as a singular prerogative untranslatable across other modalities of existence. It was the place that formed a "we" unrelated to anything but itself. Yet this "we" was inscribed as the node whose interests and aspirations were to be concretized through the expropriation and enclosure of critical metabolic relations. The city's formation of the "human" also required the occlusion of a wide range of human activity before it became labor, activity that could not be easily translated or reduced to laboring bodies.

Here, the figure of the black body looms large as something that cannot be settled even as it clears the way for settlement. Here, the unsettled, dismembered, taken apart body, not immediately convertible into the figure of sheer labor, elaborates an almost phantasmagorical space of intersections – part human, part vegetative, monstrous, demonic, exotic, liminal, libidinal. Here is the interweaving of the body with bush, dirt, swamp, rain and cacophonies and rhythms. This is a space beyond inhabitation, but yet one that can be lived-with. This is a geography that is displaced from any certain utterance or exposition. It is a "wild" geography constituted from the lapses in a surveilling and punitive gaze that cannot maintain its sovereignty if it looks too long or too longingly. It is constituted by the illusions of self-assurance of domination's efficacy, where the masters think that there is no need to look upon what is essentially nothing anyway. The job of subjugation is already done.

The conversion of blackness into forced labor and a monstrous form of human exceptionality in the long march of "moderns" to a bell jar existence in rarified enclosures of sense and domesticity has kept cities alive. In contrast to the white urban body with its sense of individual responsibility and free will, black bodies were to intertwine themselves into thick fabrics of complementarity and affordances, of dust becoming flesh and flesh neon; with everything packed into a density of contact, of the discrepant rubbing up against each other in multiple frictions, sparks that ignite chain reactions. Without these webs of many crammed causations looking out for any possible vehicle of release, there would have been no city. Blackness was not simply then a vehicle to space things out, to engender order, but also to connote the chaos of intermingling, the loss of boundaries and the dissipations of propriety. The black body was an urban body; forced to extend itself into various manifestations to preclude exhaustive extractions. It is a body renewed beyond the form of the contract, beyond discernible modalities of social reproduction. It is the "real inhabitant" of an urban surrounds.

PC **You are involved in education since long time, with many experiences across Europe, Asia, USA etc. How do you see the state of African universities? How would you shape a course on black urbanism in a school of architecture based in Africa ? In which way are you sharing your African knowledge with your non-African students? How would you imagine a decolonised approach to urbanism education?**

AMS Mahmoud Mamdani has written extensively on the significant role specific African universities played in the elaboration of particular orientations and critique of decolonial projects. While often being reigned in by shifting political regimes, they provided a crucial intellectual underpinning to significant struggles around the viability of different socialisms, liberal ethos, and valuation of knowledge. During the past decades many universities have faced severe budgetary and political constraints, become sites of prolonged militarized conflict, or have simply become warehouses for youth without prospects. Some border on resembling vast informal settlements; others have tactically brokered all kinds of partnership arrangements that maintain multiple spaces of advanced scholarship. As evidenced by the recent pandemic, once sclerotic bureaucratic apparatuses are sidelined, universities are revealed as holding inordinate capacity for invention. The frequently highly skewed generational and gendered arrangements often undermine the capacities of universities to make productive use of their intellectual resources.

That said, most universities demonstrate an inordinate desire to be part of the larger academic world in ways that exceed simply demonstrating their ability to mirror Northern knowledge production. Often with few resources they manage to make significant contributions to a range of social and scientific thought, of which the Les Ateliers de la pensée in Dakar, under the stewardship of Felwine Sarr and Achille Mbembe are exemplary. Here there is a determination once again to engage the generativity of the heterogenous ways in which various settings and actors attempt to come to grips with the different ways in which contemporary Africa endeavors to configure contemporary ways of life that draw upon long histories of engaging the world in its entirety – rather than simply revalorizing notions of cultural tradition. Urban life, with its continuous and tumultuous transformations particularly reflect the interweaving of heterogeneous technical, cultural, and religious contributions that embody orientations to pedagogy and collective living that offer an enormous archive of thought and practices essential to a broader understanding of the urban. This is an archive that extends beyond considerations of building technique and materials, beyond the logics of spatial arrangement to a fundamental reconsideration of what urban life is and does.

Francoise N' Thépé

Museum of Slavery, Benin

Francoise N' Thépé
born in Douala, Cameroon, Françoise N'Thépé has lived in Paris since 1975, and been working as an architect for more than twenty years. She graduated from Paris's Ecole Spéciale d'Architecture in 1999. After 17 years at the head of the Beckmann-N'Thépé agency, Françoise N'Thépé set up Françoise N'Thépé Architecture & Design in 2018. Having worked on the design and construction of many major projects in France, she is now keen to turn her skills and experience to international projects. She is currently working on projects in Africa (the museum of the Kings and Amazons of Danxome in Benin, a mixed-use building in Cameroon...), and has developed links with the purpose of setting up new gateways and responding to major issues that affect the continent, including the responsible use of resources, need for housing, and the development of culture and tourism.

PC Despite the economic growth and the need for basic infrastructures in Africa, there is still a lack of African architects. How do you explain this? Unfortunately, women architects are still struggling to emerge worldwide. What are your thoughts on the condition of African women architects? You were born in Douala (Cameroon) and grew up in Paris, where you founded your office. How and why did you gradually decide to take on projects in Africa?

FN'T Only nine out of 54 countries in Africa train architects (Algeria, Cameroon, Ivory Coast, Mali, Morocco, Democratic Republic of Congo, Senegal, Togo and Tunisia), with schools of architecture being mostly linked to universities. We also observe that many students go to study, or complete their studies, abroad and few return (although this trend is gradually reversing) because there are fewer work opportunities on this continent. The number of architects per inhabitant is therefore very low compared to Europe, and, as a result, African women architects are all the more rare.

This problem – which also exists in Europe – is often linked to social pressure in societies that have remained predominantly patriarchal, and especially in a very male sector of activity. Women architects therefore often abandon their careers, or are relegated to secondary roles, in order to devote themselves to their family lives, the education of their children. As a result, African women act more at a local and community level. In addition, although the trend is once again being reversed, international media coverage is not very representative of the work of women architects, African or otherwise.

Personally, I decided to (re)turn to Africa because I have acquired the experience and the 'credibility', which means that I can present myself as a woman architect and an African, coming from two cultures. I currently feel that the evolution of contemporary African architecture is underway, and I legitimately want to participate by contributing my expertise and my sensitivity.

PC Looking at the statistics, African cities and economies are growing faster than expected. What are the problematic social and environmental aspects of this dynamic? How can the new generation of African architects address this growth by evolving the pre-colonial culture and translating the logic of unplanned settlements and spontaneous design into a more contemporary design agenda? Could you propose three key concepts for this agenda?

FN'T Africa is facing an exponential increase in its demography. This implies a rapid need for housing and infrastructure. Today, few African governmental bodies have a managerial vision of this problem, both in terms of development and concrete responses. They lack a clear understanding of the economic, ecological, and social impacts that will result from it. However, we can see that this subject is more and more present, especially in sub-Saharan Africa. Consequently, architects (as well as landscape designers, town planners, etc.) have a major role to play in this situation in order to guarantee architectural quality and urban coherence. The new generation must be able to support this change, knowing that all eyes are currently on this continent.

Beyond managed urbanization, there is also a form of spontaneous urban planning, an informal micro-architecture that represents a significant part of the evolution of African cities. The question of land ownership is at the heart of this issue because it nevertheless presupposes control over constructions, their viability, and sustainability. (These are often self-financed constructions, initiated by poor populations or people unfamiliar with building codes.) This is why architects must be able to take part in this process.

The first action would be to put architects – specifically African architects – back into the role of expert with regard to communities and politicians, in particular by becoming a relay in the field. It is necessary to adopt a contextual approach in order to redefine the bases and the needs of future populations while making use of existing local resources (materials, know-how and labour, a bioclimatic approach, etc.). This will make it possible to put in place the levers essential to an ecological transition, which must take place in the short term, and to analyse the investments necessary for its proper functioning.

The second action would be to focus on the training and transmission of constructive knowledge, even the kind associated with a so-called 'colonial' heritage, while combining the ancestral cultural heritage present and specific to each culture. New builders (in the broad sense) must innovate by developing these techniques towards mastery in terms of the management of future infrastructures in the medium and long term. The third action would be to develop a real comprehensive city policy by adopting a long-term and large-scale vision, and by ensuring that the governments support the housing sector (financial aid for the population, support in terms of bank loans, etc.). But the question of the long-term borrowing capacity of the banks themselves is also often a hindrance to this.

PC In two of your African projects, the Slavery Museum and the Voodoo Museum in Benin, you were confronted with the question of cultural spaces in relation to colonial history and pre-colonial identity. How did your African/French background inform the creative process when dealing with such delicate topics? What is the African notion of cultural spaces, and how can it contribute to the broader debate on museums as community/urban spaces? What kind of tactic did you develop in order to organise spaces to attract the public to cultural institutions? How did you interact with the local community and institutions during the design process? What are some of the problematic issues when these projects reach the construction phases?

FN'T I can actually talk about three African projects since I am currently developing the Museum of the Kings of Danhomè, in Benin. It's a country that I didn't know at all before. But carrying a dual Afro-European culture has made me feel more comfortable, especially with the issues of colonialism and what has come from it. I didn't have any prejudices or preconceived notions, but rather a critical perspective on both sides of the same story.

African countries have very few cultural facilities; the heritage is primarily oral rather than material. The establishment of museums or cultural spaces is very recent, and it is aimed at a new generation that wants to be able to speak proudly of their history to as many people as possible, to those who are retracing the history of their ancestors, etc. These places are also powerful tourist attractions and financial vectors for the cities in which they are located. They create jobs and a new social and cultural dynamic.

But for this to work well, new institutions need to be formed, supported first and foremost by government authorities so that these institutions ultimately have a real public vocation. In that sense, even before construction, the success of these projects depends, first and foremost, on the establishment of programming and tools for management.

Then, what I'm looking for is to create a constructive mix: to be able to mix modern construction techniques with traditional techniques, and especially local ones. This is what takes the longest when you don't know the country where you are developing a project. You have to find the right partners and interlocutors (often thanks to a local architect) and forge a common history. You have to understand the 'customs' and rules of the market. Because we can also come up against obstacles or complications: the workers are not always trained in certain regulatory requirements, the quality of materials is not the same everywhere, etc. There needs to be constant oversight.

It is also to important to respond to the environmental issues by promoting the work of artisans, the use of local resources, bioclimatic techniques... things that are often lost to make way for an energy-intensive, decontextualised 'international' architecture.

PC Informal housing seems to be one of the main issues to tackle in African cities in the near future. What are your views on the question of providing accessible housing solutions in Africa? How did this vision inform your design for the Ville Nouvelle de Yennenga in Burkina Faso? How did you develop your social and environmental agenda? What was your source of inspiration, and how did you manage the question of scalability and incrementalism in your design strategy?

FN'T Today it is important to find an alternative to the so-called 'international' architecture that has been developed in Africa in recent years. The goal is no longer to adapt urban layouts borrowed from references in industrialised countries, but rather to develop an architecture specific to each culture. However, sustainable construction methods resulting directly from ancestral practices are not the only guarantee of success, and energy resources must increasingly be optimised.

The pressing demographic expansion results specifically in a need for housing. Given the low purchasing power of the majority of African populations, we must be able to offer affordable or even social housing models. And the question of vertical construction is a significant problem in the face of urban sprawl, given that collective ownership is still poorly perceived culturally in most African countries.

The concept of the new town of Yennenga stems both from an anchored cultural reference (the warrior princess Yennenga) and from the existing territory and its potential. By developing a mixed and multifunctional city core, the idea was to create major economic axes and ecological corridors as a link to less dense residential areas. This project, developed in association with Arcade Architecture, architecturestudio, Coldefy et Associés, and Hardel + Le Bihan, aimed to offer a model for a sustainable African city in Burkina Faso, supported by a new strong economic centre.
But the first questions in terms of implementation involved access to water and the creation of road infrastructures.

PC **You were born in Africa and, like many others, you moved to Europe, where you trained as an architect and then also became involved in cultural and educational activities. How does this mix of cultures influence your practice and your cultural activities? How do you share your African knowledge with your colleagues and partners? How would you focus your educational agenda if you were asked to teach architecture in Africa? How would you imagine a decolonised approach to architectural education?**

FN'T I can say that I am more European than African in my training and my education. Despite everything, Africa has always been there for me, at first through my family (and my occasional stays in Cameroon), through some of my friends, and through a culinary and artistic culture that my mother passed on to me. So I am relatively 'comfortable' in both cultures, and I can talk about them with full knowledge. It is all the richer and more natural for me, as a result, to draw my inspiration in a very cosmopolitan way. However, I continue to learn techniques that I did not know and in contexts I was once unfamiliar with, such as, recently, the use of raw earth (and its properties and constraints, depending on the location).

If I were to teach in Africa, it would undoubtedly be either for a short intervention of the 'workshop' type, or on an intermittent basis, anchored by a local colleague, which is the conventional approach. My teaching would clearly reflect what I defend: making the most of existing techniques to offer an architecture with ties to its context. I think there is a midpoint between the 'all vernacular' and the 'all modern', and that is where innovation should take hold.

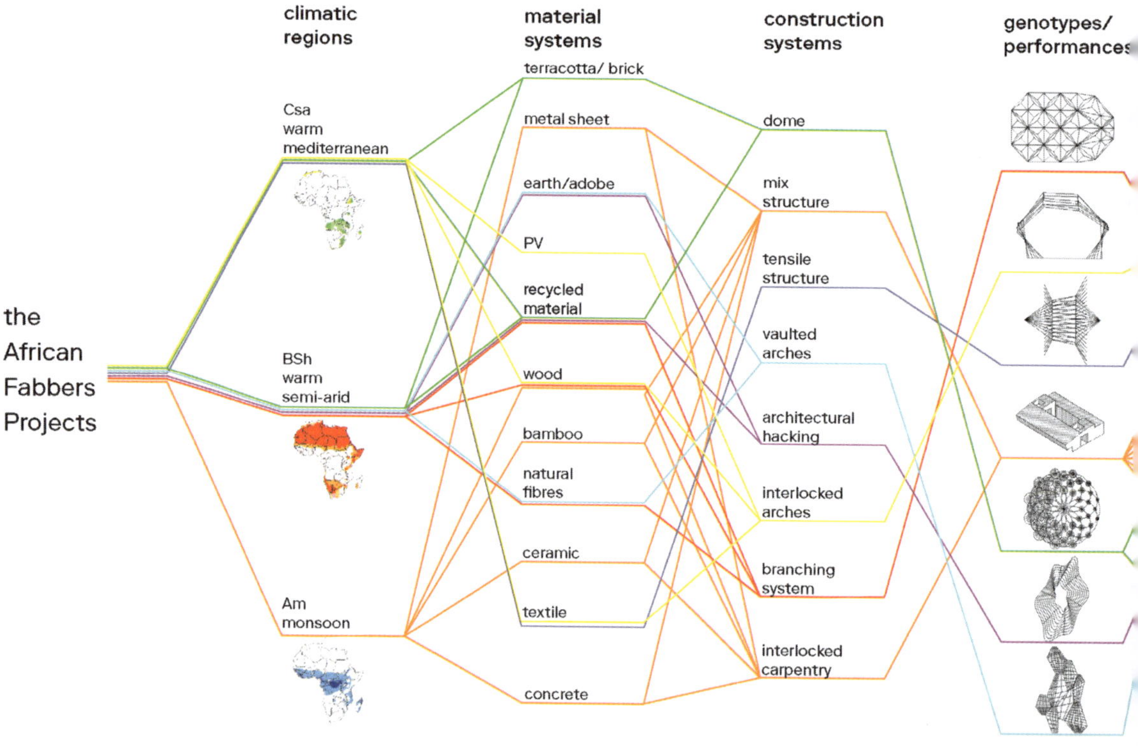
the
African
Fabbers
Projects
climatic
regions
Csa
warm
mediterranean
BSh
warm
semi-arid
Am
monsoon
material
systems
terracotta/ brick
metal sheet
earth/adobe
PV
recycled
material
wood
bamboo
natural
fibres
ceramic
textile
concrete
construction
systems
dome
mix
structure
tensile
structure
vaulted
arches
architectural
hacking
interlocked
arches
branching
system
interlocked
carpentry
genotypes/
performances

III
African Fabbers taxonomies. Connecting high and low-tech cultures

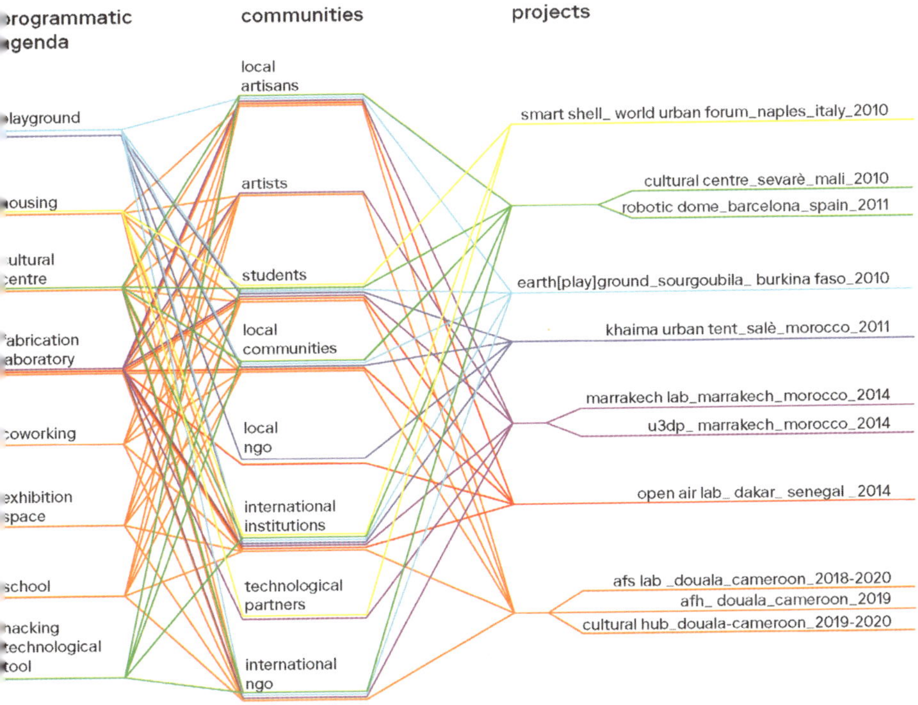

Intro

Since the very beginning, the African Fabbers project has aimed to overcome the dichotomy between manual and digital practices and between theory and practice. There has been a continuous interaction between different skills to create that extra value that we have lost in Western society: the knowledge of how to build together. As the Senegalese economist Felwine Sarr explains in his book Afrotopia, we need to think about African economies in their cultural substratum to avoid the mistakes of the past. This does not mean dismissing the opportunities of new technologies; on the contrary, we felt it necessary to acquire awareness of the local culture while, at the same time, integrating digital culture in order to investigate endogenous solutions. As a matter of fact, there are several studies that demonstrate the great familiarity with digital technologies of the new African generations. For instance, it is enough to look at the mobile phone diffusion maps of the continent to understand just how fast digitalisation is occurring in these countries. What distinguishes these phenomena is informality; and that is why it is crucial to investigate cultural and economic models that can support themselves in osmosis with their territories. Manufacturing is intrinsic to the popular culture of many African countries, and our approach considers production as a tool for anthropological investigation, as a practice with the potential to knit together disadvantaged social fabrics, making a virtue out of necessity.

The AF project derives from a cultural journey that began almost 15 years ago as an itinerant and independent programme that strategically reached very different countries, including Senegal, Morocco, Mali, Burkina Faso, and others. The result of that initial activity has gradually generated an information-based methodology through a taxonomy of climate-sensitive and community-oriented projects, in which we have experimented with the connection between "advanced" technologies and local vernacular knowledge. The AF project was intended to fill in the gaps due to the scarcity of research-by-design programmes in Africa and the lack of joint (African-European) applied research activities on these specific issues, as well as the lack of projects going beyond the rhetoric of the typical paternalistic humanitarian cooperation initiatives. At the same time, we have always viewed Africa as a continent that, despite the colonial aftermath, is growing economically at a phenomenal rate. And new cultural and productive processes that intersect with local demands are needed in order to respond to this development. The main generative drivers of AF projects were the relation between the social scenario and a collaborative form of re-shaping public spaces, as well as the relation between the climatic context, the material systems, and the local construction techniques. All this with the added aim of learning from the African legacy to develop alternative solutions for Western countries to address issues related to climate change based on an ecological and sustainable approach. The fil rouge of these paradigmatic projects is based on an evolutionary way of bridging and sharing different knowledge within a learning-by-doing methodology.

The richness of this initiative lies in the fact that we created a network of actors operating between Europe and Africa, which includes regional and art institutions, prestigious universities and artisan cooperatives, NGOs, private foundations, and individuals interested in the project. Nevertheless, our main interlocutors were local, small-scale craftspeople and young students interested in studying design and architecture. That said, we have also involved European students and researchers who wanted to develop their research with us in Africa. This idea of bringing together people with different backgrounds is one of the key concepts in the effort to overcome the dichotomy between knowledge from the West and from the Global South with the aim of creating a common ground in the response to the challenges of climate change. Although the different projects were developed over time without adhering to a linear path, the systematic approach in dealing with site-specific climatic and social scenarios followed the same causal logic.

That logic is based on the connection between climate, the material systems available on site, and local tectonics, generating a new form of contemporary "regionalism". This systematic approach was clearly emerging as we were working on the exhibition for the 2021 Venice Biennale of Architecture, and we decided to represent the whole effort using a sort of ramified diagram to connect the different projects into a single system of relations. This climate-based diagram was the best way to diachronically explain the kind of common ground that linked each project in a sort of generative archive, where the first sessions informed the more comprehensive experience we developed in Cameroon. For the above-mentioned reasons, the first projects are introduced by theoretical themes, and subsequently a comparative approach explains how the issues were addressed in different cultural and climatic contexts.

3.1 FROM GENERATIVE COMPONENTS TO LIVING INFRASTRUCTURES

Some of the AF projects explored the concept of difference and repetition in architecture through redundancy and optimisation, reiterating the use of modular construction components for diversified solutions conceived as living micro-infrastructures. Two projects in particular explore this topic using different material systems and assembly techniques following the same logic. The first was the result of a series of workshops on the use of bricks (in terracotta and recycled materials) as a generative component. The workshops were developed in collaboration with the Agha Khan awarded architect Fabrizio Carola, held between Mali and Paris in years 2010 and 2011. The continuation of such experimentation was developed with my Burkinabè student Stephane Tapsoba in the frame of the Smart Geometry workshop at the IAAC in collaboration with engineers and robots from ETHZ. The second was centred on the use of a small wooden modular element for flexible off-grid micro-architectures, realised in the context of the World Urban Forum organised by UN Habitat in 2012.

Herbs market in Bamako by Fabrizio Carola

CULTURAL CENTRE — MALI 2010

SITE
Sevarè (Mali)
34°02'24"N
6°48'36"W

CLIMATE REGION
Hot semi-arid

CLIENT
N:ea

PROGRAMME
Cultural Centre

TEAM
Paolo Cascone with Fabrizio Carola (architects), Stephane Tapsoba, Helena Agurruca

STRUCTURAL SYSTEM
Dome

MATERIALS
Terracotta bricks

Fabrizio Carola and Paolo Cascone

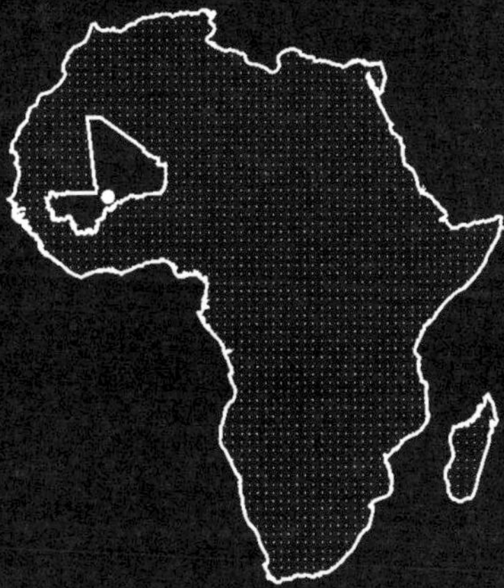

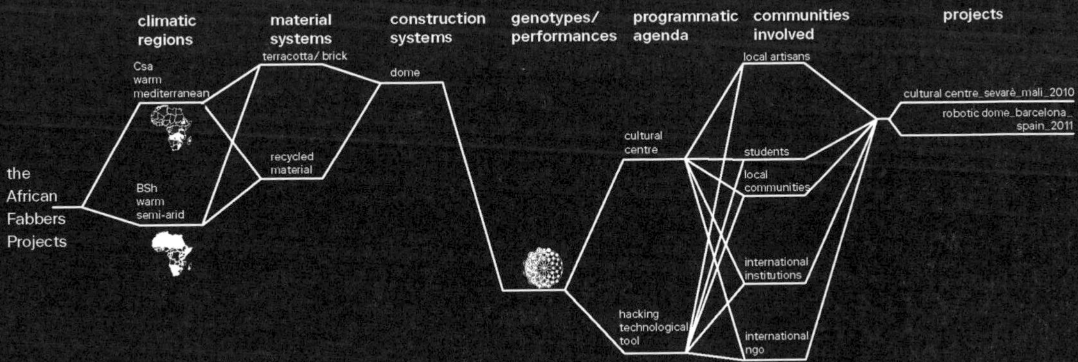

1

Although we were unable to finalize the construction of this project, meeting Fabrizio Carola was probably the most inspirational experience I have ever had in my cultural career. In this article, published in Domus no. 940, I explain how it all began:

Casablanca, 8 august 2010. I am a 34-year-old architect/ engineer who studied at the Architecture Association in London. For the past ten years, I have been traveling around Europe to develop my research on environmental parametric design for performative architectures. This may sound distant from the world of Fabrizio Carola, who has built and experimented with traditional construction techniques in distant lands. In reality, though, I grew up with Fabrizio's work, when as a child I followed my father around Africa and first heard of a Neapolitan architect who was building "new African hospitals". I was fascinated by the idea of a white architect designing African buildings. I come across Fabrizo's work again on a cold Sunday in London, where I had taken shelter in the AA's library. That day it all seemed clearer: I began to understand everything I had been nurtured on and which I had called "ecologic design" (associating the study of form with environmental performances, the generative use if modular structural components, and experimentation with complex geometries and recursive systems). Come from a distance: from people who, like Fabrizio, without the aid of digital technologies or pseudo-avantgard theories, had used construction ad point if knowledge and experimentation. In search of a delicate balance between nature and tekne.

It was a lukewarm April day when I met Fabrizio in Brussels. We spent four hours together in a Japanese restaurant behind the Stock Exchange, taking and drawing as if we had always known one another. I was almost afraid to show him my world, and scared still of not being able explain it to him. However, with his boyish enthusiasm Fabrizio thoroughly understood everything. He made it possible to reach that turning point which, to paraphrase Guattari, I call the "fourth ecology": a sort of generation-cultural pact of knowledge and production processes shared through an evolutionary approach. This is where new technologies integrate processes that have been passed down for centuries, to make them still more sustainable and reproducible on different scales. The urge to put our enthusiasm to the test helped to create the immediate conditions for collaboration on the project for the cultural centre at Severe, in Mali. Fabrizio had already begun working on this task in 2007. When he spoke to me about it he pulled out a plan and said: "this is what I have begun: use it as starting point to develop it according to your own techniques. Hence, the idea of considering this opportunity as a case study in a wider survey. I am developing this in Paris with my study on "high-tech design process and low-tech construction", in which I have involved my French architecture student (half of whom are of Africa origin).

The project for the Severe Cultural Centre, in its ecological being, is intended to become a construction site/school involving, in addition to my student, young people from other international universities, the local population, and other partners whom we are finding along the way. It is participatory construction experiences aimed at uniting people of different background and experimenting, with the new points of contact between traditional construction techniques and advanced design processes for a post-vernacular architecture.

The design process we developed starts from the initial genotype of Fabrizio's 2007 project. From t we abstracted what Deleuze calls the "material system" (a series of principles governing morphological, tectonic and bioclimatic aspects) and then developed in according to a recursive, evolutionary process of his morphology. The restraints set by Fabrizio's initial idea on the development of a series of cupolas, linked together around a central space, guided the creative process. The result is the development of a series of successive generations (phenotypes) of design solutions through what I call "contextual algorithms". The help of parametric instruments and environmental simulations (thermal comfort, passive ventilation, natural light, etc.) enabled us to generate and test families of different solutions in a correlated way, the morphology in the scale of the centre was differentiated according to the programme's spatial and ergonomic necessities: library, reading rooms, IT room, creative workshop, cafeteria and open-air theatre. The objective of this strategy is therefore to alternate a sequence of semi-covered patio/impluviums in clusters of terracotta bricks cupolas, differentiated in their dimensions and forms on the basis of the various activities spatial requirements.

This alternating of solids and voids channels and accelerates the prevailing winds in order to cool the air. On the scale of the architectonic component –the cupola- the strategy is to regulate the porosity of the outer shell and the variation of its form in relation to its exposure to sunlight, to optimise natural illumination and improve thermal comfort. We tested the whole thing during the "smartGeometry" symposium in Barcelona last March, with an initial 1:1 scale prototype realised in collaboration with engineers and robots from ETH in Zurich. Fabrizio, submerged by this "computational tide" was at firs puzzled. Then he called me one day and told me he was very interested in the prototype that we are developing for its realization. He talked to me about the nests of certain giant insects that populate the project zone, which adapt to context by varying their form and optimising matter and resources. So you see, this is why I am at Casablanca Airport now, waiting to board a plane to Bamakò, where Fabrizio will be meeting me, ready to embark together on this adventure.

My first and only visit to see Fabrizio was not just a discovery of Mali and its incredible heritage, but also a sort of initiation into his work, his family, and his friends. For this reason, before starting to talk about our project, Fabrizio organised strategic site visits to different neighbourhoods in Bamako and the Medine Herb Market, the first project he completed in Mali. At the same time, he wanted to introduce me to his world, peopled by friends and collaborators who had supported the different projects over the years. After a few warm-up weeks in Bamako, he invited me to follow him to Sevare, where he had established his headquarters after completing a large number of projects in the Mopti region. For many reasons, much of this work is still unknown, and I was really impressed when I discovered the variety and richness of the building typologies – from research laboratories to guest houses, etc. – always conceived as living infrastructures. I was also very surprised when he first asked me to visit Djenne and the Pays Dogon before I was familiar with the site. That trip on its own would probably warrant another book because of the warmth of the people, the landscape, and the fascinating traditional architectures. It is hard to accept that these places are no longer accessible because of the recent conflicts in the region. After our return, we visited our project site many times at different hours of the day, to familiarise ourselves with the extreme climatic conditions in order to experiment with new forms of domes according to the constraints of the self-made bricks and the construction technique. One evening after dinner, when everyone was tired after a long hot day, we were sketching together and updating the digital model. Fabrizio was anxious to begin building the project and, despite his age and some health issues, he wanted to accelerate the construction. He put me in touch with his young local assistants to shift the generational ratio. I suppose he felt that the whole region was heading for some serious troubles. As a matter of fact, after a few experiments involving environmentally performative domes, the project was unable to continue, and Fabrizio's family asked him to return to his hometown of Naples, where he died just a few years later:

That was probably Fabrizio's last time on the African continent, the conflicts of that region unfortunately did not allow us to develop beyond our collaborative project. But what he has transmitted to me in those weeks spent together, I will always bring to me with pride and a sense of responsibility. I set many years later the African Fabbers School project that I am developing in Cameroon on its human and cultural principles.

Carola's was the story of an independent thinker, one of the few who have been able to develop theory via practical work, anticipating contemporary themes that are crucial for new generations – and for more than just architects. I'll try to put in order a series of notes taken during conversations I had with him – now several years ago – between Sevarè, Paris, Brussels and Bamako.

At the age of 19, he decided to leave his native Naples to go and study in Brussels, despite having a guaranteed future in Italy as the son of a major developer. In 1950s Belgium, he would find in La Cambre – the architecture school founded by Henry van de Velde – a cosmopolitan environment, but above all an approach to design centred on the relationship between form and structure. An inclination to design in order to build was evidently in his make-up. But the school in Brussels, with its close connections with art nouveau, may well have prompted his interest in the links between architecture and the natural world. One thing is certain: his decision to "study outside", his feeling that his identity was primarily European, and his desire to pursue a career independently of his origins anticipated what many of us have tried to do since.

From the time of his professional training, Fabrizio developed his own, highly innovative understanding of the architect's vocation and his social role. Without exaggeration, his projects – first in Morocco and then in sub-Saharan Africa – increasingly became the central elements in a tightly focused research agenda, one equally experimental and rigorous.

Fabrizio very quickly understood that Africa was the right place to test an ecological approach to architecture, in which social, mental and environmental ecology could flow into one another. He grasped that technology would have a fundamental role in this by making building processes sustainable. Above all, he understood – once again, before everyone else – how important it is to work in a state of osmosis with the landscape and the people living there. From this point of view, his interdisciplinary approach can be seen today as very advanced, despite the "primitive" techniques used.

In his work, the building site was also his studio – an applied research laboratory focused on an idea critical in Africa: self-sufficiency. Using this simple concept, he developed a method that could generate concrete responses to problems created by climate change, such as deforestation and impoverishment. Via a simple yet integrated process, he was able to transform the critical environmental and economic issues of a context into generative elements in his designs. Equally, his tendency to see the construction site as a place of production and dissemination contributed to giving his work its subversive character.

His idea of evolving Hassan Fathy's compass to create building shells (such as domes and vaults) created entirely using "0 km" materials was just one product of this. Fabrizio, with his profound understanding of African society, understood how important it was to transform the construction world into an opportunity to redistribute wealth more equally through a community (such as a village or a town district). By reclaiming the vernacular sub-Saharan culture, he saw the potential for interpreting construction as a collective practice able to hold a community together, as happens in Djenne, in his beloved Mali, at the end of the rainy season.

The building site as a factory (of bricks, above all) became a strategic element in the definition of a sustainable approach keeping the dependency on imported materials to a minimum and asserting a model of the circular economy long before we had a name for this idea. This holistic approach generated extraordinary buildings promoting the collective good, such as the hospital in Kaedi (Mauritania), the medicinal herb market in Bamako (Mali) and the research centre for traditional medicine in Mopti (Mali).

However, I believe that it is worth underlining another aspect central to his work: sharing. Although he kept his distance from academia, Fabrizio was always an educator. Above all, he understood how important it is that rising generations "learn by doing". To pass on his wide-ranging knowledge, he invented a system of "building site schools" that over the years trained many young men and women, European and African, even before architects. To have done all this, needless to say, you need to be more than an architect of genius – you need human qualities that are out of the ordinary.

Among the many that I like to recall are his cultural openness, his consistency and his contagious enthusiasm – the same enthusiasm which prompted him, at the age of nearly 80, to jump on my Vespa to go around Paris and explain to me the ups and downs he'd experienced when creating the set design for Werner Herzog's film Cobra Verde.

For the rest, there are theoreticians and academics able to praise his buildings better than I can and describe the role of his compass and the performance of the domes within domes.

For me, and for all those who had the privilege of getting to know him in the field, there remains the promise of continuing his teaching and the invitation to love and respect Africa by going out and physically touching his work.

This was a text I wrote after his death, published on the Domus website in January 2019. I can only imagine how he was celebrated in Mali by his people. Today, although it may be hard to frame his tremendous work in the current debate on the diaspora, Fabrizio's projects still arouse keen interest and astonishment among my African students.

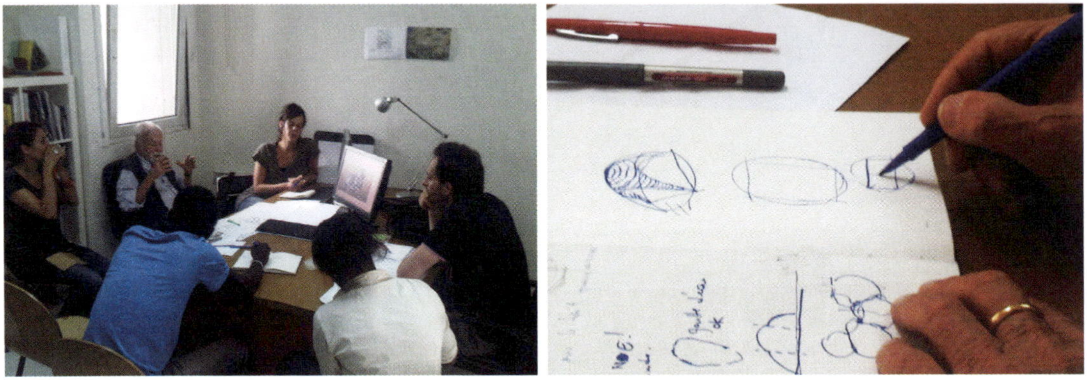
Workshop with Fabrizio Carola in Paris

Workshop with Fabrizio Carola in Mali

Fabrizio Carola's house in Mali

ORIGINAL GEOMETRIC CONFIGURATION

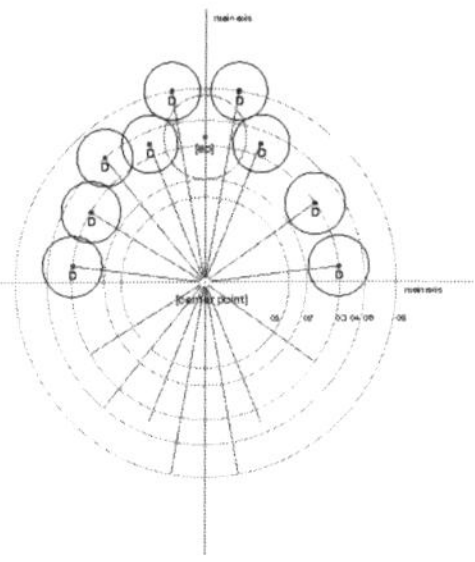

GENOTYPE

01 System geometrical variation {A1}

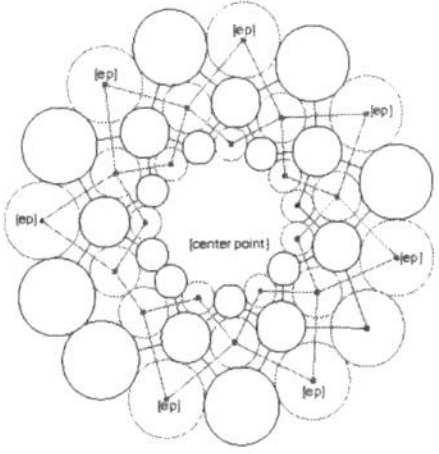

01 System geometrical variation {A2}

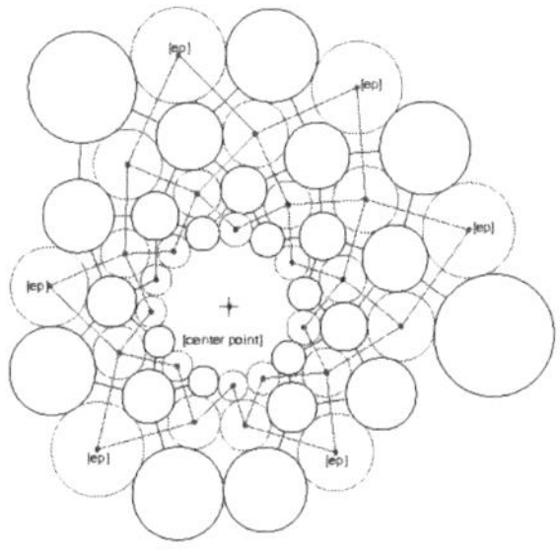

01 System geometrical variation {A3}

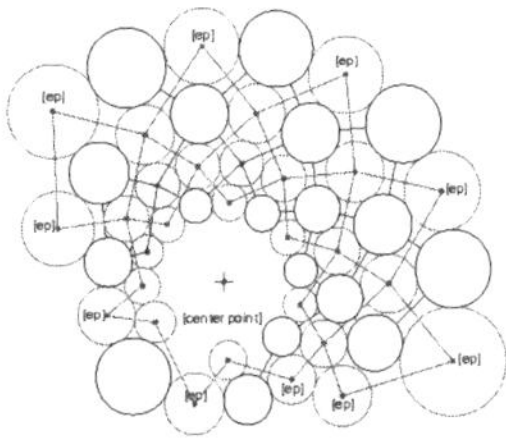

01 System geometrical variation {B1}

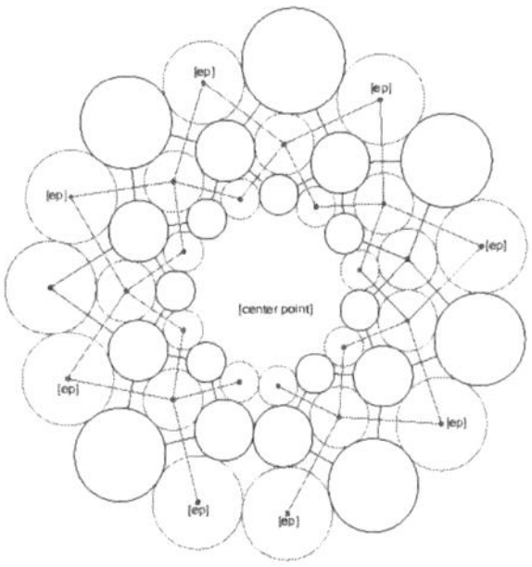

01 System geometrical variation {B2}

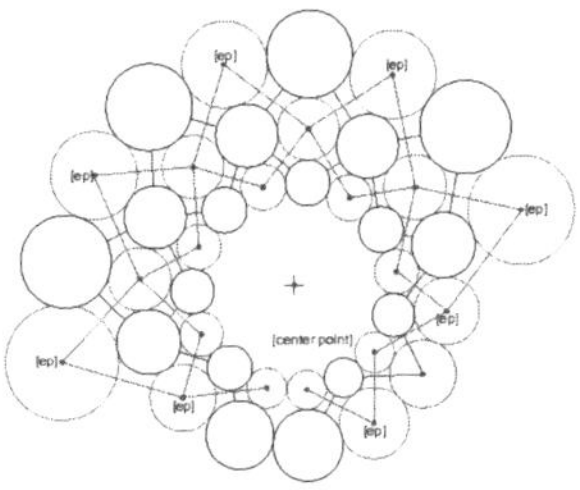

01 System geometrical variation {B3}

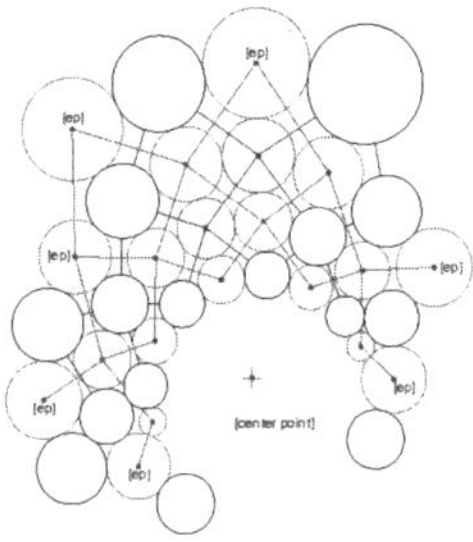

01 System geometrical variation {C1}

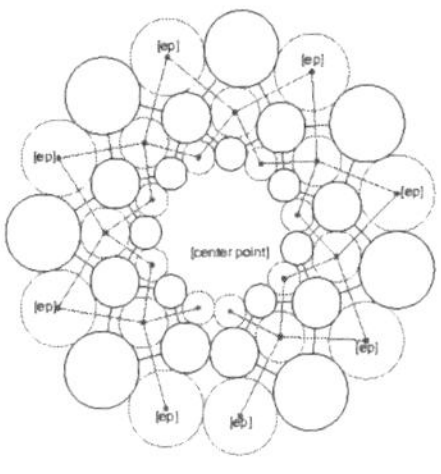

01 System geometrical variation {C2}

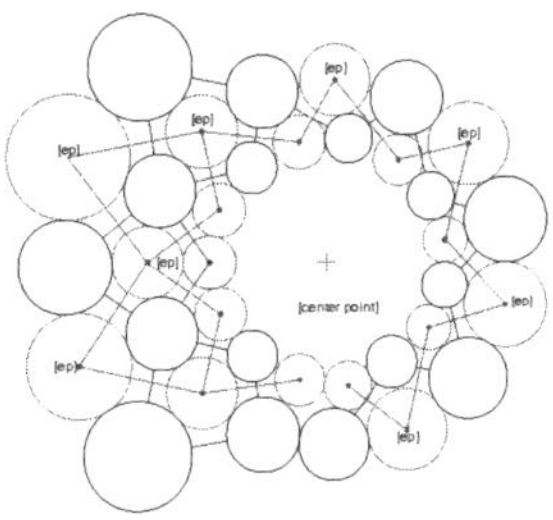

01 System geometrical variation {C3}

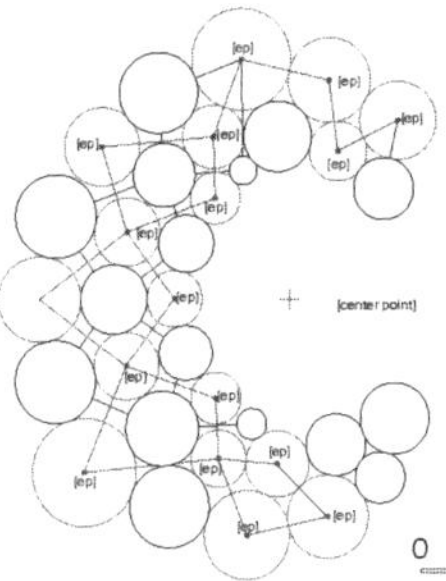

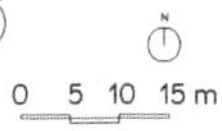

Evolutionary Configurations. Exploration of System Articulation According to Center Position. Extraction of Networked Eco Ponds and Points of Distribution

Geometrical Variation A01
Total Occupation: 530 M^2

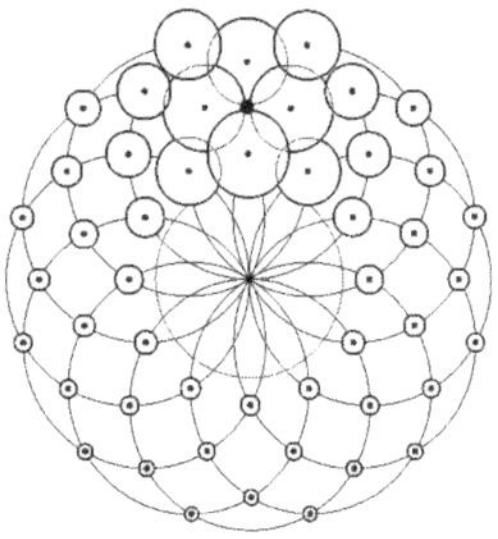

Geometrical Variation A02
Total Occupation: 530 M^2

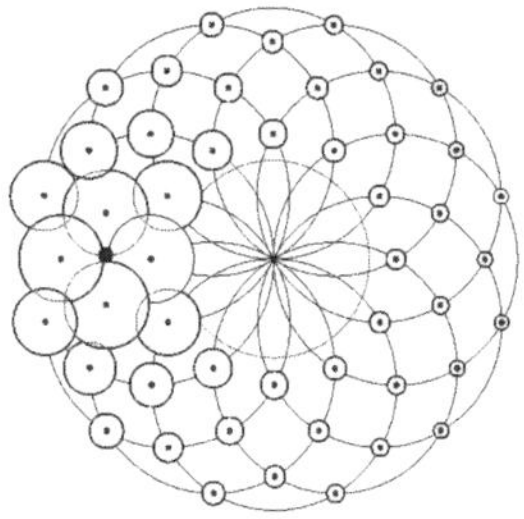

Geometrical Variation A03
Total Occupation: 530 M^2

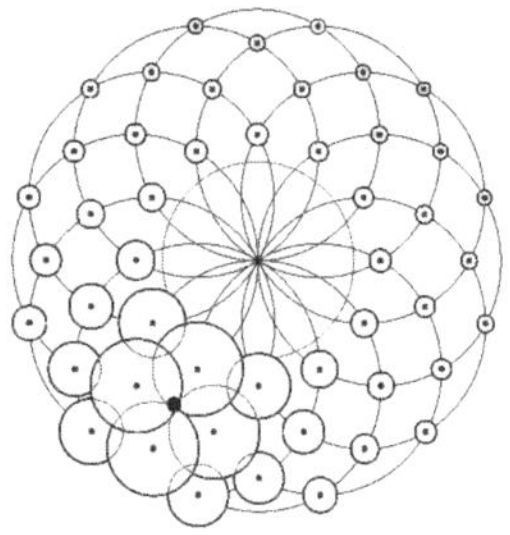

Geometrical Variation B01
Total Occupation: 700 M^2

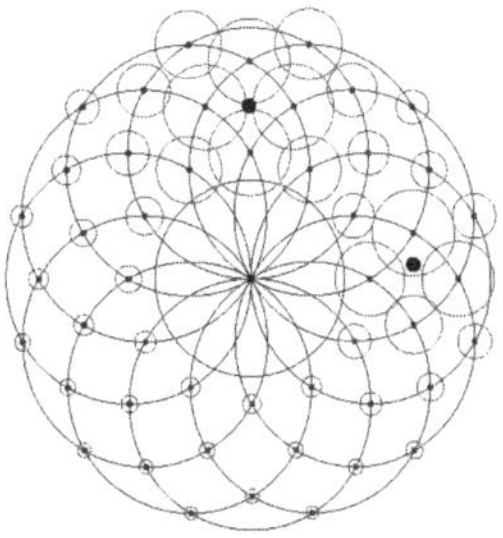

Geometrical Variation B02
Total Occupation: 700 M^2

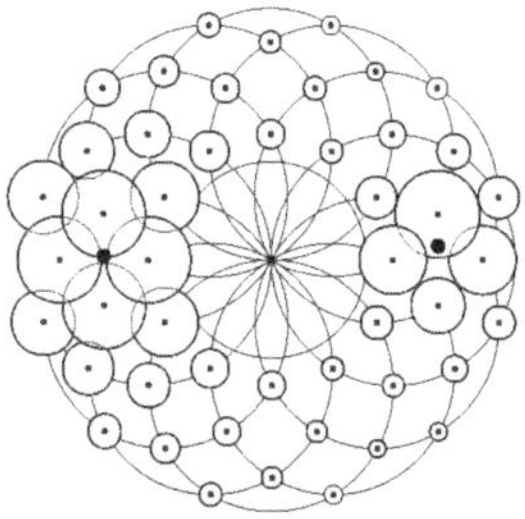

Geometrical Variation B03
Total Occupation: 715 M^2

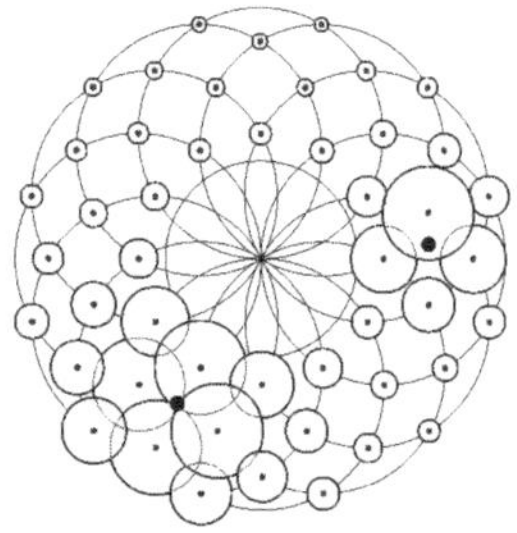

Geometrical Variation C01
Total Occupation: 654 M^2

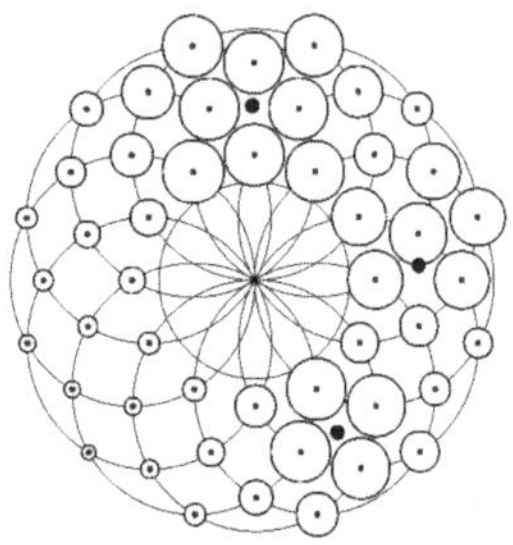

Geometrical Variation C02
Total Occupation: 680 M^2

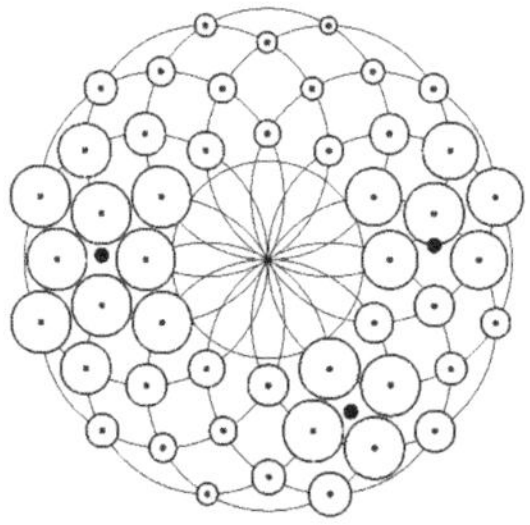

Geometrical Variation C03
Total Occupation: 637 M^2

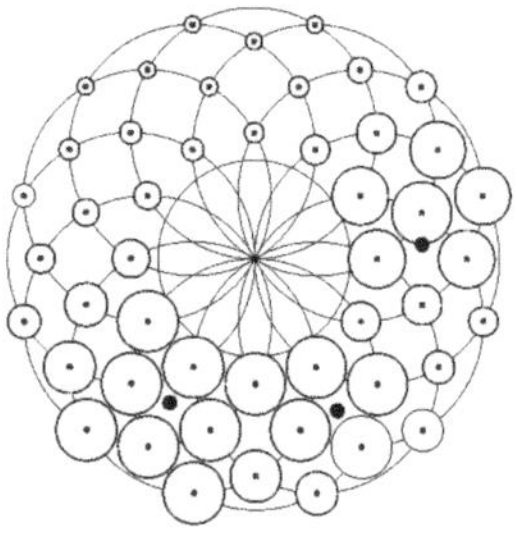

Network Exploration 01
Total Occupation: 530 M^2
Domes Occupation: 225 M^2

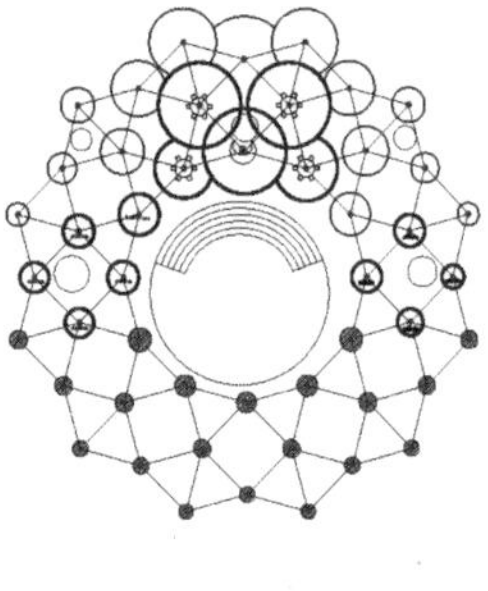

Network Exploration 02
Total Occupation: 530 M^2
Domes Occupation: 225 M^2

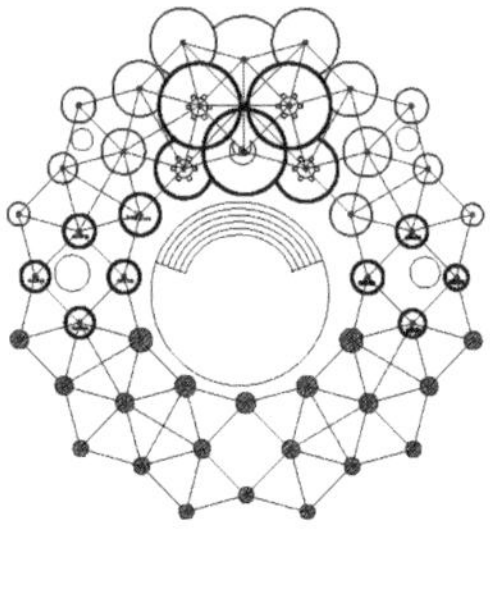

Network Exploration 03
Total Occupation: 530 M^2
Domes Occupation: 225 M^2

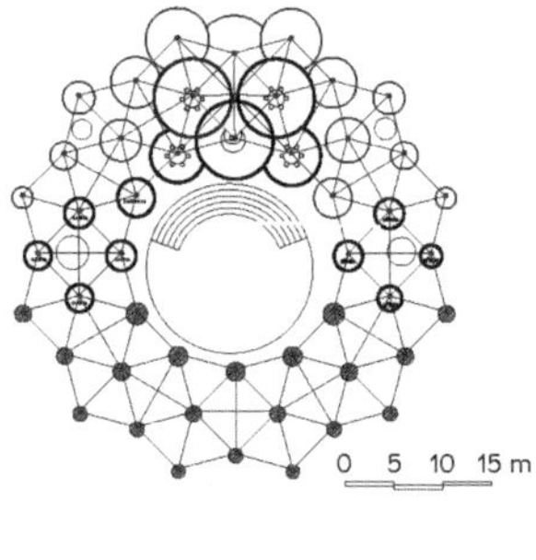

Geometrical type and variation of the original *type_01* point of attraction

A1 Courtyard Network
226 linear meters

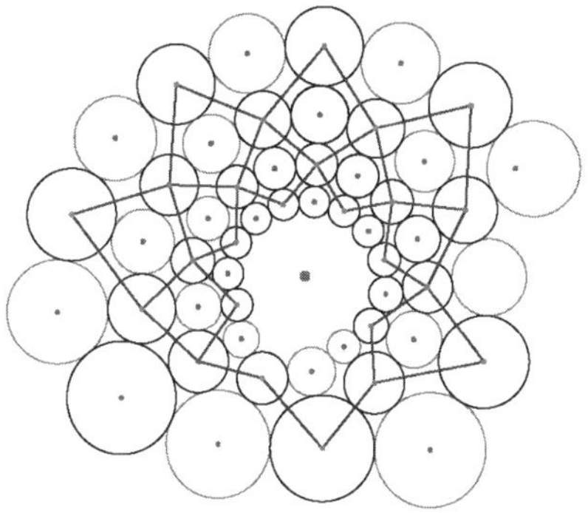

B2 Programatic Network
249 linear meters

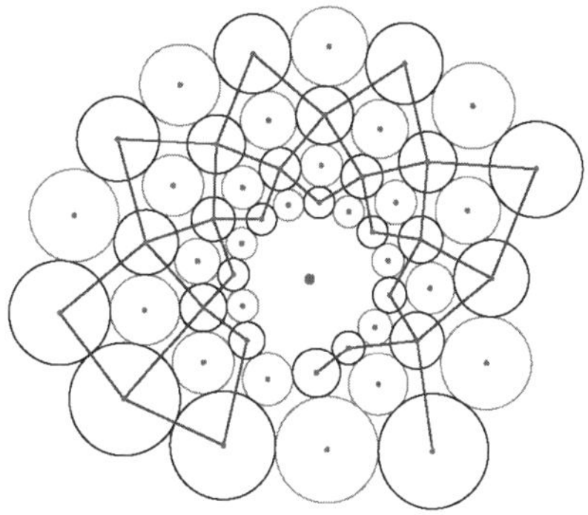

C1 Water Network
Network: 188 linear meters
nb of tanks: 19

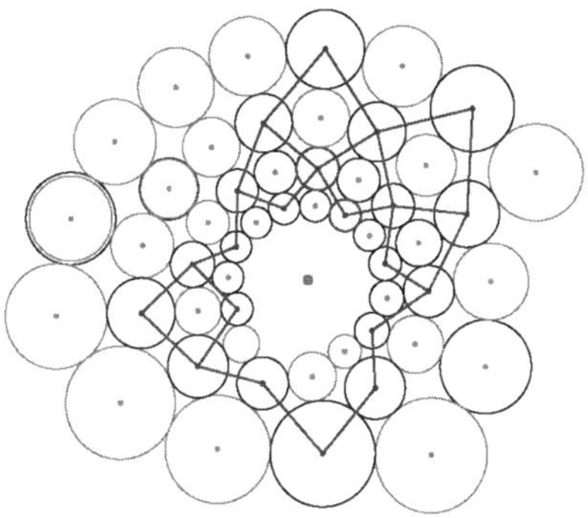

D1 Programatic Clusters
607 M^2

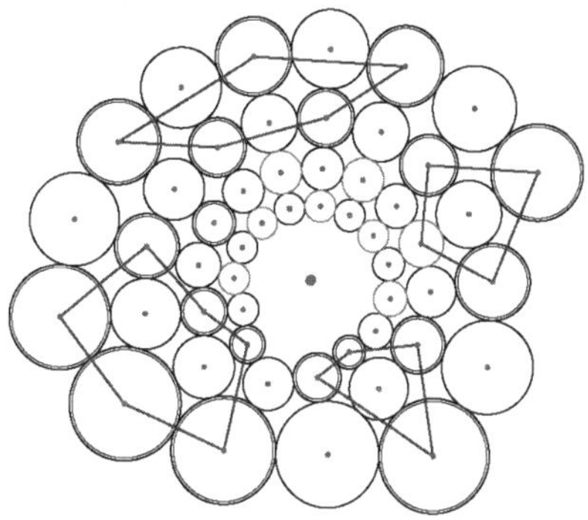

E1 Ecological Ponds
nb of ponds: 20

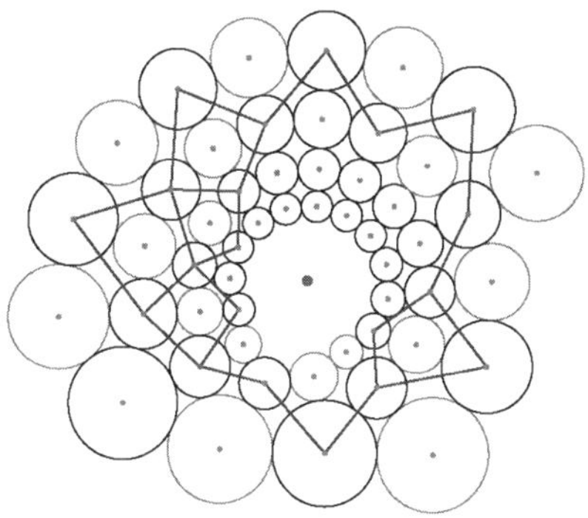

D1 Volumetric Morphologies

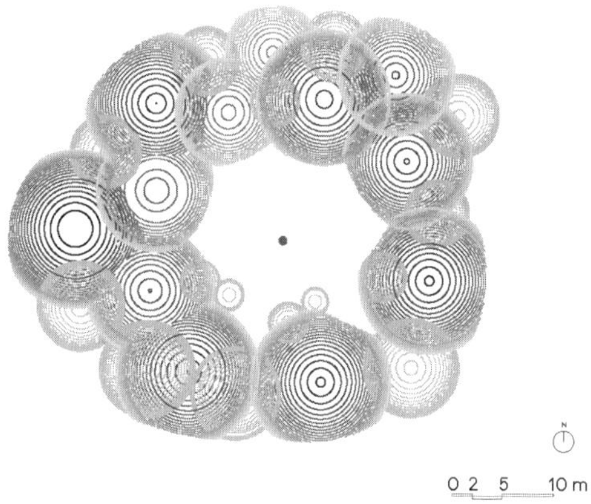

System network diagram

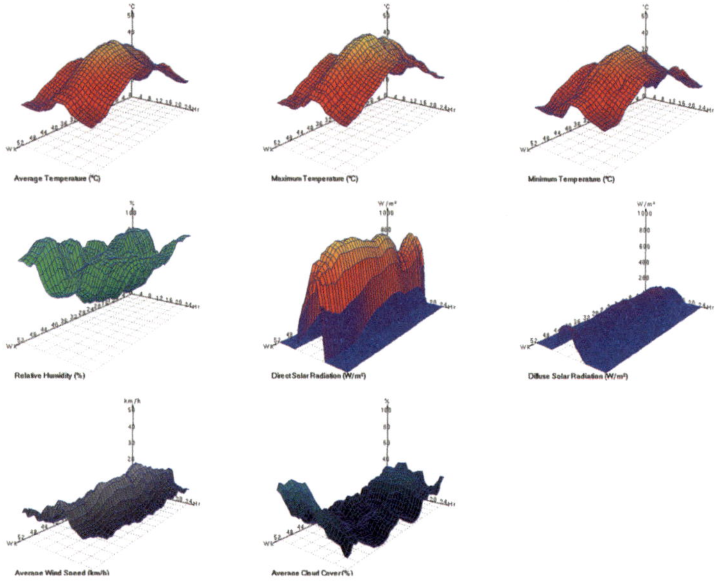

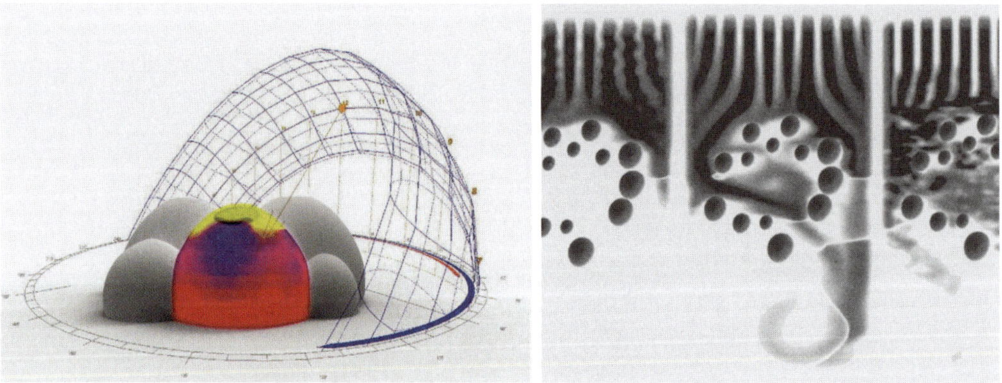

Environmental analysis

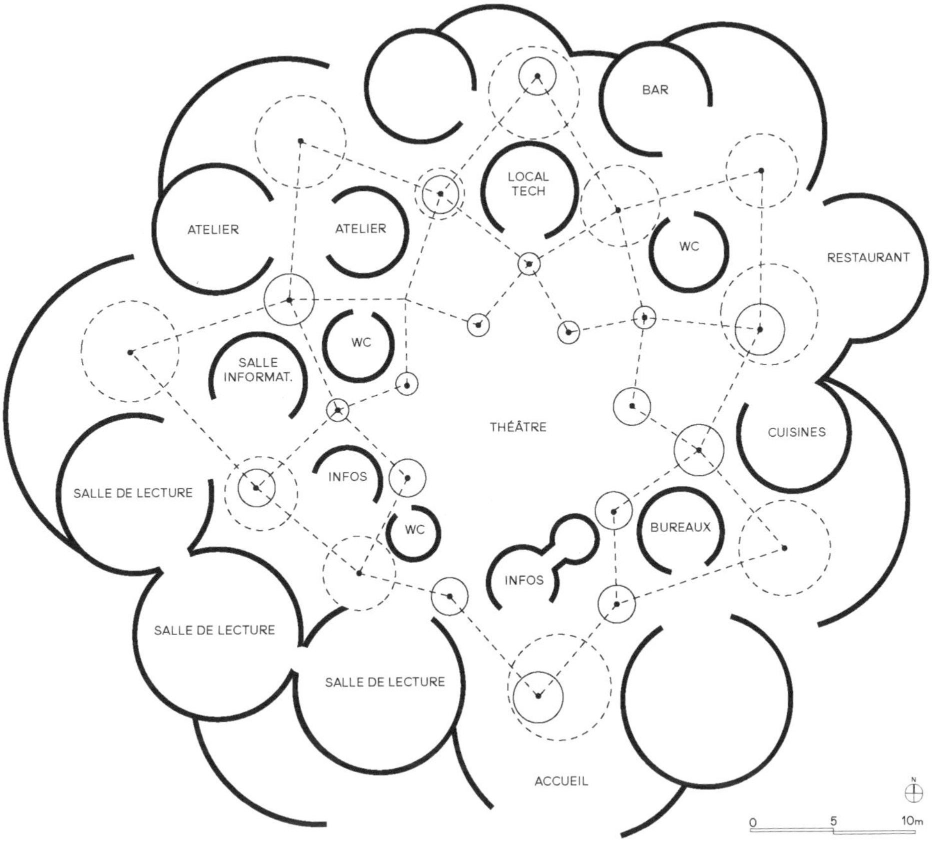

Project plan

Project volumetric view

Workshop with Fabrizio Carola in Mali

3

ROBOTIC DOME

SITE
Barcelona
Spain

PROGRAMME
House unit

TEAM
Paolo Cascone
with
Ionut Anton
Eleni Kolovou
Alessio Loffredo
Sven Pfeiffer
Stephane Tabsoba

ETHZ
Tobias Bonwetsch
Ralph Bärtschi
Andrea Kondziela

STRUCTURAL SYSTEM
interlocked bricks

MATERIALS
Polystyrene

PARTNERS
Smart Geometry
IAAC Barcelona
ETH Zurich

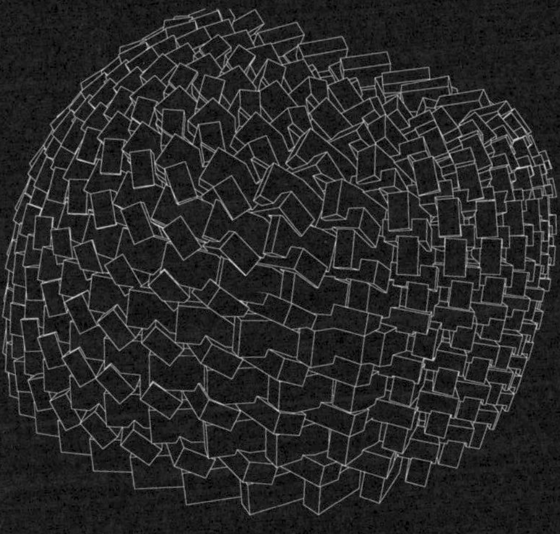

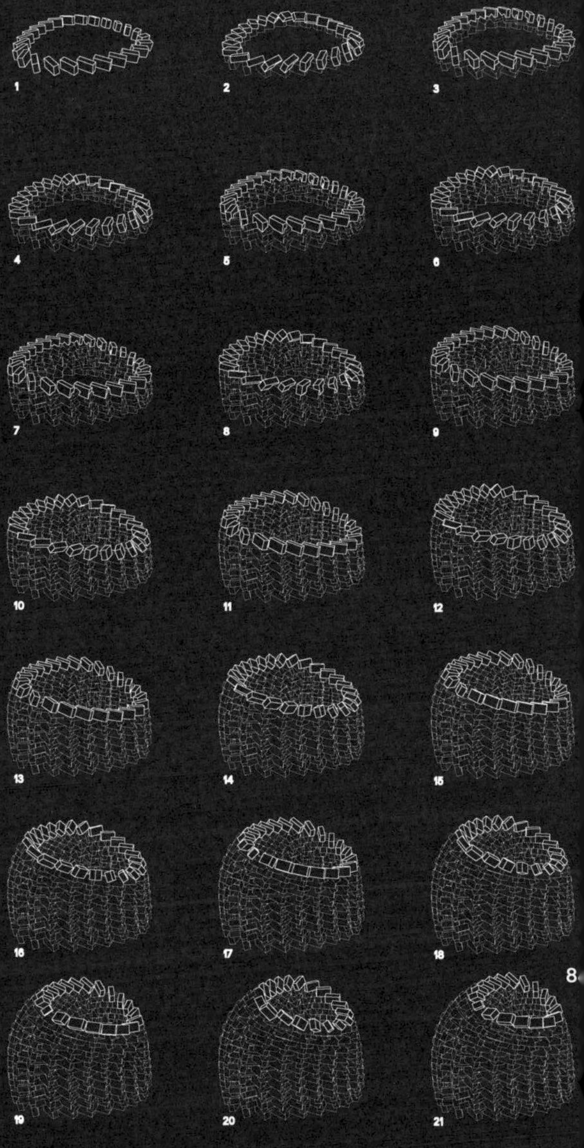

Studying drawing project robotic dome realized by a robotic arm

Evolutionary process

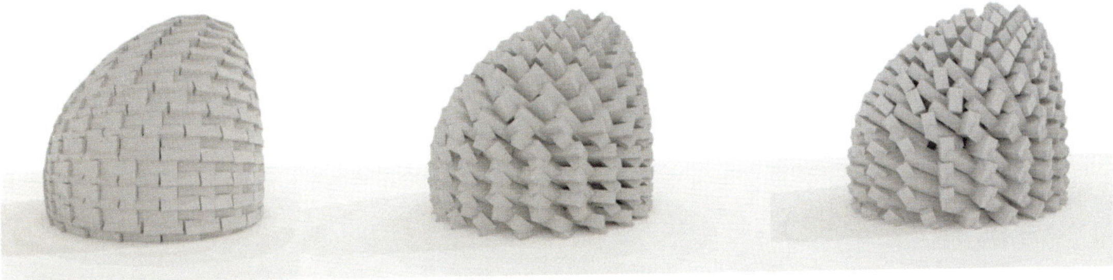

Daylight performative testing

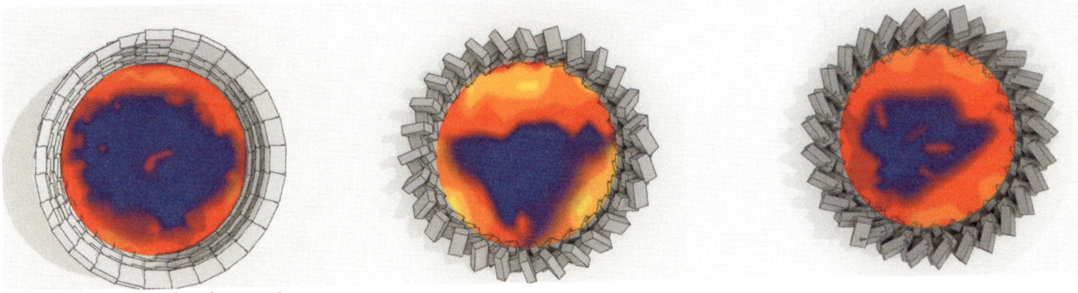

Units evolutionary development

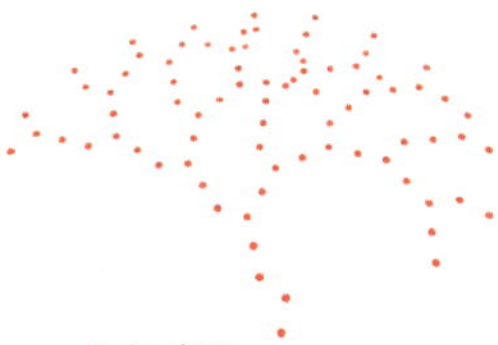

occupied points

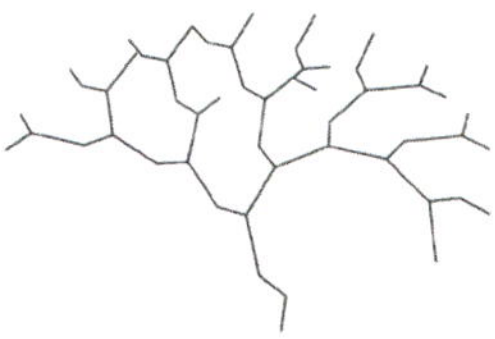

paths network

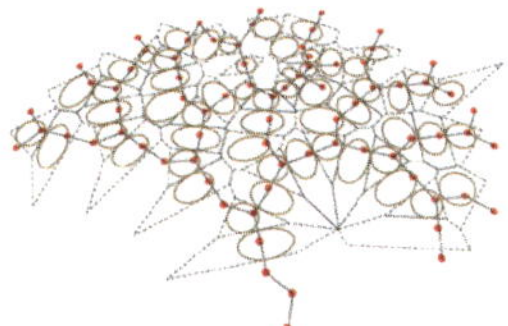

colonised network

differentiated morphology

SMART SHELL WORLD URBAN FORUM — UN HABITAT 2010

SITE
Naples (Italy) /Africa

CLIENT
STRESS Consortium

PROGRAMME
Emergency Pavilion

TEAM
Paolo Cascone (architect) with Elisabetta Corvino, Pietro Nunziante, Silvia Piccione (environmental analysis), Massimiliano Fraldi (structure analysis)

CONSTRUCTION TEAM
Paolo Cascone, Elisabetta Corvino, Elena Ciancio, Imma Polito, Andrea Giglio, Giuliano Galluccio, Delia Evangelista, Silvia Piccione, Rossella Siani, Claudia Balestra, Achille Piroli

STRUCTURAL SYSTEM
Interlocked portals

MATERIALS
Wood, photovoltaic textile

PARTNERS
selve del balzo sas, aurora, nhp

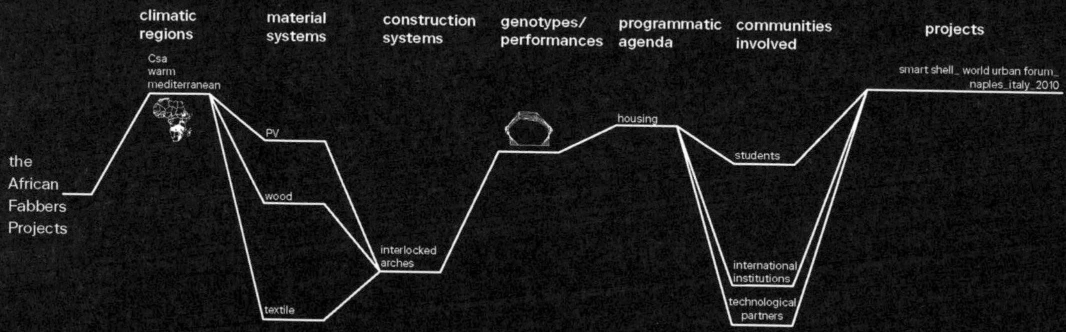

The experiments on generative components developed with Fabrizo Carola for the hot and dry sub-Saharan Africa climate were then adapted speculating on the use of small timber elements. This move took inspiration from lattice and cage structures, aiming to develop them as a building component that could be replicated in different regions according to the material available on site. In this case, the goal was to avoid using large trunks for beams, instead developing more intricate and lighter structures for temporary and adaptable dwellings that could also be built in deforested regions. Beyond the question of emergency in architecture, with the Urban Fabrication Laboratory we began working on the idea of temporary housing as a tactical solution for African slums to gradually upgrade precarious dwellings while avoiding the need to remove inhabitants from the neighbourhood during the process of refurbishment. For this reason, we developed a design-to-build protocol for a "smart shell", an affordable housing solution conceived as a transportable, rapid-deploying, and energetically self-sufficient structure. The design process investigated the relation between high-tech design and low-tech construction, exploring kinetic systems that could offer a catalogue of different shapes and dimensions according to site-specific needs. The project provided flexible solutions for different uses, from low-cost dwellings to off-grid health centres, etc. The digital variations represented a sort of structural skeleton that could then be panelised using local materials depending on the specific climatic conditions. For this reason, we began collaborating with different Italian industries interested in investing in the topic, from the areas of timber construction and photovoltaic textiles. Thanks to support from the Stress consortium and the team of structural engineers at the Naples Polytechnic, we analysed the structural efficiency of the whole system through a series of physical 1-to-1 scale prototypes. The result of this architectural investigation consisted of foldable modular structural portals made of wood and covered by strips of photovoltaic membrane. The 1-to-1 scale prototype of the smart shell was realised in collaboration with a group of architecture students from the University of Naples. The project was presented at the 6th World Urban Forum, where we were invited by the former Executive Director of UN-Habitat, Joan Clos, and his team in Nairobi to discuss possible applications in Africa. The drivers of the project included the following principles:

Ecological: the structural components made from chestnut wood are joined together by interlocking systems and customised wooden diagonals. Assembled dry and directly on the structure, without any chemical glue, the system technology offers opportunities for closing the loop by reusing the components.

Transportable: the lightweight material and the modular dimensions make the structure easy to transport. The elements can be folded, linked together, and stacked one on top of the other. Due to its feasibility and potential for fast deployment, it can be quickly sited and set up, offering portable and incredibly versatile solutions.

Adaptive: the configurations that can be made from its basic shape are almost limitless. It can be modified in a variety of ways to suit specific functional purposes. Conceived to provide temporary or semi-permanent accommodation (infrastructure and skin), the system works where traditional building methods are impractical due to cost, time, or logistical conditions.

Energetically self-sufficient: the skin is made from a PV textile (PW 90, amorphous silicon) that can be adapted to complex shapes, providing an impressive energetic performance and shaded indoor conditions. The conversation with the directors of UN-Habitat brought up the question of the use of local technologies to support the mass customisation and scalability of the system. Consequently, we discussed the possible implications of transforming the "smart shell" system into a more permanent architectural device, improving the structural and environmental performances, including water collection and ecological sanitation, etc. As a matter of fact, the dialogue with many African experts at the WUF informed the next steps in the African Fabbers projects, especially in the field of affordable housing for upgrading slums.

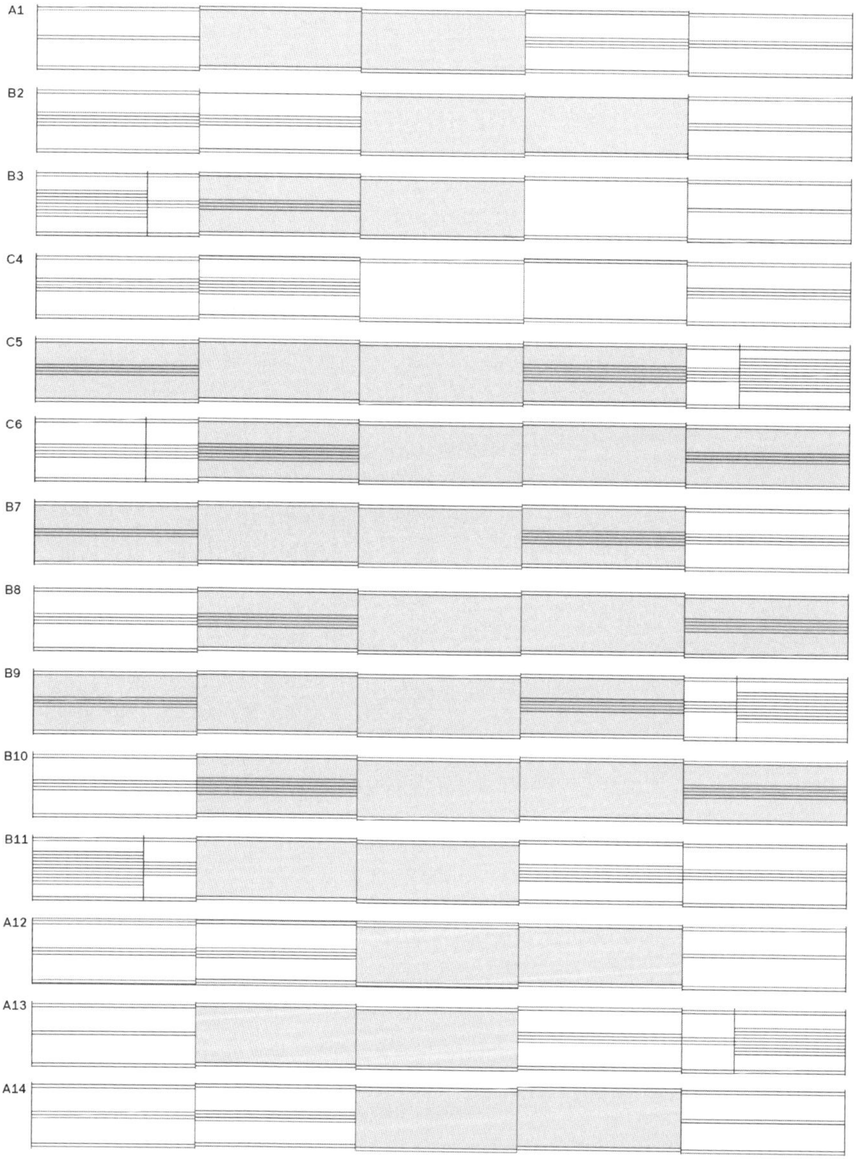

Concept design

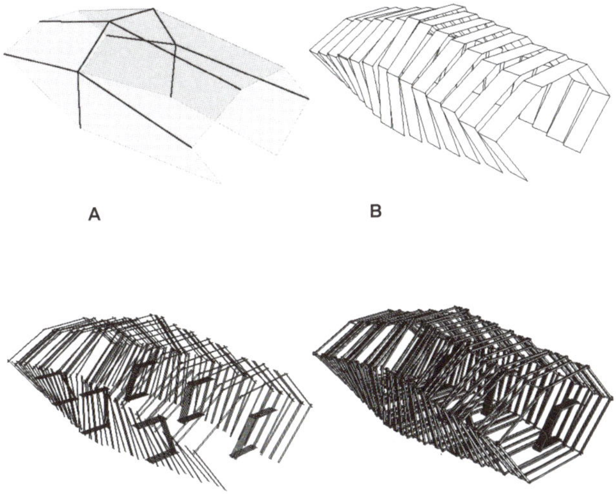

Project development: A Prototypical sections, B Modular stripes, C Wireframe model, D Structural system

YEARLY MODULE PRODUCTION	W/h
a	59.768
b	44.917
c	75.172
d	60.931
e	61.312
f	61.713
g	46.777
h	63.345
i	63.701
l	62.876
m	30.960
n	46.185
o	61.083
p	60.598
q	59.928
r	60.607
s	60.491

MONTHLY ELECTRICAL PRODUCTION	W/h
Jan	31.074
Feb	35.794
Mar	54.968
Apr	82.688
May	102.358
June	118.506
July	139.729
Aug	111.219
Sept	80.424
Oct	73.365
Nov	33.072
Dec	27.607
Total W/h	890.800

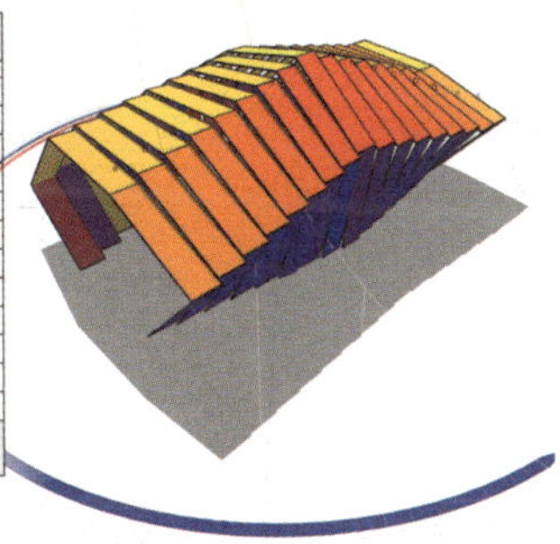

Tab. 1.1: Yearly electrical production per module.
Tab. 1.2: Electrical production from the give structure (W/h).

Solar radiation analysis

OVERSHADOWING ANALYSIS AND DAYLIGHT DISTRIBUTION

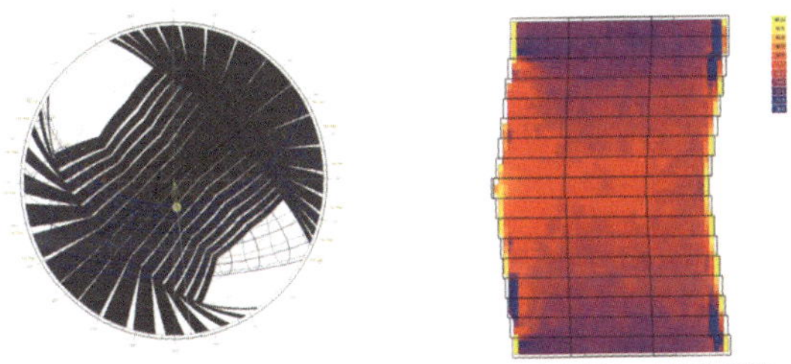

Fig. 4.1: Stereograpich sun path and shadow distribution diagram.

Fig. 4.2: preliminary study: daylight factors calculaton (SC, ERC, IRC)

Overshadowing and daylight distribution analysis

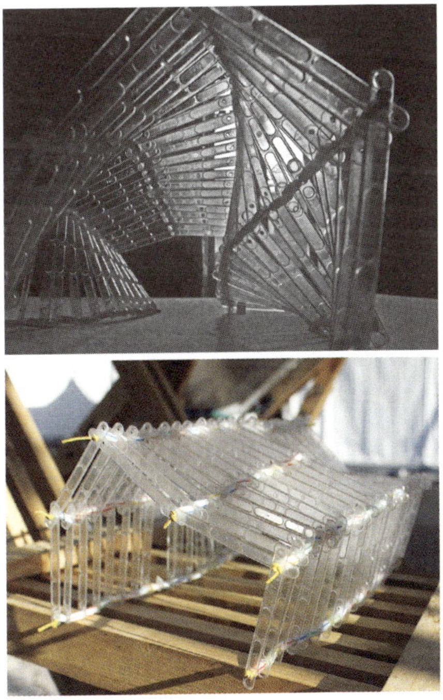

Physical prototypes

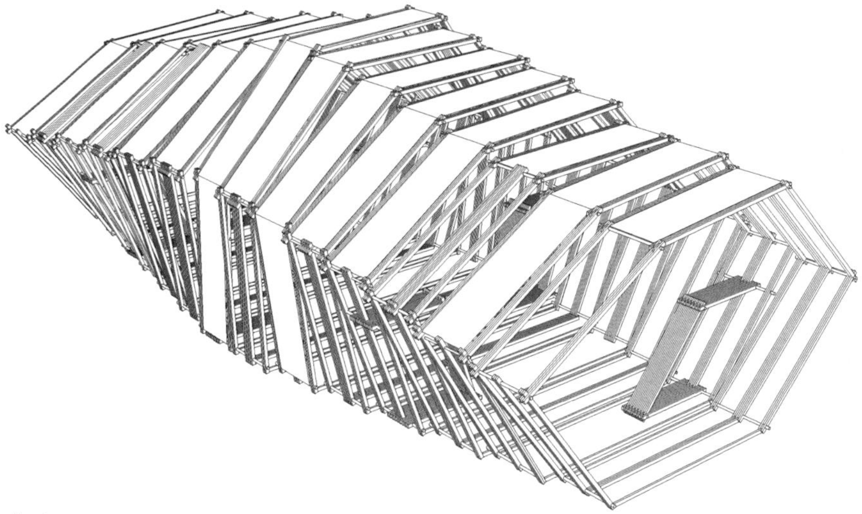

Axonometric view end prototypical sections catalogue

SECTIONS CATALOGUE

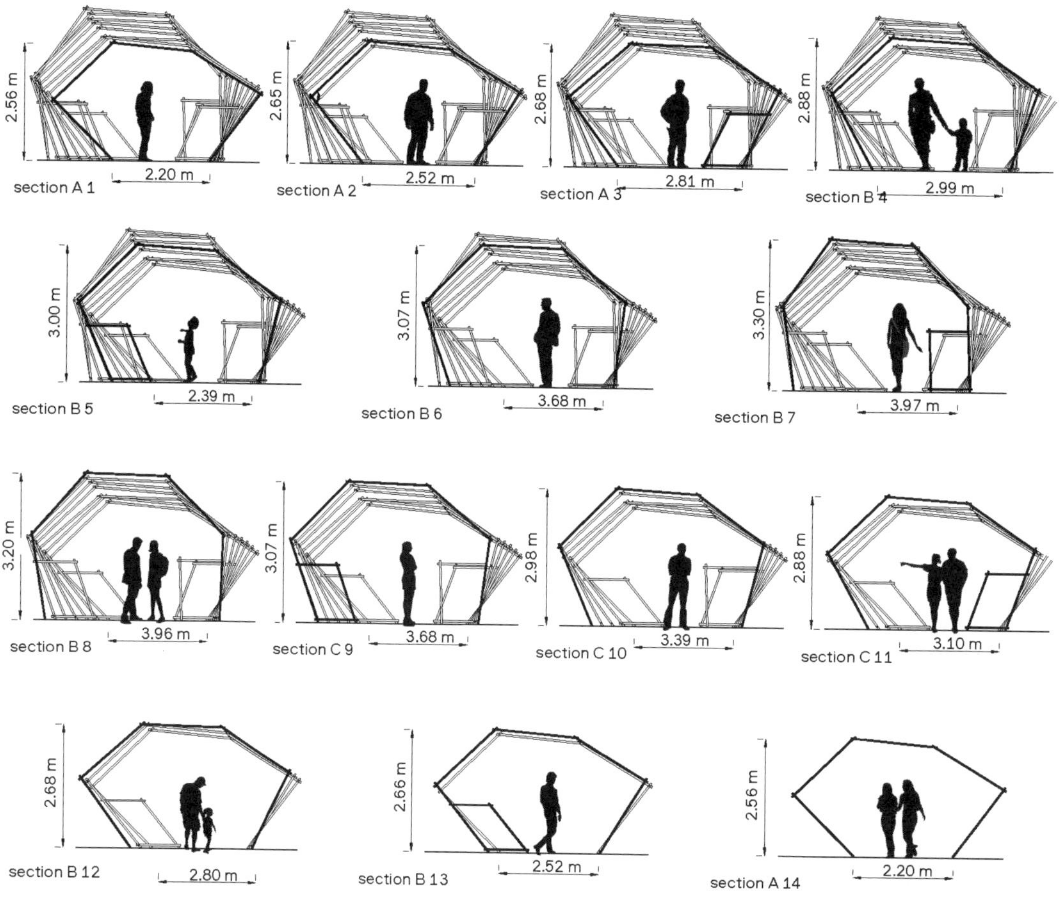

1 Smart shell installation at the World Urban Forum 6

Construction process and structural details

3.2 THE SELF-CONSTRUCTION OF RELATIONAL SPACES

The second topic investigates self-construction as a strategic approach for the regeneration of public and relational spaces. The two projects, Earth Play the Ground - Burkina Faso and Khaima Urban Tent - Morocco, adapt the same modus operandi according to two different cultural and climatic conditions. The collaborative involvement of the local community becomes a tactic to empower neighbourhood residents to use and maintain the public spaces for social and cultural activities. The two structures respond to a similar brief but with two completely different architectural solutions according to the local materials and the knowledge available on site.

EARTH PLAY THE GROUND — BURKINA FASO 2010

SITE
Sourgoubila
12°22'07"N
01°31'39"W

CLIMATE REGION
hot semi-arid

CLIENT
Sourgoubila village

PROGRAMME
Playground

TEAM
Atelier Paolo Cascone – ESA Students: Pascal Angel, Stephane Tapsoba (assistant), Geoffroy Griveaud, Christophe Lefevre, Matthieu De Lacvicier, Ali Benabdellah, Ayda Bennani-Smires, Edouard Fenet, Mathieu Quilici, Fatou Dieng, Youssef Haddadi, Victor Du Peloux, Nadège Guion, Océane Patole, Murielle Teguel, Omar Ghaiti, Juliette Rubel, Loubna Touzani, Marguerite Bureau, Nina Rotter, Salwa Essoussi Nadège Guion, Océane Patole, Omar Ghaiti, Murielle Teguel, Mathieu Quilici, Fatou Dieng, Youssef Haddadi, Victor Du Peloux,

CONSTRUCTION TEAM
Atelier Paolo Cascone with local community
La Voute Nubienne construction consultant

STRUCTURAL SYSTEM
Arches

MATERIALS
Adobe bricks

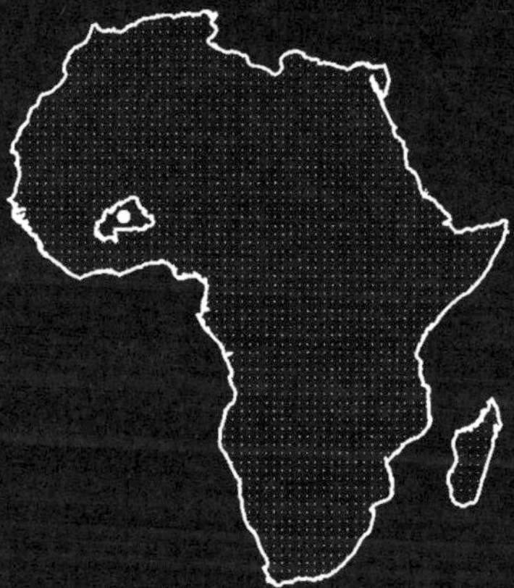

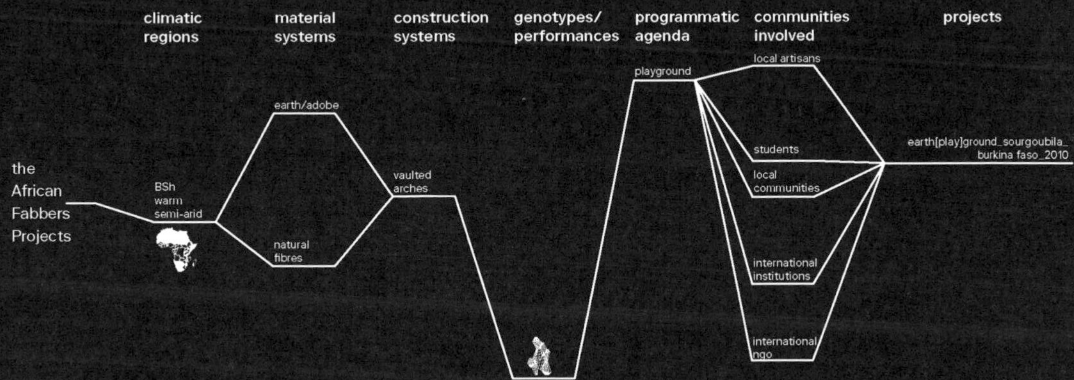

5

This project emerged after many reflections on how to translate the experience with Fabrizio Carola into a more research- and teaching-based agenda involving my students of the design studio Atelier Paolo Cascone at the École Speciale d'Architecture in Paris. For this reason, I transformed my second-year design atelier into a sort of laboratory of post-vernacular design, where students started to investigate a computational approach to traditional sub-Saharan architecture. At the time, I had taken an interest in Ron Eglash's work on spontaneous settlement and indigenous computing. The students' experimental work on contextual algorithms and evolutionary design, published on the atelier blog http://esa-ateliercascone.blogspot.com/, was probably one of the first times this kind of digital approach to the evolution of informal sub-Saharan architecture was disseminated widely, eliciting very broad interest. At the same time, the debate on the topic in the atelier was incredibly engaging intellectually. The majority of the students were originally from Africa, and with my assistant and former student Stephane Tapsoba, we organised a real-life project in his village in Burkina Faso to share our ideas and learn from the local community. Stephane's design thesis, on earth architecture in Ouagadougou, was probably the best I supervised during my teaching experience in Paris. The whole preparation of the initiative engaged the students to self-fund the project by organising a series of cultural events and social dinners in the school's courtyard in Paris.

At the same time, through Stephane's family, we started to dialogue remotely with the people of the village to discuss the function and the materials of the proposed architectural device. Since the village did not have any kind of outdoor relational space apart from the big tree outside the school, we decided to develop a sort of rural playground, a performative pavilion where children and adults could play and meet, protected from the sun. Since we had decided with the chiefs of the village to use the local earth as the main construction material, we established a collaboration with the La Voûte Nubienne association, which supports training programmes in sub-Saharan Africa to help local communities self-build their own dwellings using the technique of the Nubian vault. The story of these initiatives is well described in an interview by Lucia Tozzi, published in Abitare n° 509 in 201:

> The Sourgoubila project is a participatory building initiative in Burkina Faso organised by APC (Atelier Paolo Cascone) with the students at the ESA in Paris and the local community as part of a wider post-vernacular design project. The basic idea is to try out new forms of sustainability that go beyond the narrow confines of green architecture, exploring every possible interaction between advanced technology and local building practices. The outcome here is 1:1 scale prototype playground for the children of a school in Sourgoubila village.

LUCIA TOZZI **One of the most interesting things about thus initiative is that, against all expectation, and bearing in mind we are talking about self-construction in Africa, it isn't a humanitarian aid project. How did it develop, and what are its aims?**

> **PAOLO CASCONE** Culturally speaking, the project makes no humanitarian claims, because its basic concern is the complexity of local construction methods and ways of developing them further by combining high-tech design and low-tech construction. In this sense, leaving aside all Third-World rhetoric,

I think that Africa and the others regions with similar climates can provide extremely instructive examples of this kind of work for anyone researching sustainable production processes in the field. During the years I spent in Africa ad a child, following my father around, what impressed me most wasn't the misery and the poverty so much as the sheer creativity of people accustomed to doing a lot with nothing. Later, while studying at the AA in London, I became interested in environmental parametric design, i.e., a computer-based approach to a new ecology of architecture. At a time when computer-assisted construction was mostly high-tech (kinematic or robotic systems, and so on), it was only natural that people like me who were interested in contextual dissolutions based on the optimisation of energy and materials would start experimenting with the Third World's enormous heritage of local low-tech construction method. One can't and shouldn't have to fall in with the "emergency" rationale of these institutions and those NGOs who work in these countries, where of course they are doing an admirable job. PVD operates independently by creating real application points in direct contact with the workshop in Sourgoubila which would never have got off the ground if we had waited for funding from above. This makes for great flexibility and freedom of actions, and all this is often helped by the presence of a network of former students from Africa.

Post-Vernacular Design (PVD) is a response to the need for high-tech design processes capable of generating performance architecture that develops around local traditions in regions where the social and climatic conditions are extreme.

LT **What is precisely, post-vernacular design?**

PC Even today, Western countries enthuse over more native aspect of the applied arts in these countries, and ignore the incredible complexity of cultures which are sometimes centuries-old and which tend to reconcile nature and tekne. The production process of vernacular rural culture are also are also "open systems" endowed with intrinsic intelligence and the ability to reproduce structures on a variety of scales using the same structural components available on site, which results in differentiated and flexible spatial solutions and often leads to the best use of resources. This is why post-vernacular design processes try to make explicit the casual relationship between materials, morphology and the environmental performance of these structures using cutting-edge parametric design and simulations. In architecture the need to develop low-tech solutions has opened the way to "emergent" construction system and methods that function well in extreme climatic and economic conditions, and often with the surprising results.

LT **How many and what kind of people were involved in bringing this process to fruition?**

PC The Sourgoubila workshop involved 20 of my second-year ESA student in Paris. They began by studying the microclimate and developing prototypes that took account of deforestation so that a number of the village activities could be integrates. In parallel with this, through my Burkinese assistant Stephane Tapsoba, we contacted the local community and village elders to learn about their needs and their willingness to cooperate. Their response was enthusiastic and in the end we agreed on an open-air after-hours playground pavilion for children at the local école primarie. So we engineered the initial prototype and developed a group of my student to produce an easy-to-assemble structure in which repeated use of one simple component (mud-bricks) generated a flexible, hyper-articulated system. The prototype thus became a collective project whose outcome was a semi-covered playground structure based on a differentiated series of ogival arches. In the month before work began we asked "consultants", structural engineers and NGOs in the field to discuss ways of taking the project a stage further. We built scale models in the school garden and organised community-wide self-financing initiatives, and the entire school came on board, with great enthusiasm.

LT In championing this kind of architecture you met with obstacles, an cultural contradictions, in terms of both your students and the end-users of the structure. Why was this? How did you remedy of these situations?

PC At first it took a lot of effort to persuade my students, especially the Africans ones, that high-tech parametric needed to be combined with local materials and vernacular construction methods. Students sent by their families to study in Europe usually have a very standardised notion of progress – concrete building, glass, iron, air-conditioned and like – which is far removed from the prospects of working with" humble" materials using traditional methods. Betraying these expectations entailed, sooner or later, a certain amount of soul-searching regarding one's origins and culture. Suggesting computer-assisted design helped me to persuade them that experimenting with was already there on site could result in something truly "innovative" and contemporary.
When we got to Oudagoudou via Niamey in the middle of a sandstorm, the 38°C temperature and ochre sky told us to once that things wouldn't go exactly as our computer models in Paris simulations had side they would. In Sourgoubila we were met by dancing women, drums and welcoming songs from the school children. Later my 20 students and I looked each other in the eye and realised that this was no longer a divertissement.

Although the village chief had placed a squad of men at our disposal, things went very slowly at first: it became difficult to get water and stones.
I went over the figures with the elder's time and again and together we agreed that if we replaced local materials with cement and zinc sheeting, the structures would cost ten times more than ours because all the materials would be to be imported. We talked for hours under an enormous mango tree about what a great resource it would be for them if they could be self-sufficient in building, water storage and purification, electricity generation, and so on. At this point the women (some with babies in tow) and kids, who are the real driving-force in the village, swung into action, using bicycles and improvised wheelbarrows to fetch the water and the limestone we needed to keep on building. Though not all the details of the structures were what we had envisaged, morale was high. The school kids got over their initial silence and shyness and were attracted to the building site like magnets. Word got around and kids came from other villages to see we were doing. Overcoming their earlier scepticism, the elders in Sourgoubila asked me if we could also build their own houses this way, using the lads who were helping us to learn the traditional methods that had been lost. In Short, it was all a matter of trust. Once persuaded, no one doubted the need to get the project finished.

LT Can the structures like the one you designed be recreated by local people without you help? Is it possible to create interest in buildings in this way?

PC I can only repeat that Sourgoubila was an experiment carried out by second-year students working with the local community. Obviously, this encouraged me to develop a network of fellow-workers and draw up a more organised research workshop programme.

Clearly, cultural initiative on the ground is essential to persuading local communities to resurrect traditional building methods and put them to modern use. If nothing else, the Sourgoubila project showed us and the people of the village that can build at zero cost without using imported materials by returning to self-sufficient as far as possible. The social and economic impact of this approach cannot fail to arouse the interest of the people who lives this region. Obviously, the impact would be truly significant if it were applied on a wider scale to the urban growth Africans metropolises are currently undergoing. In this context, post-vernacular design is concerned with new forms of sustainable urban planning based on understanding how unplanned settlements from and grow, and enhancing the performance of the process involved.

For the above-mentioned reasons this project was bridging both educational and environmental issues anticipating many topics that are now becoming popular also in western schools of architecture. At the same time, it is important to highlight the completely different approach of the communities of rural areas, where the lack of resources is compensated by an extraordinary willingness to collaborate and exchange knowledge compared to the more urban scenarios. Looking at this experience after many years it is interesting to notice how this experience was affecting the African students' paths, once graduated in France most of them decided to go back in their own country to gradually establish their practices and professional careers. Some of them are still maintaining the trans African network we were creating in our design studio sharing opportunities, some others once back started to play a key institutional role in their community in the field of architecture and social design. Beyond the design process and the construction aspects of such project the human and cultural impact of such knowledge exchange experience is a key factor to shape an ecological shift in our society. Therefore, we are still dialoguing with some of the former students with the aim to push forward our project of collaboration towards community-oriented initiatives.

Project development with the local community

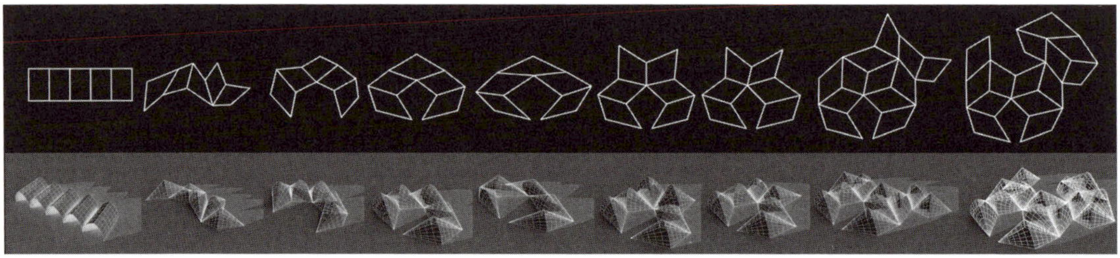

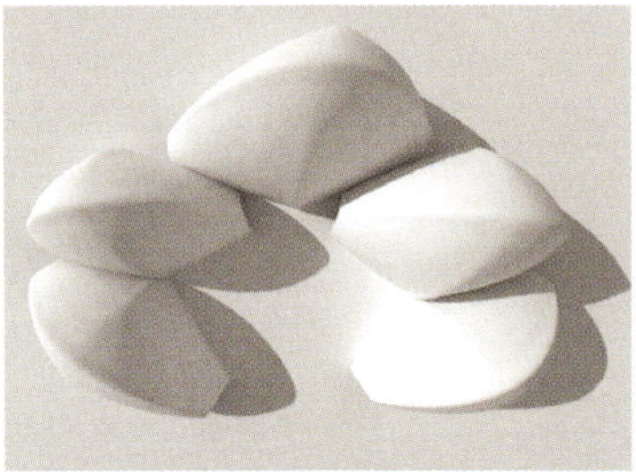

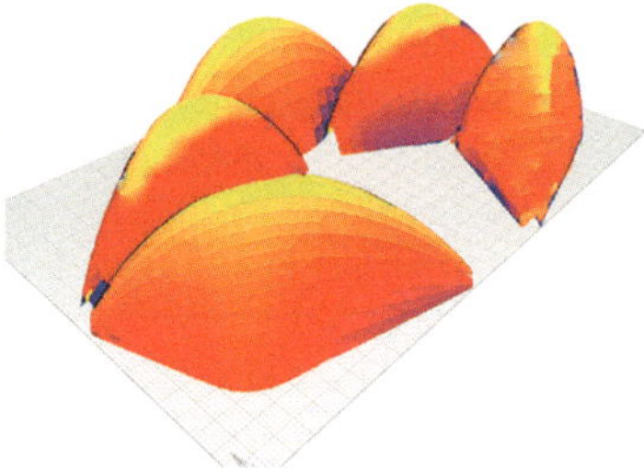

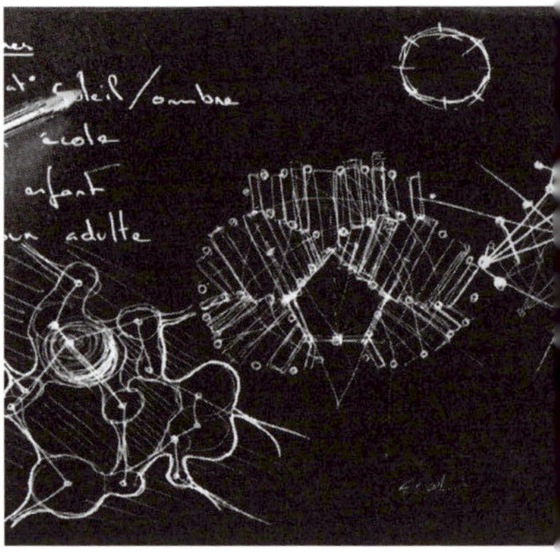

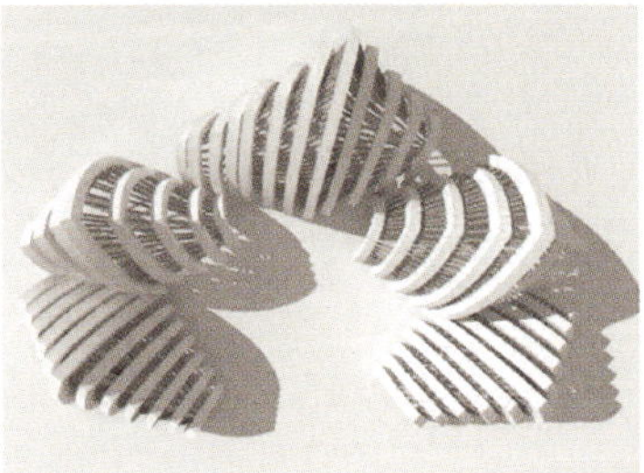

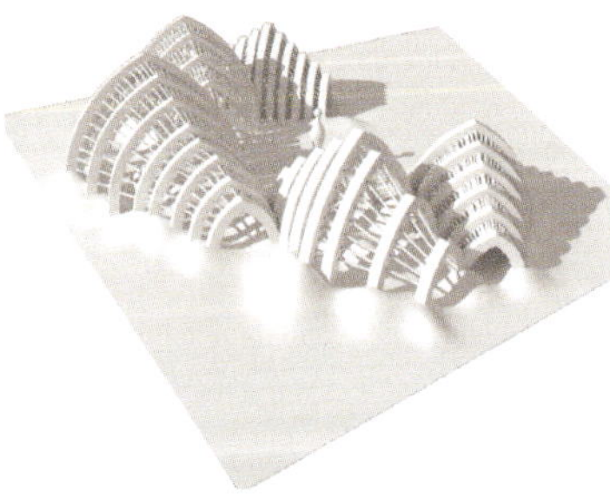

Digital and physical study models

Fabrication process with local material

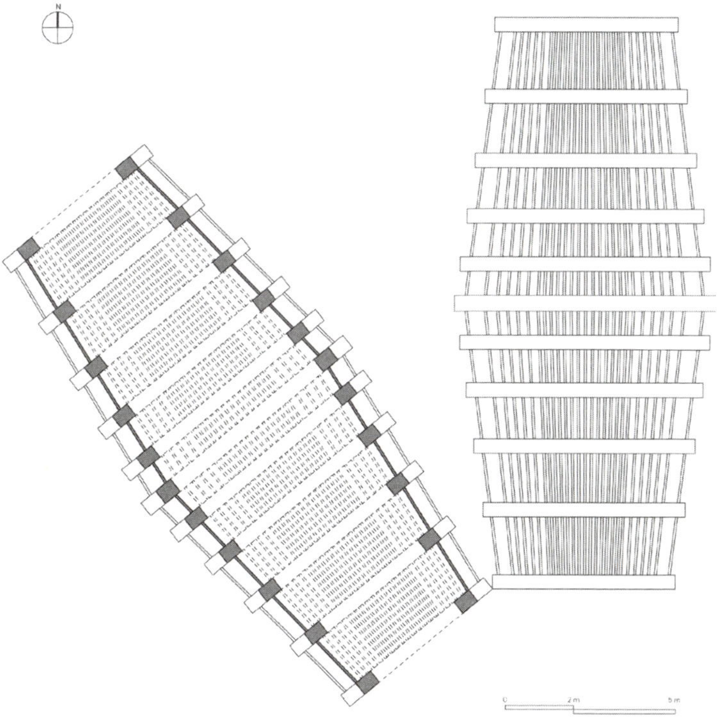

Structural testing and self construction sessions

Playground inauguration with the local community

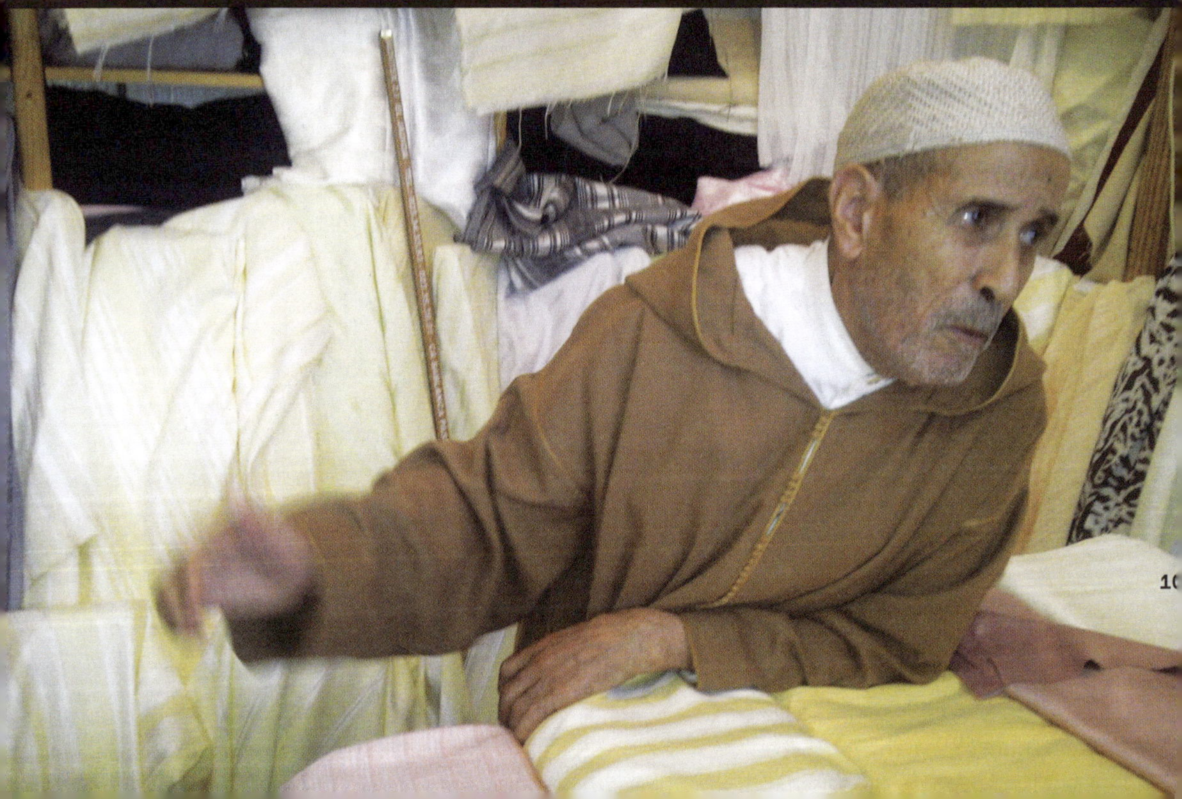

KHAIMA URBAN TENT — MOROCCO 2011

SITE
Salè,
34°02'N 6°48'

CLIMATE REGION
hot summer
Mediterranean

CLIENT
Ciss

PROGRAMME
Relational
space

TEAM
Paolo Cascone
with
Tamara Vecchione
and the local community
Karim Balliz,
Ahmed Boukri,
Jalal El Fabkh,
Nabil Ftita,
Abdel, Ahmed,
Toufik From Salè,
Jihad Houmi,
Achraf Choukr,
Abdelilah Kadiri,
Abderrazzar Chahouawi,
Rachid Talaalout,
Nabil Kaboury,
Houda Zerraf,
Dado Sidibe,
Camara Kadidiaton,
Nabila Metaïr,
Mohamed
Zakariya Agha

STRUCTURAL SYSTEM
Structure tensile

MATERIALS
Cables and fabrics

PARTNER
Quartiers du monde

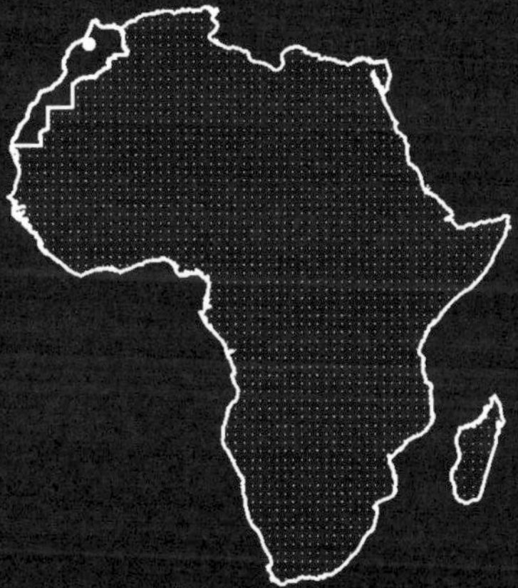

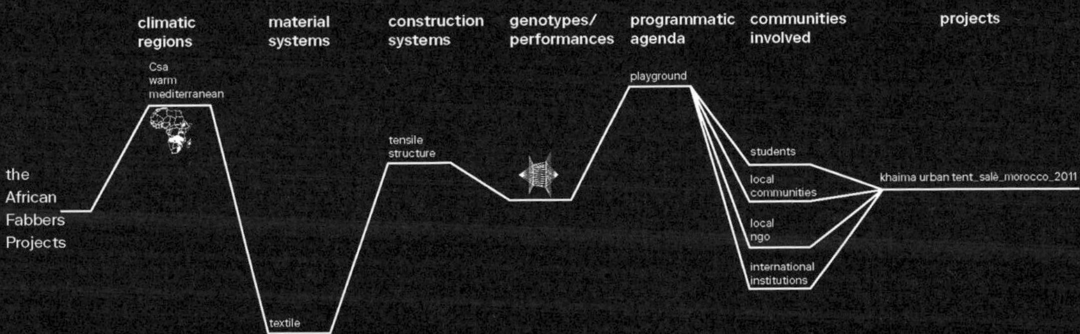

The question of public space in the north African context is quite controversial and, in any case, difficult to compare with the Western notion of relational space. For many cultural and religious reasons, the question of citizenship in these contexts follows different dynamics, in which people are not often directly involved in the governance of public spaces, including the maintenance and the public use.

At the same time, the social life – beyond mosques and public markets, which follow some very precise rules – mainly takes place in private courtyards and semi-public gardens. In Morocco, although such dynamics are changing, especially in the city's modern suburbs, for the most part parks and public spaces imposed by Western urban planners are abandoned or under-used. It seems like, since they are public, they do not belong to anyone, and therefore no one really takes care of them.

Regarding this very delicate topic, we were invited by the NGO Quartiers du Monde to work with the local community in a poor neighbourhood in Salé, Morocco. In collaboration with a network of my Moroccan former students in Paris, we started to analyse an abandoned area, which a group of local associations wanted to regenerate. During the week, the desolate open space was mainly used by goats as a sort of urban pasture and by children as an informal playground. On weekends it was a pedestrian path for people going to the mosque.

At the same time, we studied the medina of Salé as the paradigm of a traditional Islamic city, looking at the very relevant issue of urban morphology. In these cases, the most successful public spaces and busiest streets are the narrow ones, for both commercial reasons as well as for their environmental performance. The orientation, as well as the proportion between the building heights and the width of the streets, generates a very tall, dense urban fabric that provides naturally ventilated and shaded spaces. At the same time, we were fascinated by the urban "envelopes": informal structures that were made out of textile and tensile systems protecting the streets of the medina like a sort of bioclimatic urban tent. Our research also focused on the more complex Bedouin tents used as "sitting spaces": lightweight vernacular structures known as *beit al-sha'r*, or "house of hair." These tents were woven by soldiers or herders who ventured across the desert for long periods of time. They would weave the hair of their sheep and goats into strips of coarse cloth, known as *fala'if*, which were then sewn together.

The Caidal tents were the result of a collective fabrication process, typically hand-made by a group of artisans who lived and worked together for a month. Thus, we proposed a collective project to the local associations that would merge the urban and the rural methods of developing textile structures in order to regenerate an area of their abandoned public park. At the same time, we were starting to study homeostatic structures, taking inspiration from the Frei Otto's experiments with tensile structures, evolving traditional Bedouin techniques. Thanks to the collaboration with a group of young tailors and artists, we visited the local fabric market and selected the material to use for our 1-to-1 scale installation. Accounting for the physical constraints of the chosen material system and the dimensions of the fabric strips, we developed an initial study model based on cable systems, merging the most interesting aspects of both the urban and rural types of textile architectures in Morocco. The environmental strategy was to develop a temporary shelter to protect part of the abandoned park, with no trees or shaded areas, allowing people to meet during the hottest hours of the day. We adapted our study model to the site, attaching our network of tensed cables to two unused electric poles for the highest points of the tents. This intricate work involved dozens of young people from the neighbourhood and when a group of people decided to destroy the cable structure during the night, their reaction clearly showed their engagement. Thanks to mediation from the people at the mosque, we were able to involve those who were destroying the structure out of spite, since they felt excluded from the project, in order to complete the tent on time. This experience taught us to address conflicts related to the social dynamics of public space by using self-construction as a tactic to help the whole community take ownership through a collaborative approach. This capacity for social mediation is probably one of the most relevant added values of turning the street into a pedagogical and research laboratory. As a matter of fact, the next generation of designers and social drivers would be wise to learn such real-life mediation skills in the interest of creating a real ecological shift, especially in Global South contexts. *The khaima* structure was inaugurated on a Friday, and people were invited to pass through the temporary structure after prayers and to look at the photography exhibition installed beneath the shelter.

Project design workshop with local community

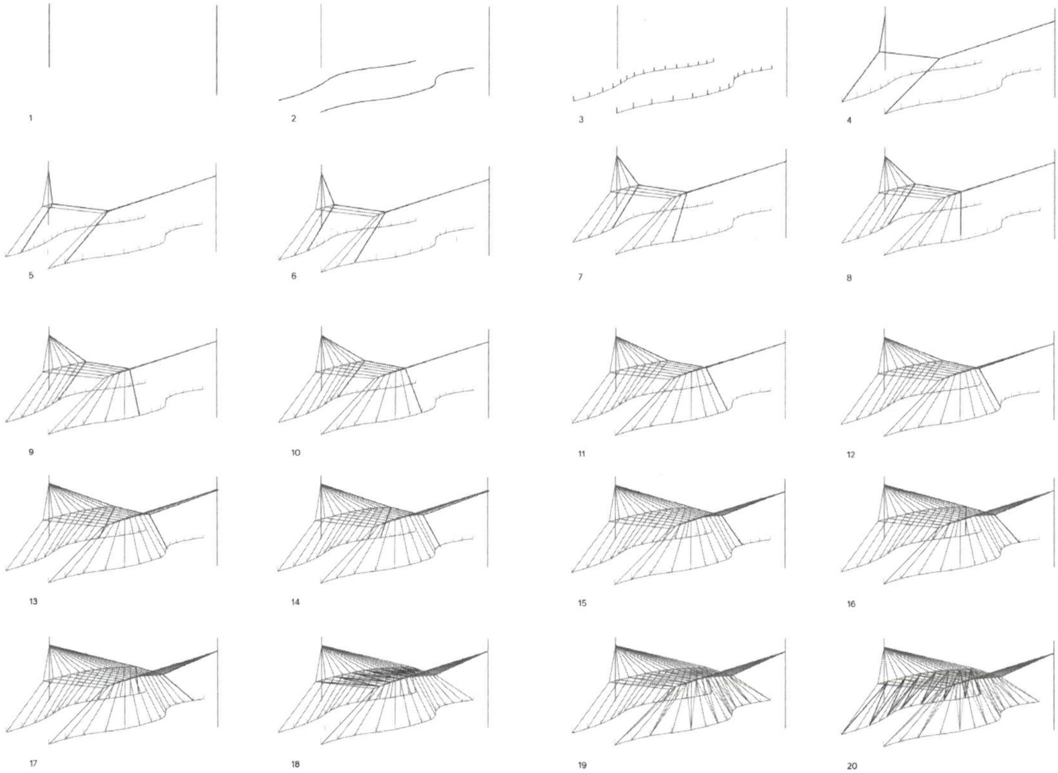

Construction process diagrams

First stage of community self construction

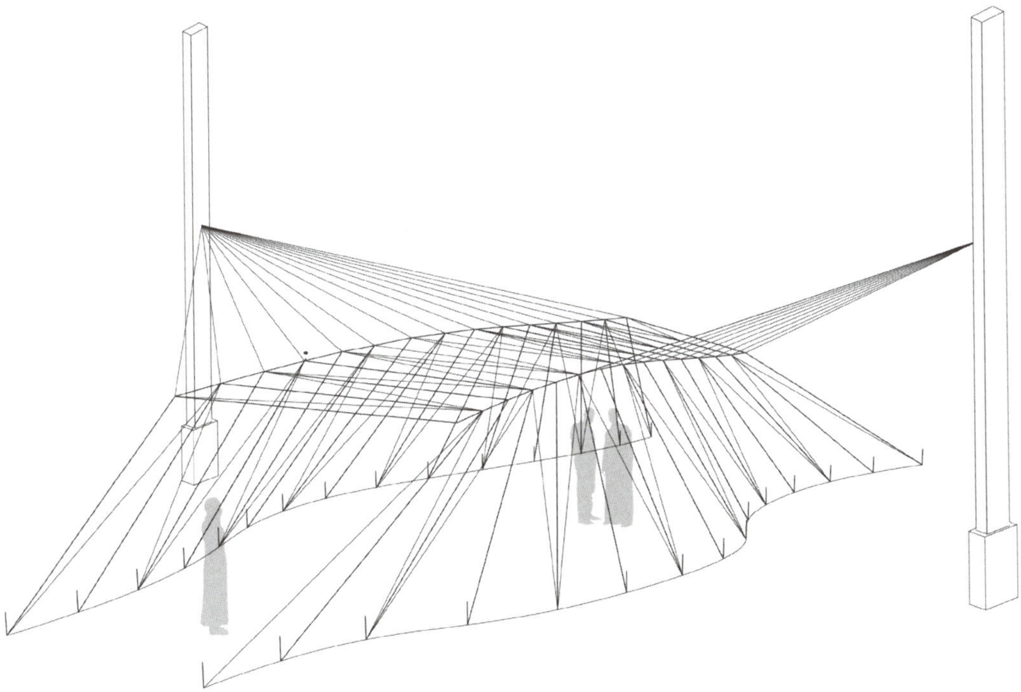

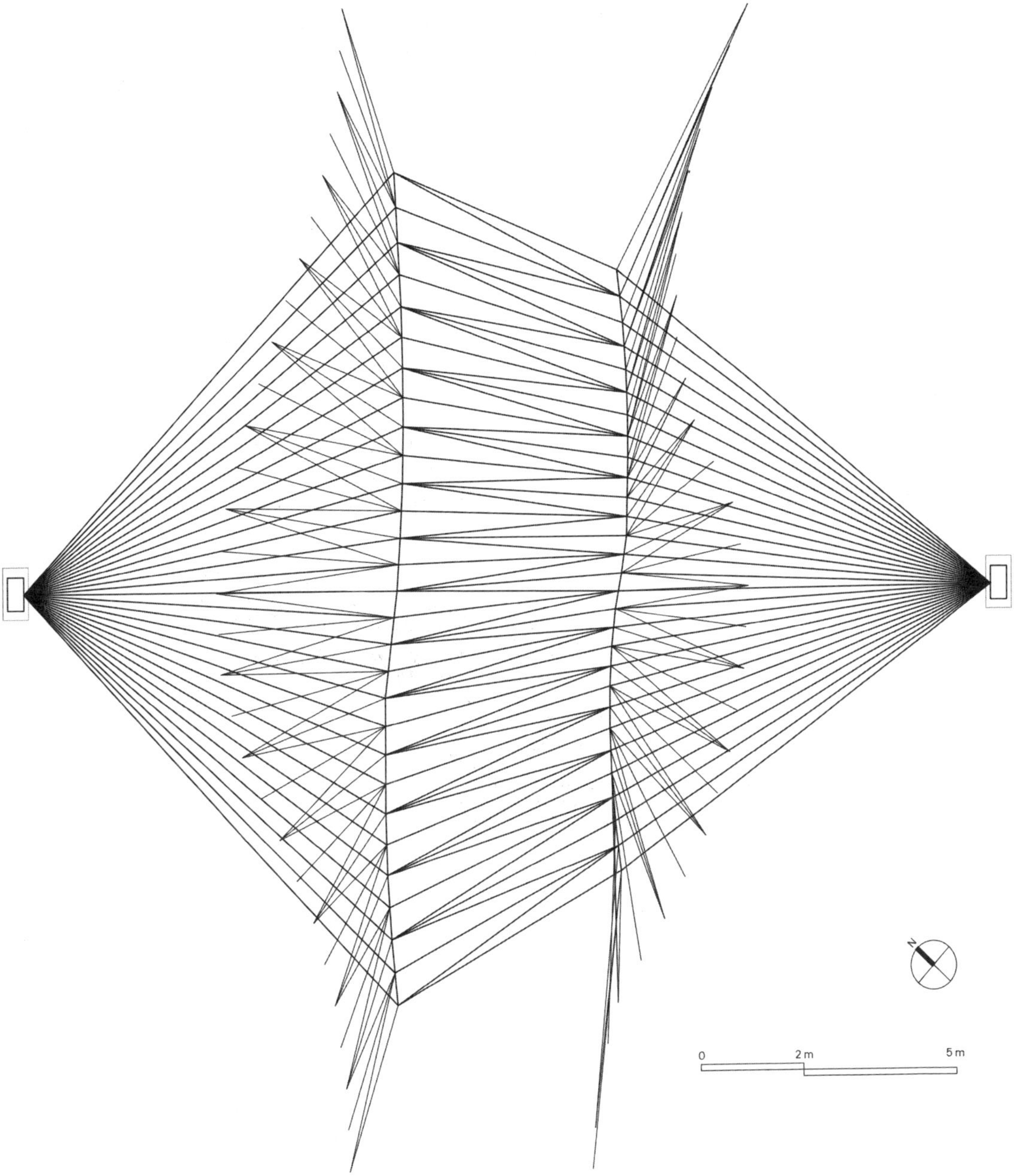
N
0
2 m
5 m

Second stage of the self construction workshop

Urban tent inauguration with local community

3.3 ON CITIES AS FACTORIES AND LOCAL INDUSTRIES

As Mohsen Mostafavi pointed out in his book Ecological Urbanism, "The fragility of our planet could be an opportunity for speculative design innovations rather than technical legitimation for conventional solutions." Meanwhile, open-source technologies are gradually affecting the global economy, supporting the development of low-cost CAM (computer aided manufacturing) machines and creating new economic and social opportunities using traditional manufacturing processes for customized solutions. With this premise, according to the interesting scenarios mentioned by Saskia Sassen in her essay "Global City 20 Years Later", we considered African cities as factories and digital manufacturing as a possible driver for a new paradigm of local industry.

Given the lack of industrial activity on the continent, we investigated the potential role of open-source technologies in minimising the economic dependency of sub-Saharan Africa on other economies, connecting digital manufacturing with local craftsmanship to generate new forms of on-demand affordable production. Setting aside the Western rhetoric of "fablabs" and "startups", we were interested in this self-organised network of small manufacturing activities and their impact on the economic and urban development of African cities – in opposition to the crisis of the top-down Western model. These networks are completely integrated into urban fabrics, generating diffuse open-air factories and creating new forms of hybrid spatial typologies. Because of their promiscuity, these 24-hour open spaces should be considered precursors of the fablabs as knowledge exchange accelerators. These manufacturing platforms are mainly based on upcycling and repairing existing devices, disseminating a sort of open-source culture that combines traditional and digital techniques to develop diversified outputs: affordable housing components and second life solutions for different kinds of domestic devices. Therefore, it was not surprising to us that the second fablab opened worldwide, after the one at MIT in Boston, was in Kumasi (Ghana).

We strategically accepted invitations from both the Marrakech and Dakar Biennials as an opportunity to develop two urban fabrication laboratories, exploring similar logics in two different contexts. Although we have never considered ourselves artists, we found these African biennials to be quite different from Western ones, for their capability to deal with informal urban dynamics as well as for their multicultural and interdisciplinary approach. The idea behind these initiatives was to focus on the social role of tools and open-source technologies to test their cultural and environmental impacts from a long-term perspective and to explore alternative manufacturing approaches as a way of generating new ideas for sustainable local industries.

MARRAKECH LAB — MOROCCO 2014

SITE
Marrakech
31°37’48”N
8°0’32”W

CLIMATE REGION
Hot semi-arid

CLIENT
Marrakech Biennale

PROGRAMME
Urban Fabrication Laboratory

TEAM
Paolo Cascone with Elena Ciancio, Flavio Galdi, Giuliano Galluccio, Andrea Giglio, Imma Polito

WASP TEAM
Massimo Moretti, Nicola Schiavarelli, Francesca Moretti

LOCAL COMMUNITY
Zaim Abderrahman, El mehdi Agharsane, Sharif Anouar, KenzahAtif, Ramia Beladel, Mehdi Belhajjam, Elena Bellantoni, Aahd Benchaouch, Mohammed Amine Chafai, Klara Gaia Chastan, Nada Dhaiba, Taoufiq Edday, Abdelhakim el Hamime, Hatouch el Houssaine, Mohamed Elkhaloua, Karima Elkhider, Youssef Errihan, Rachid er Rmizy, Ehsan Fardjadniya, Azzedine Fettahi, Ilhame Hassani, Abdeslam Khaloufi, Mohamed Labid, Ayoub Iharchi, Zineb nait Imaaz, Salma louise, Oussama Mahassine, Carlos Martinez, Yakubu hassan Mohammed, Youness Mouhtadi, Taha Ouilal, Hicham Ousalah, Wael Touati, Khalid beny Yakhlaf

PARTNERS
Urban Fablab, Città della scienza Naples; Inarcassa foundation; Voice gallery; Cfqmam-Centre de formation et qualification dans les métiers de l’artisanat

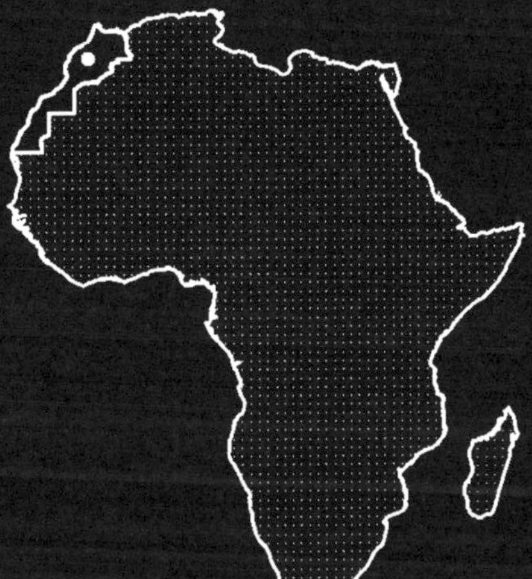

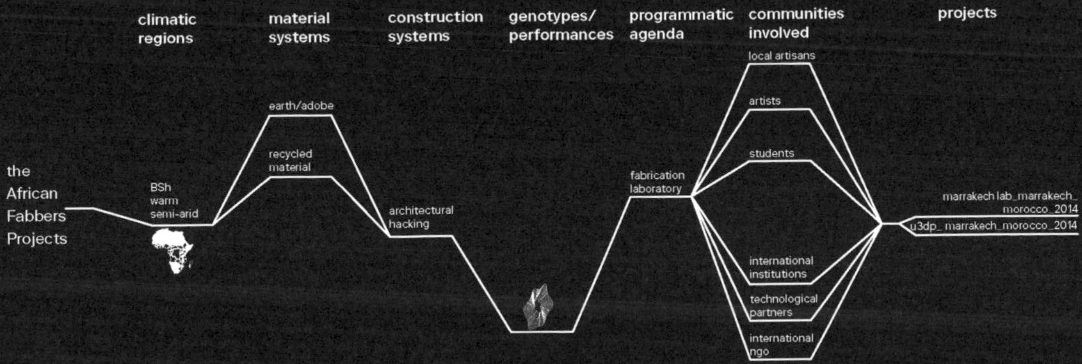

The Marrakech project arrived after many hands-on experiences with clay manufacturing processes and earthen architecture experiments developed in Mali and Burkina Faso. In parallel, we were also implementing the Advanced Ceramics laboratory in collaboration with the famous Solimene ceramic factory in Vietri (Italy), designed by Paolo Soleri.

At the same time, we began a very interesting collaboration, involving 3D printing with clay and semi fluid materials, with Massimo Moretti and his company, Wasp. The aim was to explore eco-digital fabrication protocols and test his beta version of the Delta 3D printer for architectural applications using natural and semi-fluid material systems. When we were invited to participate in the Marrakech Biennale, we took it as an opportunity to investigate the thousand-year legacy of Moroccan earthen architecture and traditional ceramics and its possible future.

We were also drawing on our previous experiences with the Italian ceramics industrial district, the most important one in the world, where we discovered that 80% of the workers were Moroccan migrants because of their specific knowledge, as well as their need for stable work. Since we have always investigated the relation between industrial revolutions and migratory fluxes, the idea of contextualizing advanced technologies in this region seemed a concrete way to generate a possible socio-economic shift, creating better job opportunities locally.

We strategically decided to transform an abandoned factory in the Medina of Marrakech as an experimental laboratory for 3D printing, preserving its role as a production space in opposition to the gentrification processes related to the dynamics of mass tourism. In order to achieve this long-term objective, we wanted to make the technology accessible and affordable to the local community of artisans. Consequently, we offered two kinds of courses: one for the self-construction of a 3D printer and the other for experimenting with the uses for a local mix of clay.

One the one hand, we developed a partnership with the Cfqmam, the training centre for artisans in Marrakech. On the other, we launched an open call on the web to involve people from different backgrounds. The response was very interesting, and a very diverse group of people were involved from the very beginning in redesigning the laboratory space and in developing a collective diagram to share the main principles of the project.

Self-construction of an Off-grid 3D Printer

The first course aimed to teach students how to design and make their own open-source 3D printer with materials available on site. We considered this a starting point to allow local artisans and students to become autonomous and to gain access to the technology, transforming it and hacking it according to their specific needs. With them, we developed a construction kit inspired by an open-source delta model available online. We self-fabricated all the mechanisms, merging different techniques and using recycled materials from plastic to timber. In parallel, we introduced students to free access software to set up the machine and develop their digital models. At the same time, a group of artisans proposed incorporating the device into their daily activities, going from one market to another during the week. Given these constraints, we developed a series of transportable 3D printer prototypes inspired by local vendors' carts.

The technical implications of making the device transportable were quite challenging and confronted with the question of energy supply. We incorporated a PV panel into the cart structure to feed the 3D printer motors. Given the climatic conditions of the Marrakech region and the cost of a basic PV micro-panel to produce the required energy, this strategy guaranteed a low-cost solution for the first off-grid 3D printer of its time. The idea behind this movable device was based on two main aspects: first, to allow the local artisans to share their acquired knowledge with a wider community by transporting the 3D printer directly to public spaces for workshops, etc. The second aspect, more ambitious, was to allow larger scale productions on site. The question of bringing the device to sites without an energy supply would minimise the embodied carbon of the whole production chain, starting from the greenhouse gas emissions from transporting materials.

With the members of the group led by Elena Bellantoni and the team of local artisans, we organised a sort of itinerant urban fabrication performance, crossing the Marrakech medina with the 3D printer cart to reach the Jemaa el Fnaa marketplace. This attracted the interest of a huge number of people of all ages, giving them the opportunity to see a 3D printer at work for the first time. The kids in the market called the device the "magic machine". After the performance, we left the prototype for the group of local artisans involved in its construction to allow them to keep updating it for their activities.

3D Printing Experiments with Local Clay

Earth could be considered one of the oldest building materials, due to its large diffusion and shortness of time from deposit to treatment. Building with earth also offers many desirable properties: thermal mass characteristics (energy efficiency), humidity controlling properties (environmental control), and plasticity of form (structural stability). For these reasons, we focused on different architectural precedents using earth and their emergent technologies, mainly from the history of Islamic architecture. Given the correlation between hot and dry climatic conditions, deforestation, and earthen tectonics, the Moroccan vernacular offered some of the most interesting examples.

Rammed hearth is the main material used for different structural typologies, which is then decorated with local geometric motifs. Certain geometric patterns are typical of the Atlas Mountains and the Sahara and pre-Sahara regions dominated by the Amazigh culture. In these rural regions there are many built examples of traditional ksour (fortified villages) and kasbahs (fortresses) like Ait Benhaddou, which has some interesting terracotta elements.

At the same time, we began to investigate the possibility of evolving the traditional additive process using a mix of traditional and advanced tools, such as computer numerical control (CNC) machines. Our aim was to improve the environmental and structural performances, optimising material consumption and generating a scalable approach to earth architectures for contemporary living. Our on-site explorations in Morocco began with a journey to the south of Marrakech towards Ouarzazate. Systematically, we collected a catalogue of earth samples from different inland desertic and semi-desertic areas. The field trip helped us to learn more about the earthen villages and kasbahs in the region, and to understand the local additive techniques and the resulting types of tectonics.

The result of this investigation was an initial local material archive based on the physical characteristics, granulometry, etc. This gave rise to a series of possible mixtures that could be extruded following the additive processes based on the sedimentation of layers. This material archive was processed in our Marrakech lab thanks to the support of local artisans, and it was tested through different 3D-printing protocols. These tests were used to analyse the interactions between the characteristics of different local clay samples (mixed with different water quantities) and the machine's parameters (extruder dimension, velocity, flux pressure, etc.). We drew on our initial investigations developed in southern Italy with our Big Delta 3D printer, which we dismantled and transported to Marrakech. At the time, the machine powered by Wasp was one of the first affordable prototypes worldwide to extrude semifluid materials. The features included a 60-cm diameter bed for a printable height of 50-60 cm maximum; the extrusion diameter varied from 0.3 to 1.2 cm.

Thanks to the technical support of Massimo Moretti and his team, we began to fine tune the settings on our machine and the extruders, hacking them according to the site-specific materials and thermal conditions. The machine featured a small external tank containing the clay to extrude; due to the hot and dry conditions in Marrakech we had to hack this device to avoid fast water evaporation inside the tank. Meanwhile, it occurred to us that we could mix the clay several times during the printing process in order to keep the material extrudable. Once the machine was set, we looked at several initial tests made with different forms and clay mixtures. We found that the printer worked better on shapes with wide, circular cross sections following a harmonic spiral movement during the extrusion. Therefore, taking inspiration from traditional Moroccan patterns seen in spontaneous settlements and other informal devices, we generated a catalogue of prototypical extruded shells and textures, from 100% to 20% infill. We also tested different filling patterns, such as orthogonal or hexagonal, to test their different degrees of resistance. With local artisans, we discovered that the cross section at the base of the object to print should be thicker and wider than at the top; the maximum angle without support that can be printed should not exceed 40°.

This catalogue of prototypes generated a very promising architectural taxonomy with ties to different kinds of African adobe architectures: from the squarer styles from the Berber culture of the north to the more circular geometries from the Musgum tradition of the sub-Saharan regions. The potential of this taxonomy and its further development was discussed at different levels, initially with the Moroccan artisans and the technical partners, and then with the scientific community at the International Association for Shell and Spatial Structures (IASS) during their International Symposium in Amsterdam (2015). For many years after the Marrakech lab experience, we tried very hard to find the resources to 3D print 1-to-1 scale affordable buildings, pushing the boundaries of the technology's future and its social role. It seems that the old-fashioned competitive approach of many Western companies and academic institutions is preventing this opportunity from being accessible for broader development, despite the collective dimension of the tradition of building with earth.

That said, we are particularly proud to have been invited over the years to share this experience in many contexts, from the IAAC in Barcelona to the Milan Triennale etc., inspiring many new courses and projects from famous colleagues. This motivated us to evolve and transfer this knowledge into the new African Fabbers projects.

Organizational diagrams of the laboratory spatial development

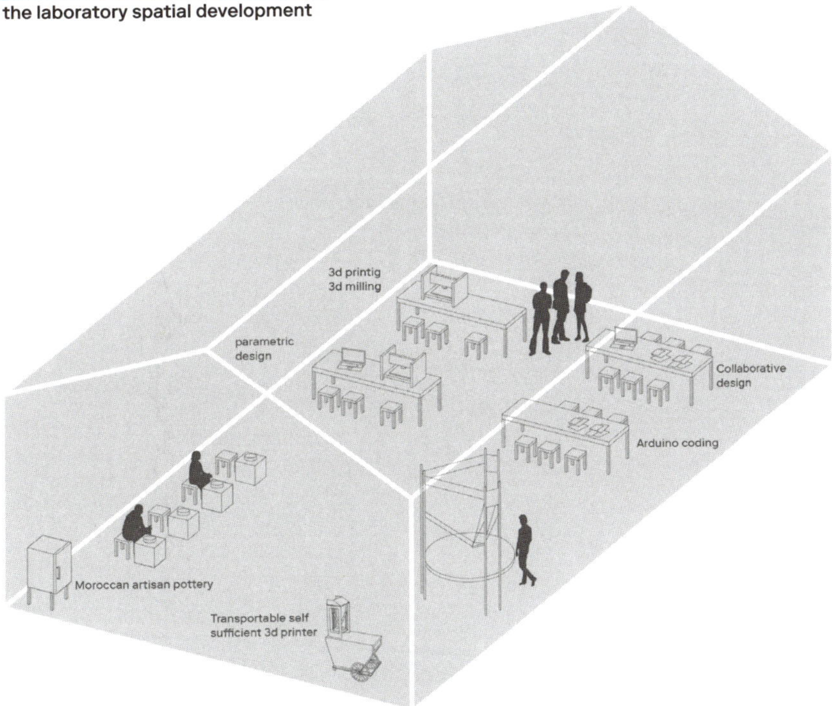

Lab space

Collecting and processing the sand of Moroccan desert with the WASP 3d printing team

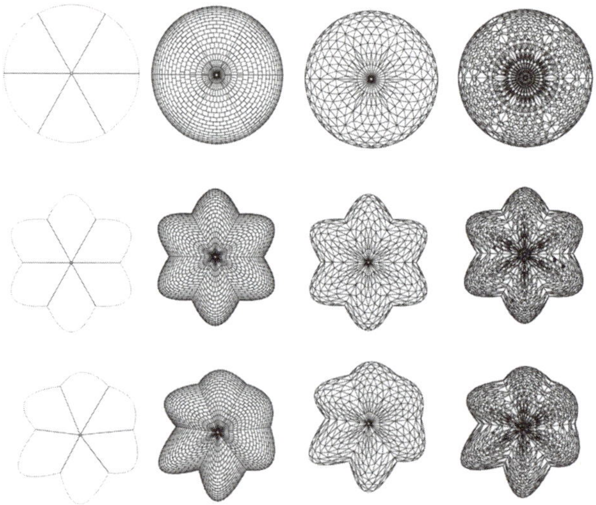

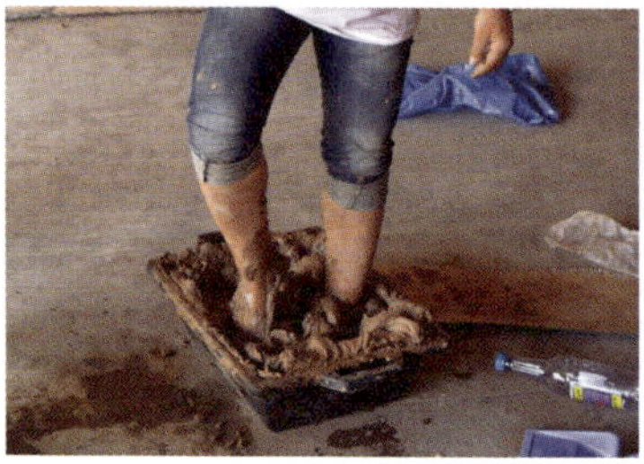

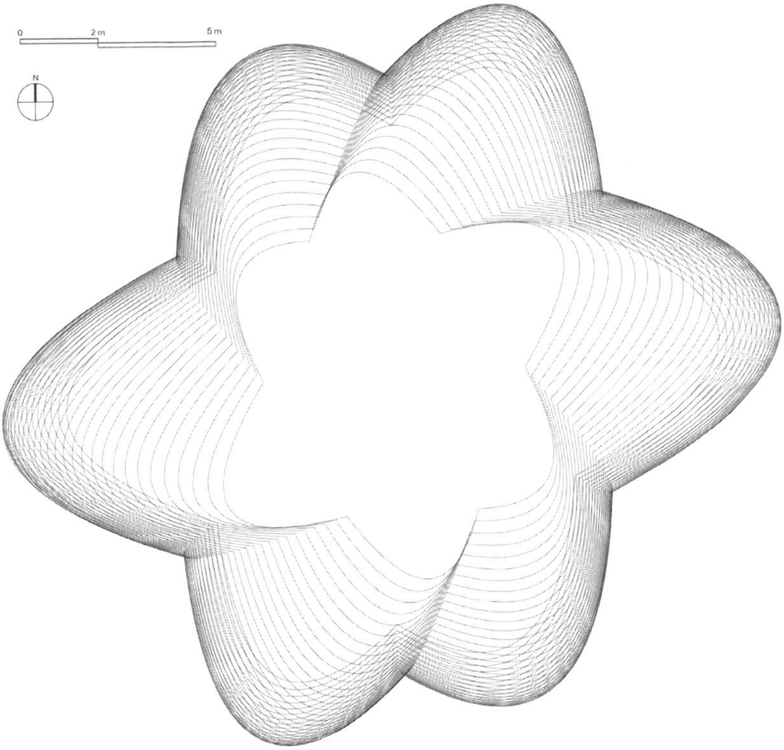
0
2 m
5 m
N

U3DP MARRAKECH

SITE
Marrakech

CLIENT
Marrakech Biennale

PROGRAMME
Mobile open source 3d printer

TEAM
Paolo Cascone with Elena Ciancio, Flavio Galdi, GiulianoGalluccio, Andrea Giglio, Imma Polito, Elena Bellantoni

LOCAL COMMUNITY
Zaim Abderrahman, El mehdi Agharsane, Sharif Anouar, Kenzah Atif, Ramia Beladel, Mehdi Belhajjam, Elena Bellantoni, Aahd Benchaouch, Mohammed Amine Chafai, Klara gaia Chastan, Nada Dhaiba, Taoufiq Edday, Abdelhakim el Hamime, Hatouch el Houssaine, Mohamed Elkhaloua, Karima Elkhider, Youssef Errihan, Rachid er Rmizy, Ehsan Fardjadniya, Azzedine fettahi, Ilhame Hassani, Abdeslam Khaloufi, Mohamed Labid, Ayoub Iharchi, Zineb nait Imaaz, Salma louise, Oussama Mahassine, Carlos Martinez, Yakubu hassan Mohammed, Youness Mouhtadi, Taha Ouilal, Hicham Ousalah, Wael Touati, Khalid beny Yakhlaf.

MATERIALS
Wood, photovoltaic panels

PARTNERS
Città della scienza Naples; Inarcassa foundation; Voice gallery; Cfqmam – Centre de formation et qualification dans les métiers de l'artisanat

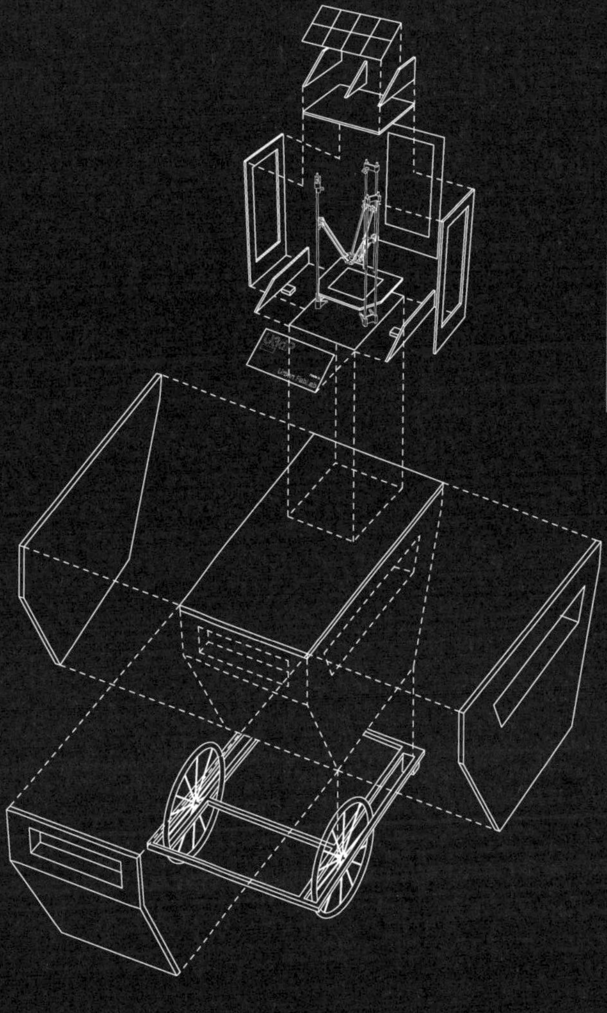

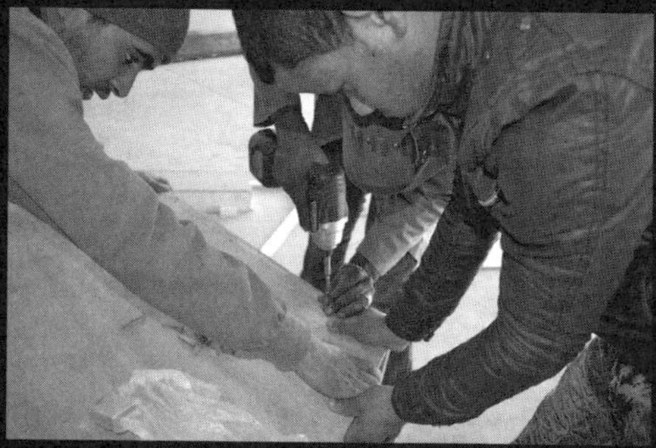

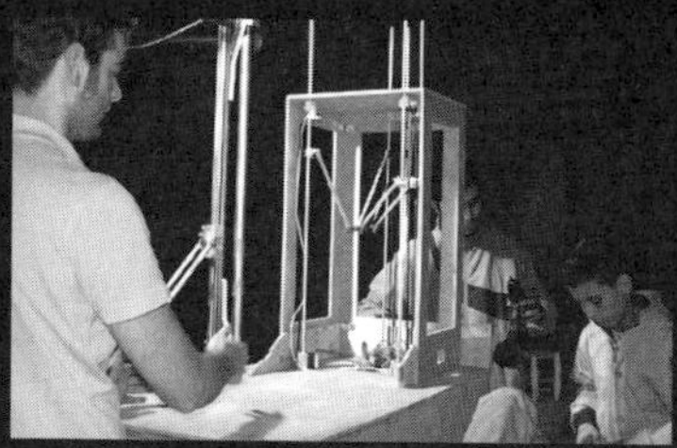

1

3d printer performance at Jemaa el-Fnaa

OPEN AIR LAB — SENEGAL 2014

SITE
Dakar
14°41'34"N
17°26'48"W

CLIMATE REGION
Hot semi-arid

CLIENT
La Biennale de Dakar

PROGRAMME
Open Air fabrication Laboratory

TEAM
Paolo Cascone with Elena Ciancio, Flavio Galdi, Giuliano Galluccio, Andrea Giglio, Imma Polito

LOCAL COMMUNITY
Roland Assilevi, Ahmadou ba, Biggiie, Demba Camawa, Ibra Cassis, Moustapha Coly, Seydou Dièmè, Stefano Ferrero, Racine Gaye, Alessia Guardo, Ariss godwill Hounkpatin, Dodji Koffihonou, Daouda Kote, Alexandre Lette, Nolèye Manè, Mariana Michalcikova, Susanna Molina, Modou Ngom, Angelina Nwachukwu, Désiré Nwaobasi, Mame less Jean Seck

STRUCTURAL SYSTEM
Branching system

MATERIALS
Local wood, bamboo and photovoltaic

PARTNERS
Ker thiossane – Defko ak niep Lab Urban fablab, Città della scienza; Inarcassa foundation

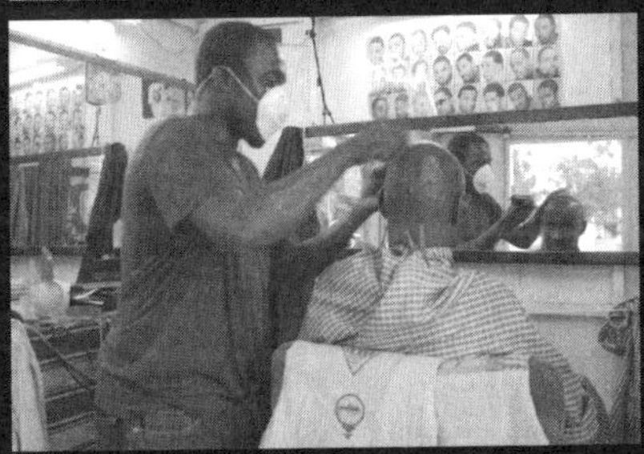

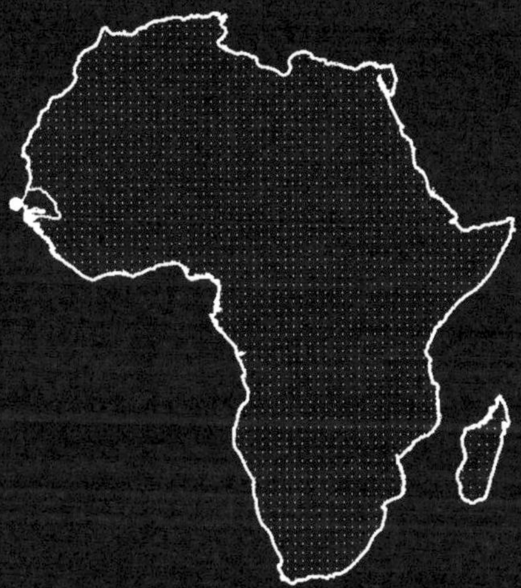

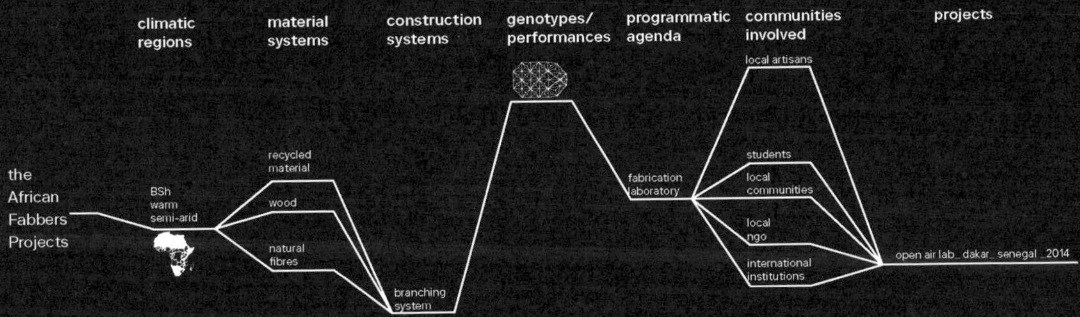

After the Marrakech laboratory, the interest in the African Fabbers proj-ect was growing widely, especially among the informal network of African makers. The idea of developing a sustainable and site-specific approach to digital fabrica-tion attracted the interest of many local NGOs that started to contact us for possi-ble collaborations. We decided strategically to accept an invitation from the Dakar Biennale as an opportunity to produce new knowledge with the local community. At the time, we were already following the work of Ker Thiossane, an independent new media centre founded by Marion Louysgrand-Sylla in the popular Sicap-Liberté neighbourhood. We were intrigued by their work and their environmental activism, involving the community in the development of a network of "resistance gardens", as well as their role as digital culture drivers in promoting Afropixel: the first festi-val of digital media, public space art, and open-source technology in Africa. Since we shared their interdisciplinary approach and their very concrete reflections on the commons, we proposed collaborating on an AF session in Dakar. The aim was to support the development of their DefkoAkNiep Lab (do it with others), the first fablab in Senegal.

The proposal was a perfect match for their objectives, and we began discussing the kind of outputs of the collaboration. On the one hand, they wanted to train a group of artisans in digital design and digital manufacturing, while, on the other, they expressed their need to expand the existing laboratory in order to host more activities. In response, we developed two sessions: the first was to map the site and develop three design solutions; the second involved the self-construction of a 1-to-1 scale version of the selected concept. Thanks to Marion and Amadou, we started to familiarise ourselves with the local community of artisans and analyse the site from the social and environmental points of view. In response to our online open call, the design workshop involved a mixed group of timber workers, engineer-ing students, and artists.

This mix allowed us to develop some very interesting computational and physical investigations, introducing open-source parametric software and learning from local techniques of woven envelopes. The idea behind the prototypes for urban canopies was based on the observation of the role of trees in Senegalese public spaces as social attractors for their ability to provide shade and well-ventilated accessible solutions. For this reason, we developed three alternative proposals to discuss and validate with the local community during an open conversation. The prototypes were explained to the public mainly through a series of physical models built using the wireframe techniques of streets artisans as a very interesting approach to test the structural performance. The final decision was to adopt the proposal for a branching canopy system, a lightweight structure that could protect the existing artisans' labs from the sun and create a new open-air lab that would be naturally ventilated and visible from the street. We developed a more accurate model, exploring different ways of contextualising the Lindenmayer algorithm. The aim was to control the branching structure using digital simulations to verify the environmental performances and fine tune the chosen configuration before moving on to the construction phases. The final result of the design process was a network of interconnected artificial trees shaped around an existing tree. The branches connected to one another in order to create an undulating thatched roof intended to collect rainwater to be used by a local association to water the garden in front of the lab during the region's prolonged dry season. The structure was conceived as a living infrastructure that could perform as a double ventilated roof for some of the existing buildings underneath. This was one of the most popular aspects among the local community, in addition to the possibility of expanding the canopy over time as a growing structure that could respond to new spatial requirements. In the second workshop, the entire team focused on the selected solution with the aim of developing the construction details and testing the tectonics. At the same time, we visited the different markets and artisans' workshops in the surrounding area to map possible material systems available on site. As deforestation is rapidly affecting Senegal, we were interested in local techniques using fast-growing construction and recycled materials.

As we were fascinated by the tradition of pirogue construction, made by local carpenters for fishermen, we also visited small coastal villages outside Dakar, where piles of wood lay scattered around from the debris of old and half-completed vessels. Since the characteristic variety of rosewood used for these boats is obtained from the Casamance forest region, an area that has been plagued by illegal logging in recent years, we wanted to repurpose some of these offcuts by giving them a new life. We split the team into three groups, taking inspiration from a tree-like structural organisation, to develop the different building components. We used different sections of small local timber elements for the "roots" /foundations, the "trunk"/pillars, and the recycled wood "branches" /roof frames. For the "foliage" of the artificial trees, we developed a catalogue of panels, taking inspiration from traditional artifacts made from split woven bamboo of different sizes. Once the material arrived on the site, we organised a production chain to fabricate the different architectural elements and to assemble the system from the ground up: attaching the "roots" to a new geo-concrete slab and the "trunks" to the foundation points.

The branching system was developed by a very talented carpenter who created tailor-made three-dimensional nodes connecting the structure to the existing buildings while protecting their roofs. The paneling was made from woven fibres, assembled as sort of sandwich system sometimes integrating corrugated plastic sheets to provide waterproof zones underneath. The result of this collaborative self-manufacturing process was a very solid, open structure developed to endure and grow over time. The project was displayed in the context of the Dakar Biennale, and we invited the neighbourhood to a public event to disseminate the entire construction process and discuss possible improvements and further developments. To our great satisfaction, we still receive updates from the Ker Thiossane about the activities developed under the canopy, which is still standing after many years thanks to the systematic maintenance on the part of the local community. Beyond the physical output, no doubt the most valuable result is the number of similar projects that the team of local carpenters has developing as a result of this training experience.

Bibliography

Airoldi, Silvia. "Urban [FabLab] Ecologies." Ottagono n° 273 (2015): 120–125.
Cascone, Paolo, "Architectural Fabrication. Towards eco-digital design to build process in Architecture." In *Computational Morphologies*, edited by Michela Rossi, Giorgio Buratti, 1–22. Springer, 2018.
Cascone, Paolo. "Decolonising performative architecture, Towards alternative models of climate sensitive design in *Post-normal design: Emergent approaches towards plural worlds*, edited by Alastair Fuad-Luke, 135–143. Porto: esad-idea, 2022.
Cascone, Paolo "Fabrizio Carola: the social role of technology." *Industria delle Costruzioni* n° 465 (2019): 120–123.
Cascone, Paolo." Structural Eco-system" *L'Architecture d'Aujourdhui* (2011): 93–97. Cascone, Paolo. "Talking about architecture bores me – I prefer making it instead." *Domus web* 2020. https://www.domusweb.it/en/architecture/gallery/2019/01/29/fabrizio-carola-obituary-africa.html
Cascone, Paolo. "The fourth ecology." *Domus* n° 940 (2010): 47–49.
Cascone, Paolo, et al. "Architectural self-fabrication". *International Journal of Parallel, Emergent and Distributed Systems*, 32, 2017, S39-S53.
Cascone, Paolo and Laddaga, Maddalena "African Fabbers Cities: new opportunities for self-organisation and self-production in the African urban context". At the frontiers of the urban: thinking concepts and practices globally-UCL University College London.
Cascone, Paolo, Sossa, Jaun P., Louisgrand, Marion. "How can we create a together creolization of protocols." *Folios* n° 4 – 2022. Moleskine Foundation: 76–109.
Claypool, Mollie, "The digital in Architecture. Then, Now and in the future" Space 10 Journal, 2019.
Flow of Forms / Forms of Flow: Design Histories Between Africa and Europe. Germany: transcript Verlag, 2018.
Keuning, David. "*Paolo Cascone combines high-tech design and low-tech construction techniques in Africa*." *Mark* n°29 (2010): 210–211.
Maditla, Neo. "Merging architecture, entrepreneurship and digital fabrication in Cameroon." DesignIndaba 2019. https://www.designindaba.com/articles/creative-work/merging-architecture-entrepreneurship-and-digital-fabrication-cameroon?fbclid=IwAR398KxJ0mcYVrqQGh7PtSrM98TD9xNC6PzotNLGuelHU6h8kk1Z-O7LWcA
Mostafavi, Mohsen, Gareth Doherty, and Harvard University. Graduate School of Design. *Ecological Urbanism.* Baden, Switzerland: Lars Müller, 2010.
Peluso, Salvatore. "The first digital manufacturing laboratory for architecture and design in Africa." Domus web. 2018. https://www.domusweb.it/en/design/2018/12/26/the-first-digital-manufacturing-laboratory-for-architecture-and-design-in-africa.html
Sarr, Felwine. *Afrotopia*. USA: University of Minnesota Press, 2020.
Sassen, Saskia "Global City 20 Years Later" Diversified Solutions A New Beginning in Architecture, *a+u magazine* n° 485 (2011): 10.
Tozzi, Lucia. "Design Post vernacular." *Abitare* n° 509 (2011): 94–99.

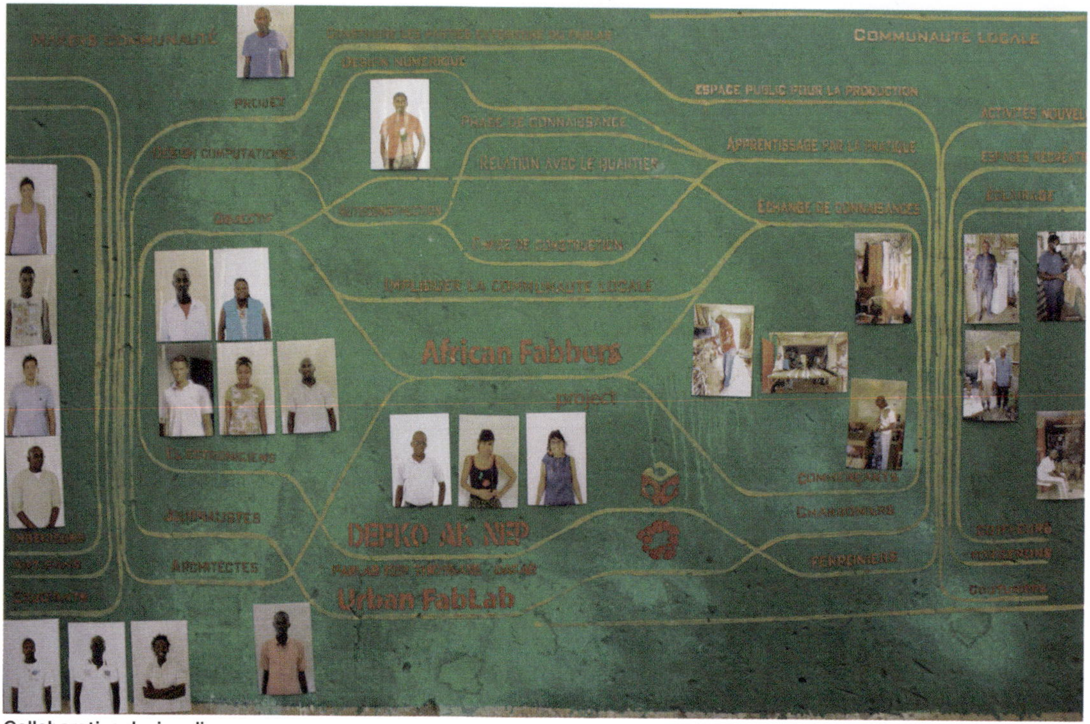

Collaborative design diagram

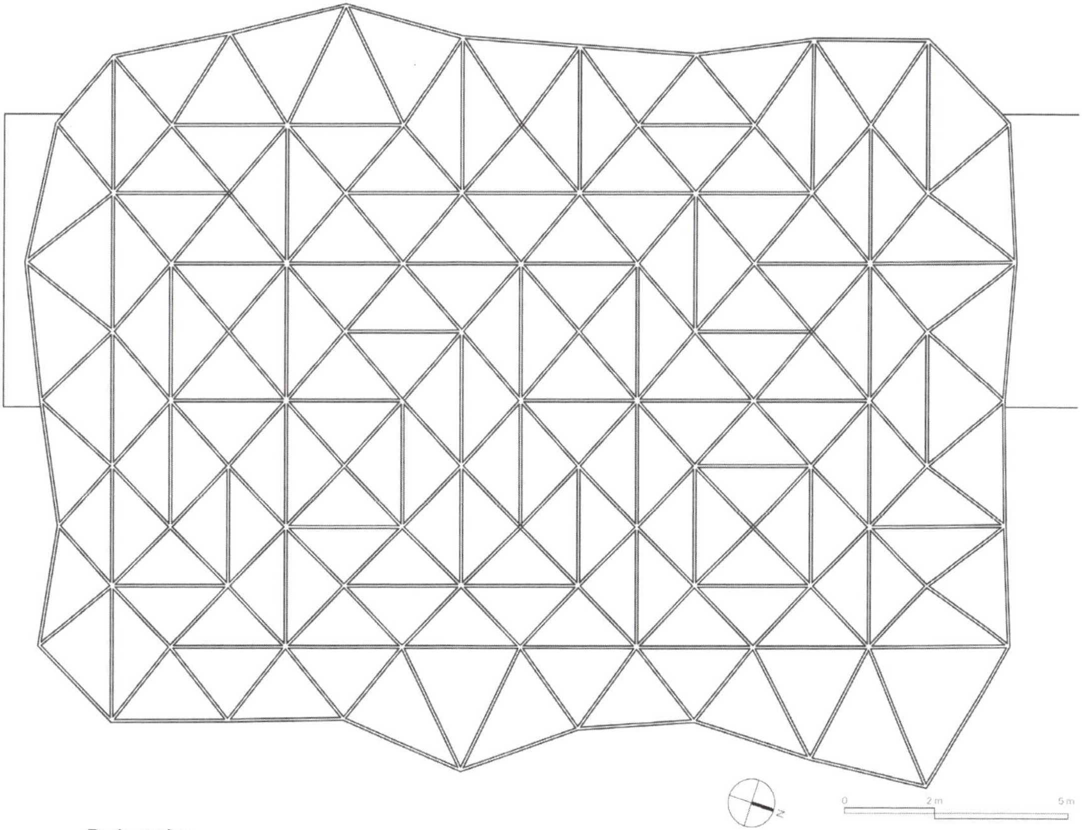

Project plan

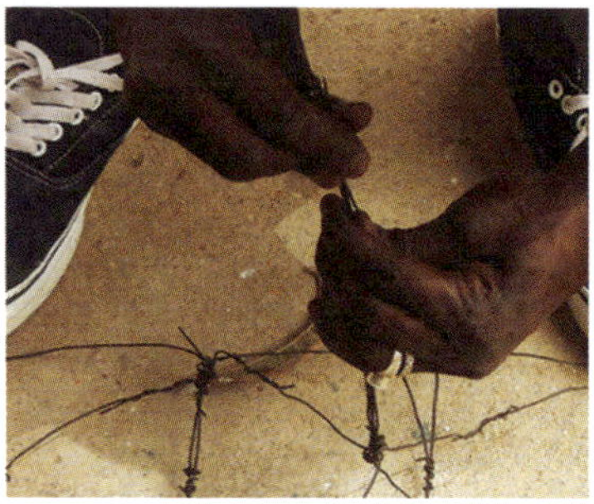

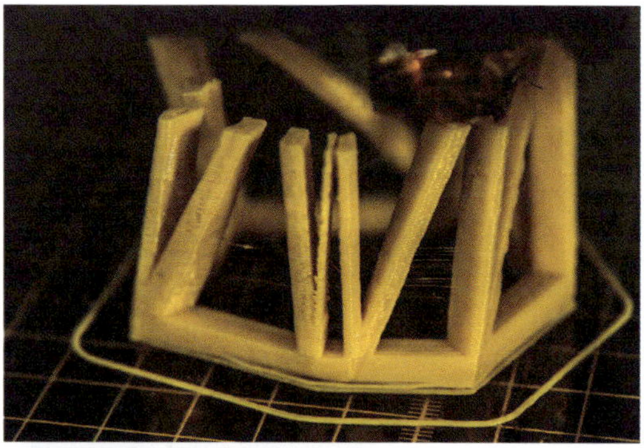

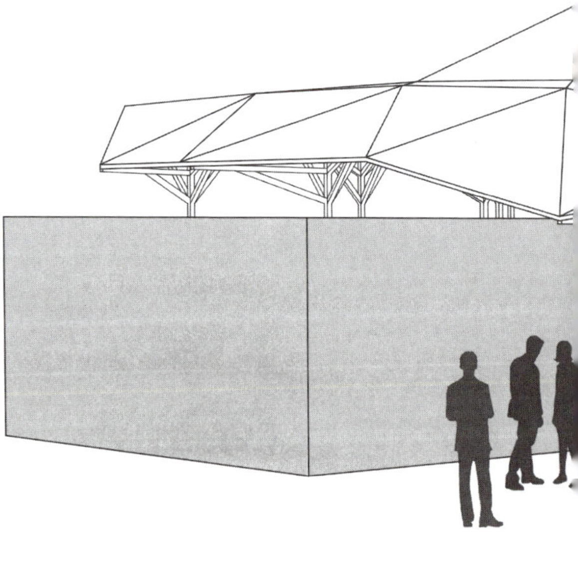

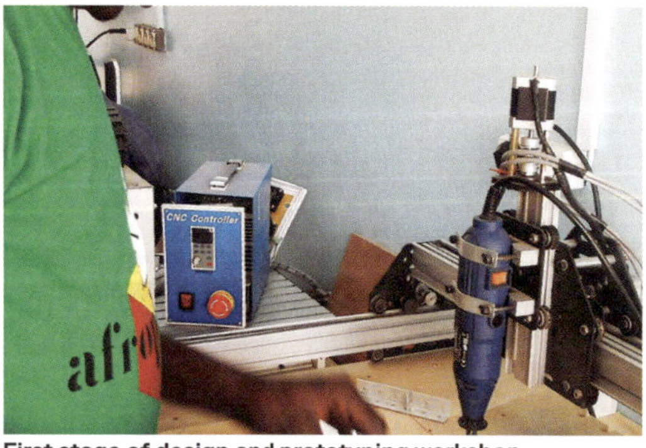

First stage of design and prototyping workshop

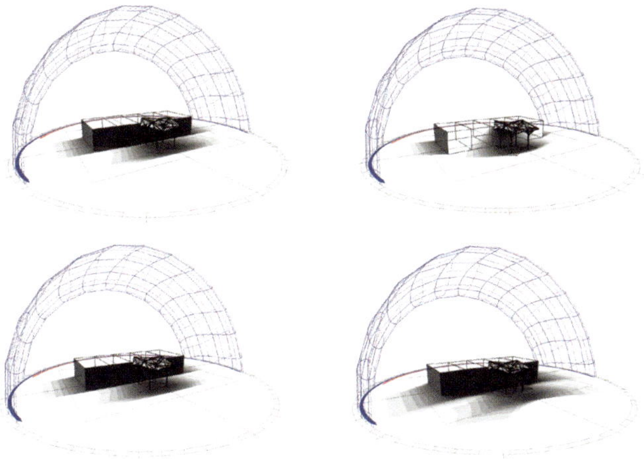

Environmental analysis of the open air lab

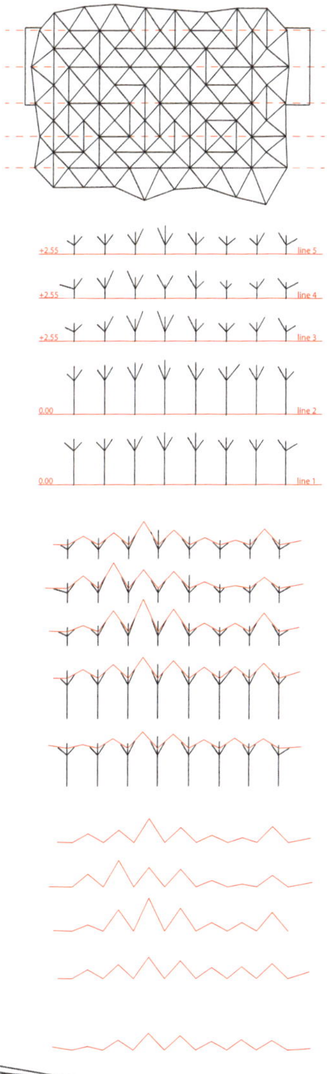

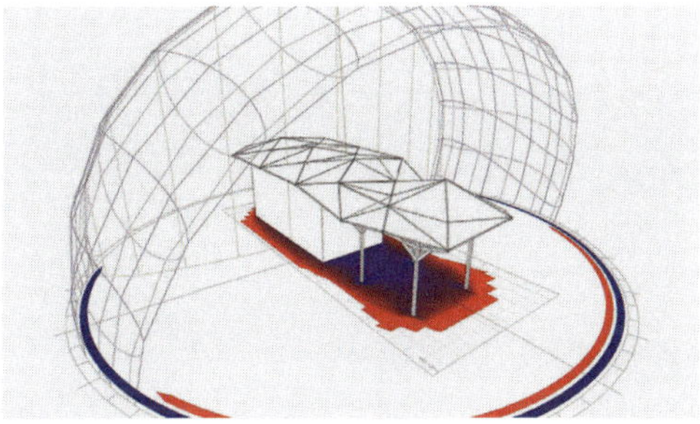

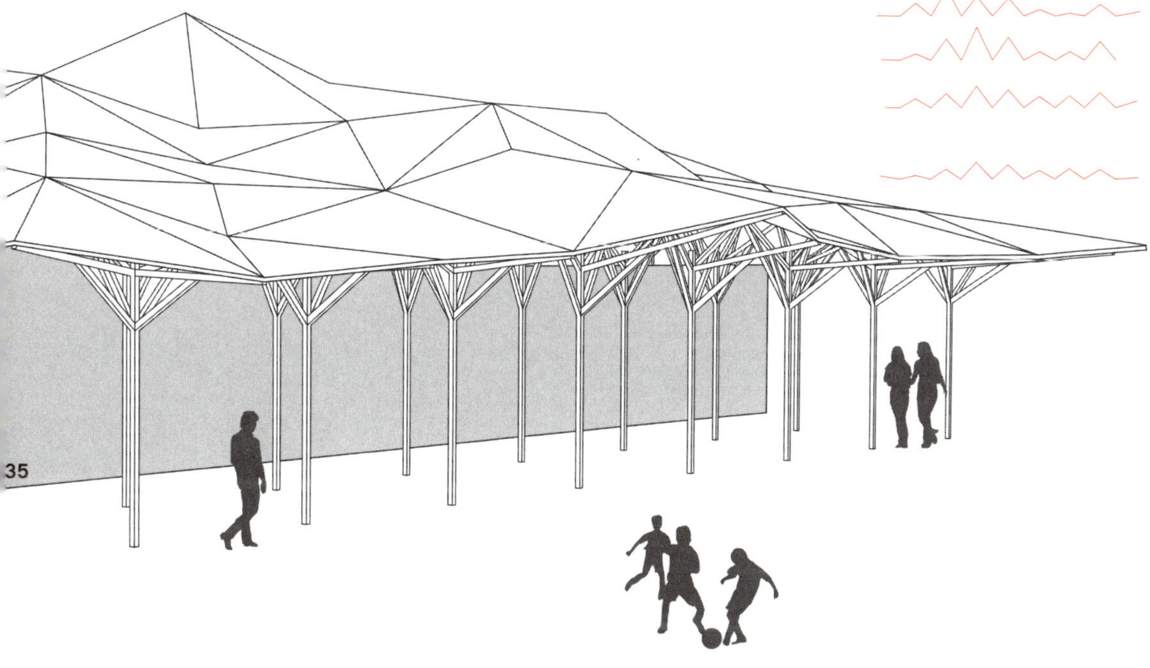

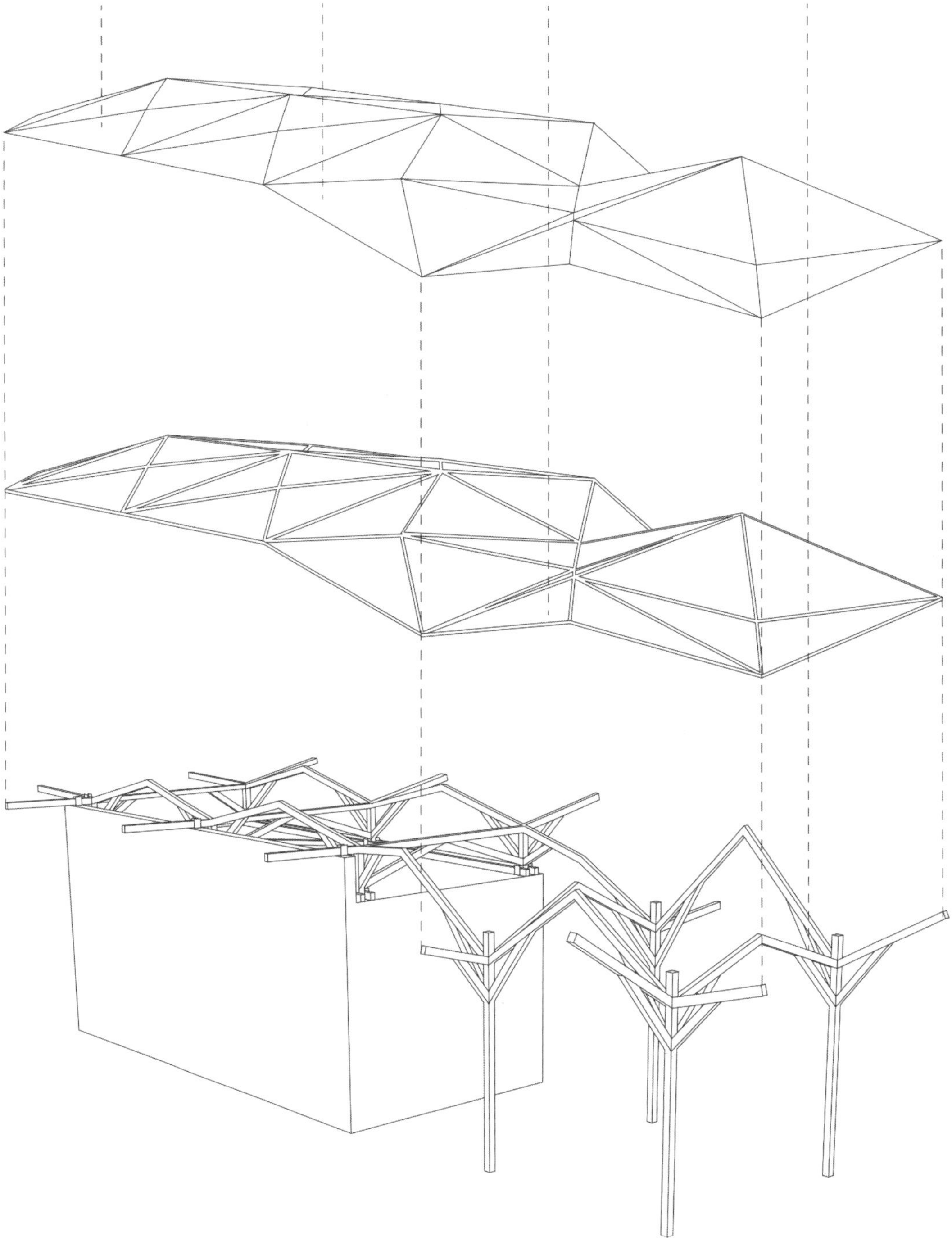

Project view

Second stage of self construction workshop

Third stage of self construction workshop

Inauguration of the Open Air Lab

Canon

IV
The Douala Cultural Platform

4.1 Educational models for independent schools

My personal, professional and academic experiences in the Global South have led me to believe that without a decolonised approach to the history of our planet, there is little chance we will succeed in addressing the current global climatic and social crisis. This ecological approach to history should include the very rich knowledge from the pre-colonial and informal cultures of the Global South. Therefore, more attention should be paid, especially by the Western world, to the alternative and hidden environmental and architectural models developed in Africa. The pedagogical models and the role of universities should be seriously called into question for their inability to produce and disseminate new, inclusive forms of knowledge that can overturn some of the dynamics of our societies. In particular, the inadequacy of contemporary architectural pedagogies is mainly related to the fact that schools perpetuate the logics of professional practice rather than developing alternative approaches. These alternative approaches should be based on the principles of social and environmental ecology to offer diversified solutions to complex issues. Instead, the issue of complexity is often delegated to technology without questioning the cultural and anthropological foundations associated with its evolution in different contexts. This cultural shift should come from new approaches to teaching architectural history and theory. In truth, the question introduced by Cedric Price in one of his memorable lectures at the AA (1966), "Technology is the answer... but what was the question?", is still very timely. In fact, in our hyper technologized society, asking ourselves the right questions is becoming paradoxically more and more difficult: the definition may require a critical reinterpretation of the history of our planet and a paradigm shift regarding to the Western idea of progress.

The Need for a Cultural Shift

The aforementioned cultural shift should begin by stressing that one of the oldest continuously operating institutions of higher education worldwide is the University of Sankoré, built by Berbers in Timbuktu (Mali) in the 1100s. From an architectural point of view, the university buildings were made mainly of clay, generating a very interesting network of courtyards, but the most important aspect was related to its governance. As a matter of fact, the pedagogy was developed as a sort of knowledge exchange platform, where classes were conducted in open courtyards without a central authority. The educational system seemed very articulated and competitive, and prior to entering the university, students pursued two degrees: one in Arabic language and the other in poetry and literature. Once they entered the university, students followed a very holistic programme based on different courses, from philosophy and Islamic law to physics, medicine, chemistry, arithmetic, and astronomy. Unfortunately, for many reasons, this sophisticated and pioneering educational model could not expand widely across the continent because of the colonial policy of imposing a Western system.

As a matter of fact, the result of the colonial influence on the development of higher education intuitions in Africa generated multiple critical effects: on the one hand, a lack of universities and, on the other, a diaspora of African students attending Western educational institutions. As shown by recent studies and statistics on studying in the UK and the fluctuation of migration dynamics, this is becoming a geopolitical issue. The third non-EU country (after India) sending the most students to the UK is Nigeria, with 21,305 students currently enrolled in UK institutions [1].

At the same time, as predicted by UNESCO's Institute for Statistics, students from Sub-Saharan Africa will remain attracted to US universities for access to a high-quality education. Last year, these students represented 4% of the international student community in the US; the main countries of origin are Ghana, South Africa, Cameroon, Ethiopia, Nigeria, and Kenya. African students make up 43.2% of all foreign students in France, with "figures for other continents now decreasing slightly". Despite growing interest in the higher education market in Africa, as explained very well by Achille Mbembe in his article "Decolonizing the University: New Directions"[2], a mix of political actions will be needed to achieve decolonisation. First of all, he highlights the question of improving the accessibility to knowledge, which (especially in Africa) is still limited to a very restricted number of people. Secondly, Mbembe proposes overturning the economic system that has transformed higher education into a "marketable product" based on standardisation, credits, and penalties. This authoritarian system discourages students and teachers from an independent and accessible pursuit of knowledge. As mentioned in his article, as a result of this dynamic universities have become very bureaucratised environments, where most of the evaluation criteria are based on a quantitative approach, considering students as customers and consumers. Mbembe proposes breaking with this cycle, in which universities' main concern is to make students happy as customers rather than involving them in the processes of knowledge production. This should occur through a process of decolonisation, which would transition the notion of a university toward a pluriversity, as pointed out by Boaventura de Sousa and Enrique Dusse: "By pluriversity, many understand a process of knowledge production that is open to epistemic diversity. To decolonize the University is therefore to reform it with the aim of creating a less provincial and more open critical cosmopolitan pluriversalism – a task that involves the radical re-founding of our ways of thinking and a transcendence of our disciplinary divisions."[3]

If we consider the field of architecture, the main principles/pillars of what is called "ecological design" are related to such cultures for their capability to generate site-specific responses to extreme climatic conditions, reconciling nature with *tekhne*. Since a paradigm shift in the architectural education system is needed widely (in the Global North as well as in the South), the first question is: What should be the foundations for rebuilding the discipline? In response is the risky decision of considering Africa as a possible laboratory for innovative pedagogies: starting by learning from very diverse experiences that represent, in a paradigmatic way, both informal African processes of knowledge production and radical educational experiments developed between Europe and Africa from the 1950s through the 1970s.

This diachronic approach, although quite controversial, aims to generate a possible cultural common ground as a synthesis between different cultural models. It should be taken for granted that the best examples for teaching pre-colonial cultures should come from African universities and their ways of learning from their heritage and producing new knowledge from it in terms of content and methodologies. Unfortunately, we quickly find that in African academic institutions, there is still a cultural resistance – paradoxically more so than in Western countries – toward shifting this paradigm. Because universities are still organised as colonial products, only a restricted elite associated with the diaspora is developing critical thinking on the topic of decolonising architectural education.

Sankoré Mosque of Timbuktu and Mosque Djenné (Mali)

Community as School: The Djenné Case Study

In order to broadly re-shape the role of higher education institutions, it would be crucial to learn from the pre-colonial process of knowledge transfer. Looking at the case of traditional African approaches, one of the most interesting aspects is that indigenous education stressed communal and social aspects rather than focusing on the individual. The teaching did not need to be deliberate; it was more implicit. In this approach, the younger generations received the tools to deal with complex material over time, rather than teaching the complex material and then giving them the tools. As evidenced by ethno-mathematicians like Ron Eglash and cultural anthropologists, even without a written language, most indigenous sub-Saharan cultures relied on a computational approach to address complex issues, developing their own techniques for elaborate calculations. This knowledge transfer, based on story-telling from one generation to the next, has always been supported by the learning-by-doing methodology, where the concept of togetherness structures how people live and work together within societies or chiefdoms. While, on the one hand, this oral knowledge transfer has provided a “static” education, conservative with little change, on the other hand, it has supported an inter-generational pact for living in harmony with nature and local resources.

As for other educational spheres in the field of architecture, the pursuit of knowledge has always been action based, considering the community as a school and the construction site as a classroom. In this educational model, construction becomes a collective practice based on a few principles of optimisation, self-organisation and self-sufficiency. For this reason, I would like to propose, as a paradigmatic example of an informal school of ecological architecture, the reconstruction of the Great Mosque of Djenné, which has involved the whole community every year for many years. The Great Mosque was designated a World Heritage site by UNESCO in 1988 as one of the most relevant examples of Sudano-Sahelian architecture, as well as the largest building made of mudbrick. The building itself is an informal manifesto of bioclimatic earthen architecture, a tangible, open-air manual on environmental design and ecological construction, from which the local community learned how to make their own adobe homes.

In response to the very hot and dry climatic conditions of the southern Sahara of Mali, the walls are made out of adobe plastering and wooden scaffolding providing thermal insulation. The roof openings are distributed to provide passive cooling ventilation during the dry season and are fabricated with terracotta devices that can be closed during the rainy season. Nevertheless, what makes the Great Mosque a contemporary example of the open-air school of ecological design is the cultural event called the Crépissage (Plastering), in which the whole community collaborates on the structural reinforcement of the building ahead of the rainy season (July - August), which concentrates almost the entire 1,000 mm of average annual rainfall. At the same time, the Crépissage is not only an important technical act of preserving the building, but it is also a festival that celebrates Djenné’s community and heritage. The night before starting the reconstruction, known as La Nuit de Veille, the people of the surrounding villages dance and sing together to celebrate the event like a kind of carnival. The Crépissage is than coordinated under the supervision of dozens of senior masons *Barey*, a highly revered profession in Djenné. The key role of the *Barey* consists in selecting, training, and guiding their young disciples from each neighbourhood, transforming the event into a sort of hands-on master class. In this informal master class, the whole community contributes to the effort, each group playing a different role; while women bring the water from the river to mix with the mud, children contribute by carrying baskets to the masons. Men usually collaborate in the preparation of the construction material (banco), a mix of fine clay from the nearby rivers, rice bran, shea butter, baobab powder, and water.

As recently explained by the mayor of Djenné, Balassiné Yaro, "The mosque of Djenné is a symbol of social cohesion every year; the communal participation in the maintenance work shows the sense of community and an expression of how to live together"[4]. Despite its centuries-long history, due to social involvement the mosque is reborn every year as a living infrastructure with a slightly different shape, preserving its cultural heritage as a fundamental part of Djenné's contemporary society. This collective experience is also a driver for teaching the community about the construction of the entire city, generating a taxonomy of very diversified architectural typologies from housing to community-oriented buildings.

From the Bauhaus to the AA's Department of Tropical Architecture

Despite the growing interest in such informal knowledge in Western schools of architecture, there is still a lack of programmes that study it systematically and view it in methodological terms. Above all, there are only a few applied research studies that analyse the pedagogical logics, beyond such knowledge as a key factor in new models of sustainable development. Moreover, there are only a few books on the history of African architecture that highlight the possible implications of its legacy for a contemporary perspective. In most cases, the most relevant contributions on the topic do not reach beyond a basic classification of precedents. At the same time, the authors of these contributions are mainly non-African, which does not helping in understanding the history from the indigenous point of view. As a consequence of this cultural gap, the titles of architectural courses in Western universities have remained almost the same for decades, mirroring a sort of cultural resistance to hybridising and evolving the discipline from other perspectives.

For the above-mentioned reasons, it is difficult to find relevant pedagogical precedents in contemporary universities that are truly engaged with informal knowledge and interdisciplinary approaches. The most interesting experiments on bridging different formal disciplines and informal practices happened between the 1920s and the 1970s. In that respect, I was not surprised to discover some members of the Bauhaus among the forerunners interested in learning from the generative aspects related to southern pre-colonial cultures. Examples include the early studies of Paul Klee in Tunis and Egypt, where he analysed spontaneous settlements as abstract, grid-like fields of colour, as well as the textile experiments of Anni Albers based on vernacular Andean weaving techniques, and Marcel Breuer's interest in traditional African chairs. It is not by chance that the core of their very innovative interdisciplinary pedagogical programme was based on a radical shift from crafting towards mass production processes, starting from their preliminary course on the study of basic material systems and experimental techniques and tools to process them. As a matter of fact, after 1933 when the Bauhaus shut its doors, only a few Western academic institutions and independent schools, such as the Ulm School in Germany or Black Mountain College in the US, were following this innovative and experimental pedagogy. At the same time, some of the most interesting and less well-known experiences were developed during the post-war period in areas of the Global South where former Bauhaus students and staff were involved in shaping alternative pedagogical models for new post-colonial schools of architecture.

It was no coincidence that, around the same time, the most reputed and independent school of architecture worldwide, the Architectural Association in London, founded by a group of students, implemented the first Department of Tropical Architecture in 1954. This initiative began thanks to Adedokun Adeyemi, a Nigerian student at the AA who organised the first Conference on Tropical Architecture in Europe, at the University College of London, in 1953. It was a period when the British colonies were becoming independent, and there was an economic and social enthusiasm related to the development of modern African states that considered architecture as a possible driver of an African identity. For this reason, Adeyemi was no doubt influenced the prevailing debate and found that his architectural education did not prepare him for building in the climatic and socio-economic context of Britain's colonies.

One year after this conference, the Architectural Association launched the Department of Tropical Architecture, whose advisory committee included George Atkinson, Leo De Syllas, and Otto Koenigsberger. At the same time, the AA appointed as course director Maxwell Fry, the importer of Gropius and the Bauhaus into Great Britain, and developed a six-month postgraduate training course mainly focused on building in tropical climates. The interdisciplinary curriculum of the Department of Tropical Architecture was shaped by climate-sensitive design issues, proposing different kinds of courses on advanced climatological studies. In parallel, the university offered specific equipment for use in the design process, such as a heliodon for calculating the values of direct or reflected sunlight, wind tunnels, artificial skies to study daylight with overcast skies, models for studying heat flow, etc. Although this experiment, especially from the Western point of view, contributed to the development of environmental design as a discipline based on bioclimatic principles, the way it imposed the modernism of Western culture onto the regions of the Global South without a real connection to the local pre-colonial culture has been often criticised.

Experimenting with Radical Pedagogies in Africa

Around the same time, as Beatriz Colomina describes it in her book *Radical Pedagogies*[5], many former members of the Bauhaus contributed to founding new schools of architecture in Africa and experimenting with alternative pedagogical models on the continent. In some cases, the knowledge exchange was more the result of a technical diplomacy, like in the case of the Ethoi-Swedish Institute of Building Technology (1954) by Ingvar Eknor, the first transnational programme between Europe and Africa. In the case of the School of Kumasi – Ghana, the first school of architecture in Africa outside of South Africa (established in 1957), where architectural education was first introduced in 1921, the idea was to develop a sort of *Cosmopolitan pedagogy* for post-colonial society. The school was created one year after the country's independence from Britain and was initially supported by the AA school: the dean was John Lloyd, and the programme was inspired by their Tropical Architecture Department. The strategy was to give an initial leading role to British academics with a gradual transition towards Ghanaian leadership. The collaboration with a group of Eastern European architects contributed to a cosmopolitan environment, and the school implemented a multi-disciplinary and comparative approach.

This approach gradually shifted away from Euro-centrism towards a study of *world cultures*, bridging local vernacular culture (a course on architecture without architects was given by Paul Oliver) with performative tectonics (Buckminster Fuller taught structural design) and environmental design (Jane Drew taught a course in tropical architecture and Eustaquio Toledo thermal comfort). The transition was completed during the 1960s when Ghanaian architects like Samuel Opare Larbi and John Owusu-Addo joined the school, developing a more engaged agenda in response to the urgent post-independence challenges. Thereafter, students and staff were involved in many community-oriented projects in the Volta region, addressing the fast population growth and the lack of industrial resources and seeking out solutions regarding affordable housing and infrastructure.

In the case of the Department of Architecture at Ahmadu Bello University (established in 1952 in Zaria, Nigeria) the post-colonial transition was less gradual. Local students and staff launched a revolt in defence of a decolonised educational model thanks to the engagement of one of the few Nigerian lecturers, Ekundayo Adeyemi. In 1968, the students called for radical change as the school, shaped by the Royal Institute of British Architects, was accessible only to the local elite, and British teachers had complained about the lack of quality in *three-dimensional drawings* by local students. This resulted in a large number of failing marks among students who felt discriminated against by the British assessment criteria and the RIBA requirements. Therefore, the school was transferred under the supervision of the Architects Council of Nigeria with a new curriculum inspired by the Ghanaian school of Kumasi.

As a result of this decolonised shift, a new Nigerian head was appointed, Augustin Egbor, and the school began to develop *real life* projects for the local communities of northern Nigeria, involving students and staff in alternative knowledge production. Beyond the creation of these more institutional schools of architecture and their processes of emancipation from the Eurocentric educational model, it is worth citing other independent and non-academic experiences that were being developed in Africa during the same period. One of the most significant was the Mbari Club, initially formed at the Dugbe Market in Ibadan (Nigeria, 1961) by a group of young Nigerian artists and writers, including the Nobel Prize in Literature, Wole Soyinka. The Club's activities included a series of summer schools on the topic of *basic design*, organised between Nigeria and Kenya by Julian Beinart, Pancho Guedes, and Ezekiel Mphahele, among others. As explained by Ayala Levin in her essay " Basic Design Toward Decolonization", the itinerant workshops were developed with the aim of bridging local art and crafts with building technology, experimenting with a sort of *vernacularized Bauhaus pedagogy*.

In particular, the workshops were inspired by the Bauhaus model of *unlearning* to liberate African students from Western preconceptions, generating three-dimensional installations with a critical emphasis on the use of readymade materials. These exercises aimed to reconnect students from different backgrounds with the resources of their environment and their local urban and rural knowledge. The purpose of the approach was to generate a new, non-tribal language that was not even modern according to Western standards. Upon studying these challenging experiments developed between the 1950s and the 1970s, two questions naturally arise:

Did these initiatives achieve their purpose of developing an alternative but contemporary educational model in continuity with pre-colonial cultures? How have those experiences contributed to the further development of African universities and schools of architecture?

Judging from the current situation of the dominant educational models in Africa, it is difficult to evaluate the impact of such radical pedagogical experiences, especially on the development of African schools of architecture. As a matter of fact, a hidden restoration was affecting most of the few African schools of architecture still referring to the Western approach. Their courses were mainly structured with a system based on obsolete European standards, building regulations, architectural typologies, etc. Most of the time, such programmes and their related curriculum are completely detached from the context, preventing the development of more independent and adequate educational and professional paths.

At the same time, recent statistics show that an increasing number of African students are often obliged to migrate abroad to access higher education programmes. In some cases, analysts are showing an interesting trend of new educational migrations to China, Turkey, and Middle Eastern countries, which have strategic and religious interests in Africa, generating a new kind of cultural/economic colonisation. In the field of architecture, the fact that the most reputed African architects, from the Pritzker prize Francis Kere to Sir David Adjaye, have all studied in Western countries where they have then implemented their professional practices is clear proof of the inadequacy of the education system. In this regard, it is interesting to highlight the formation, in continuity with the Black Lives Matter movement, of a new cultural ferment in relation to the diaspora debate.

This emerging ferment shows little similarity with what happened between the 50s and 70s, when architects actively participated in creating their new independent states. Although this new sophisticated movement, based on a cultural elite trained between the UK and the US, seems to be more ecologically and socially engaged, it is hard to gauge how much they are connected to local communities and their specific issues. It is with this hope and curiosity that we should consider recent experiences like the African Design Centre in Rwanda, founded by Christian Benimana and his office MASS based in Boston, thanks to the support of American foundations. At the same time, the statement behind the creation of the African Future Institute (Accra, Ghana), funded by Lesley Lokko and exhibited in her curatorial project for the Venice Biennale of Architecture 2023, is even more ambitious in defining Africa as *the laboratory of the future* focusing on the cultural dynamics of the diaspora. Will these initiatives be able to truly involve the territories of origin by generating a real shift and independent critical thinking? Will they be able to integrate local tradition and culture into a site-specific innovative approach?

The challenge is great, and the risk of avoiding a cultural hybridisation is concrete, undermining the realisation of a needed real shift without positively impacting local communities. In this regard, the experience of Douala posed the problem of learning from the lessons of the past by trying to generate a common ground within a more inclusive approach.

Notes

1 "International student statistics in UK," Studying in UK, accessed January 31, 2024. https://www.studying-in-uk.org/international-student-statistics-in-uk
2 Achille Joseph Mbembe, "Decolonizing the University: New Directions." Arts and Humanities in Higher Education 15, no. 1 (2016): 29–45. https://doi.org/10.1177/1474022215618513.ù
3 Achille Joseph Mbembe, "Decolonizing knowledge and the question of the archive." Accessed on January 9, 2024. https://wiser.wits.ac.za/system/files/Achille%20Mbembe%20-%20Decolonizing%20Knowledge%20and%20the%20Question%20of%20the%20Archive.pdf
4 AFP agence, "La mosquée de Djenné, restaurée, passe à l'énergie solaire" Le figaro, April 29,2019, https://www.lefigaro.fr/culture/la-mosquee-de-djenne-restauree-passe-a-l-energie-solaire-20190429.
5 Ayala Levin," Basic Deign toward decolonization" edited by Beatriz Beatriz Colomina, Ignacio G. Galán, Evangelos Kotsioris and Anna-Maria Meister. *Radical Pedagogies* (UK: MIT Press, 2022), 68-71.

Bibliography

AFP agence. "La mosquée de Djenné, restaurée, passe à l'énergie solaire" Le figaro. April 29,2019, https://www.lefigaro.fr/culture/a-mosquee-de-djenne-restauree-passe-a-l-energie-solaire-20190429

Colomina, Beatriz; G. Galán, Ignacio; Kotsioris, Evangelos and a Meister, Anna-Mari. *Radical Pedagogies*. UK: MIT Press, 2022.

Eglash, Ron. *African fractals: modern computing and indigenous design.* UK: Rutgers University Press, 1999.

Joseph Mbembe, Achille. "Decolonizing the University: New Directions." Arts and Humanities in Higher Education 15, no. 1 (2016): 29–45. https://doi.org/10.1177/1474022215618513.

Joseph Mbembe, Achille. "Decolonizing knowledge and the question of the archive." Accessed on January 9, 2024. https://wiser.wits.ac.za/system/files/Achille%20Mbembe%20-%20Decolonizing%20Knowledge%20and%20the%20Question%20of%20the%20Archive.pdf

Studying in UK. "International student statistics in UK." Accessed January 31, 2024. https://www.studying-in-uk.org/international-student-statistics-in-uk

4.2 The African Fabbers School Sessions in Douala

The aforementioned considerations were the basis for the African Fabbers initiative in Douala. After many years of itinerant sessions in sub-Saharan Africa, where we tested our learning by doing methodology and developed the knowledge exchange programme, in 2017, the African Fabbers School moved to Cameroon for a few years. This initiative was developed in the framework of the *Cam'on* project, developed with the COE ngo based in the region since decades and other international partners thanks to the support of the Italian Agency for Development Cooperation (AICS). The project gave us the opportunity to structure the programme in a more systematic way within a bottom-up approach, based on an articulated series of paradigmatic ateliers and master classes. The strategy beyond this approach was to map the context and allow a very diversified community of creative people to share knowledge and co-create their own cultural and fabrication platform as a space of production.

Therefore, having learned from our previous itinerant sessions, as well as from the cultural precedents mentioned in the paragraph 4.1, we started by addressing the question of the social role of schools in relation to their local community with the aim of shaping a non-academic curriculum that would be more accessible and transversal, able to tackle the complexity of sub-Saharan dynamics. At the same time, we wanted to create a common ground where African as well as Western students could learn from each other, creating a new sort of hybrid approach that could question cultural or social barriers imposed by more conventional initiatives.

TITLE
Mapping the context

OUTPUT
Maps on local materials, techniques and makers; AF School strategy and future agenda

METHODOLOGY
Interviews, collective mapping, co-design

STUDENTS
Daniel Ndanga,
Nickson Moukeke,
Ambang Dieudone,
Prince Ngoudafg,
Atouba Joseph,
Roddy Monguell,
Laetitia Keman,
Yann Mbella,
Kevin Boukoua,
Gabriel Song,
Landry Tamba,
Mvenga Onana,
Ebade Thelesphoz Edgar

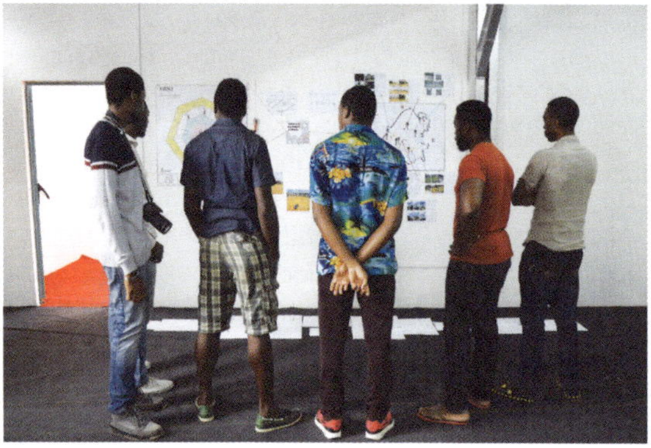

Mapping the Context

As a first methodological step to approach the project, we structured our first site visit with the aim of starting to map and study different aspects of both the pre-colonial culture and the contemporary informal creative dynamics. For the reasons cited above, we initially had two main local drivers: Paul Assako (professor of Art History at the University of Yaoundé) and the young Cameroonian architects Murielle Teguel and Pierre Marie Bissek (my former students from the ESA in Paris). With Murielle and Pierre Marie, we started to learn more about Cameroonian vernacular architecture by exchanging some interesting researches; with Paul Assako, we traveled the country to learn more about the pre-colonial cultural legacy, meeting a very interesting network of artists, artisans and independent institutions. The picture that emerged from that perlustration was incredibly rich and diversified.

Mbalmayo

In Mbalmayo, we met the staff of the Institut de Formation Artistique (IFA), a pioneering training centre for generations of contemporary artists in Cameroon. We discussed their struggles with maintaining contemporary art and craftsmanship practices without renouncing their traditions. The conversation also focused on the role of their very engaged laboratories, the relation with the material available on site (namely clay and timber), and possible ways of evolving the teaching methodologies. One of their main concerns was to make the path of creative practice more attractive to students, like it once was, possibly by integrating digital technologies in a sustainable way. For this reason, we started to imagine collaborations with the African Fabbers School, merging the different approaches and eventually supporting transforming their laboratories into a production centre, creating broader opportunities for students after their graduation.

Yaoundé

In Yaoundé, the capital, we continued to develop our map by visiting the Mission de Promotion des Matériaux Locaux (MIPROMALO), a training centre and factory using local materials (namely ceramics and terracotta) to make components for building construction. Although the centre has a growing reputation in the sector, with many projects realised by a team of in-house designers, the architectural quality and its performance appear have yet to justify the actual costs of the whole production chain. On this topic, we had an interesting conversation with their staff about learning from vernacular solutions to improve architectural quality and cost management for local industries in sub-Saharan Africa. The question of sustainability in mass production processes will need to be developed by a new generation of locally trained architects in order to generate performative solutions. At the same time, we visited the ateliers of different wood craftsmen, such as Gabriel Tegnoto, a pioneer of designers as producers who is very well known for developing his own collection of furniture, experimenting with different languages and qualities of local timber. Arriving at Gabriel's atelier for the first time, we realised how timber is central to the Cameroonian economy, even if it is systematically exported to Europe as a raw material. My strategic *naïf* question to him was: How we could develop a timber industry directly on site? Apparently, this is one of the most controversial topics for the future of many countries in the region. As Gabriel clearly explained, the main obstacle is that local governments have already sold forests to multinational companies and have no interest in transforming the material on site for the local market. As a result of this, timber products are paradoxically disappearing from the African market, and the material is mainly used by artists, such as Iyaa Enam. His paintings on the bark of local trees no doubt form one of the most ecological and poetic practices we came across in Yaoundé, where we also met the collective of environmentally engaged artists driven by Jean Michel Dissake. Their work, reflecting on the role of their atelier in the neighbourhood and raising awareness among young people on waste production and gender equality issues, showed us the added value/responsibility of being an artist in a contemporary African city.

Foumban – Bandjoun – Bafoussam

On our field trip from the capital to Foumban, on the way to Douala, we started to experience the unique vernacular architectures in the rural areas of western Cameroon, where indigenous communities have preserved construction techniques adapted to the tropical climate, using local timber (mainly padauk) for the primary structures and thatching techniques for the pitched roofs. The Musee de Bandjoun is one of the key cultural institutions of the region, where we learned more about the very rich history of local arts and crafts. The museum also presents an interesting insight into the very articulated organisation of traditional society and its significant historical events. This organisation is mirrored in the plans of the old Palace of Foumban, architecturally speaking one of the most interesting and sophisticated pre-colonial buildings (14th century) in the whole region for its system of diversified courtyards. The architectural pattern generates hierarchised spaces conceived as a sequence of private, semiprivate, and public courtyards. This volumetric configuration is still very relevant for its bioclimatic performance as well as for its ability to generate mixed-use and differentiated architectural typologies.

For these reasons, it was even more difficult to accept the possible consequences of the crisis affecting the local bronze casting activity, a valued cultural heritage of the Bamum people. Although the bronze craftsmen are very well known for their sculptures representing the collective memory of the Bamum, the future of their legacy is now in danger due to Chinese migrant competitors. Foundries are closing down, and some bronze artists are turning to farming and other trades in order to survive as most of the traditional art practice is in decline. As for other traditional activities, the only way to give continuity to this bronze legacy would be to develop new kinds of production for contemporary uses for both the local and the international markets. While this perspective may still be hard to imagine from both the manufacturing and the architectural point of view, the most interesting experiments on new forms of indigenous identity are coming from the field of contemporary art. In that sense, the Bandjoun Station, developed by one of the most influential African artists, Barthelemy Toguo, is probably the best example for its relationship with the local community as a non-profit making project. The Station is not conceived as a conventional exhibition space and residence for contemporary artists. On the contrary, it is structured around the idea of a local factory that provides work for farmers and artisans in the village. The project addresses the question of self-sufficiency, as the coffee plantation feeds the work of local artists as a sort of educational platform. As Barthelemy explains in his statement: This way of combining both environmental issues and social experimentation sets an example for the local youth; it is a way of creating a dynamic and equitable relationship between guests and hosts, as well as of demonstrating the central importance of agriculture in our quest to become self-sufficient in food production. It is a strong political statement; our artistic breeding ground will in turn give birth to a coffee plantation. In this case, this critical act magnifies the artistic gesture and powerfully critiques what Léopold Sédar Senghor has called 'the deterioration of the terms of exchange', in other words the lowering of prices for export imposed by the West which punishes and impoverishes the farmers of the South.

Douala

Following this very important introduction to self-sufficiency and independent cultural practices, we approached Douala, probably the most vibrant city in the region, mainly for its very active port that has generated a multi-cultural society over time. Our first guide in understanding its complexity was Marylin Douala Bell, co-founder, along with Didier Schaub, of Doual'art. This pioneering association was the first to engage in a very radical activity of contemporary art in public space in Africa. In 2005, the project gave rise to *SUD*, Salon Urbain de Douala, a sort of triennial festival of public and contemporary art. The very interesting format is intended to connect artists, designers, and architects with local communities to co-design and co-create multi-scalar interventions in the neighbourhood. As clearly explained by Iolanda Pensa in her book Public Art in Africa , this has generated a very interesting methodology, in which the work was strategically divided across three years of activities, emphasizing the collaborative aspects and the dialogues with the local communities to address the ecological role of relational spaces and public infrastructures.

Thanks to Caroline Nadège Ngouegni from SUD, we were able to visit the outputs of this urban strategy, a network of very diversified interventions that, at different scales, stimulated the social and the environmental debates in the local community, providing conceptual and sometimes very practical solutions. It is not surprising that the most successful interventions are urban devices such as bridges or water infrastructures, like the *Théâtre Source* project in the Ndongpassi III neighbourhood, where a group of creatives co-realised an open-air theatre that also works as a public fountain during the day. Since the approaches of Doual'art and the African Fabbers School were so similar in considering the street as a cultural platform for new ecological practices, we started to discuss possible synergies and collaborations. In parallel to these very inspirational conversations and site visits, we began working with our very first group of students from the LABA-Douala school of fine arts, generating a series of maps, starting from their different skills and backgrounds and looking at the urban informal dynamics of the city and the networks of local creative communities to collaborate with. The strategic aim was to generate our site-specific programme focusing on the social and cultural role of the African Fabbers School in Douala for the next three years. These intensive workshops generated a series of interdisciplinary courses investigating informal social scenarios, climate issues, manufacturing techniques, and local material systems, with the aim of experimenting with possible approaches towards community-oriented solutions. At the same time, with the COE, we started to discuss the logistic needs of the Cultural Hub as well as of the AFS and its laboratory. For this reason, after a series of site visits around Douala, we encouraged the COE to implement its Cultural Hub in the Logbaba neighbourhood because of its association with manufacturing, but also as an opportunity to regenerate an abandoned site.

IFA laboratories in Mbalmayo

Modernist architecture in Yaoundé, the Prime ministry building

Local artisan atelier of bark painting

Foumban local market

The Bandjoun Station, artists atelier and residency

Western Cameroon vernacular architecture, the Bandjoun Museum

Bonamouti and Ndogpassi III neighborhoods with the Doual'art installations

TITLE
Atelier de fabrication urbain

OUTPUT
Local timber archive, self-construction of the lab space and furniture

METHODOLOGY
Timber testing and prototyping, open-design, design by making

STUDENTS
Ghis's Berth Ngon, Jean Honoreau Koutou, Ulrich Fotso, Alice Penda, Ambanga Abawa Asser, Somhbe Tamba Landry, Keman Arroga Leticia, Ngouda Prince, Ongong Atouba Joseph, Song Gabriel, Tcheumann Fabien, Yvess Ddonda

Atelier de fabrication urbain

The first hands-on atelier was strategically dedicated to the design and self-construction of the AF School laboratory, conceived as an urban fabrication platform within the framework of the Logbaba Cultural Hub. The idea was to transform part of the existing building into a production space that could generate different projects for the hub itself, as well as for the people of the neighbourhood. The atelier was structured with two main goals: to co-design and self-build the laboratory space; and to build relationships with local artisans. At the same time, since we wanted to keep the school accessible for everyone, we launched an open call on social media to involve people from different backgrounds. The final results of this call were quite successful, as the initial group of fine arts students were ultimately joined by artists, local artisans, and architecture students from other cities and countries in the region such as Congo, Nigeria, etc.

Methodologically speaking, the self-construction of the laboratory with the future users was an initial tactic to empower them from the very beginning to take care of the space and participate in future developments. At the same time, the idea of involving people from other cities and countries was related to the possibility of helping them implement similar initiatives in their own communities after their return, generating a possible network of future labs. For this reason, we focused on local furniture – specifically, the spontaneous structural systems of the street kiosk – as a prototypical example to learn from. We then transformed the original model using an open design system that could generate different families of ergonomic solutions, from shelves to workbenches, etc., using an interlocking system allowing users to easily assemble and dismantle these structures as fast deployment devices. We visited different informal markets for local timber to use the same kind of standard timber elements from the kiosks as generative components to build different kinds of movable furniture using an incremental and scalable logic.

The idea from the very beginning was to create a very flexible arrangement through different lab activities – from digital fabrication sessions to more analogue wood and ceramics manufacturing workshops. Some of the video makers on the team also interviewed the different local artisans involved to better understand their interests, their expectations, and their proposals for future lab activities. This archive of inspirational interviews began to inform the school's next sessions, generating a shortlist of small paradigmatic interventions to regenerate the public spaces in the surrounding area and creating the pillars of our knowledge exchange platform, sharing tools, and expertise for collective projects.

TITLE
3d printing Africa

OUTPUT
Protocols for 3d printing with local clay, course on 3d printing wit natural materials

METHODOLOGY
Design to print

STUDENTS
Ndasse Michel Thresor, Balla Awoumau Landry Guy, Siezau Youmbi Francois Joel, Kamdoum Benoit Valery, Ngongang Ghish Lain, Atangana Steve, Domwa Christelle, Danielle Kengne, Ndounda Ndongo Yves Yvier, Ongong Atouba Joseph, Roddy Manguell, Dongmo Claire Laure

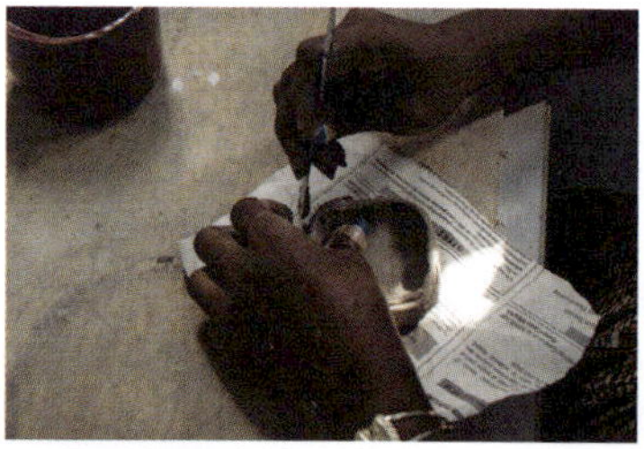

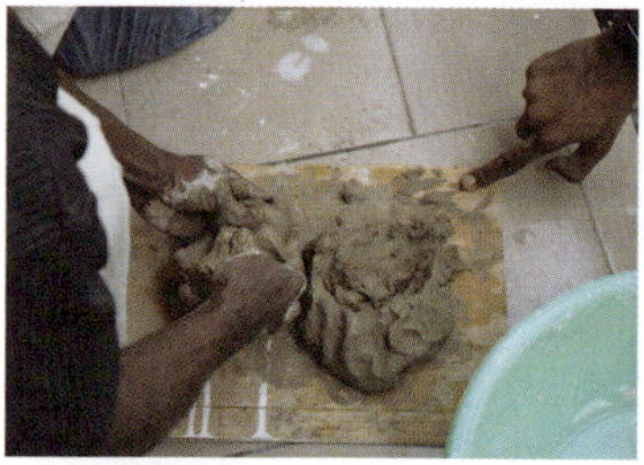

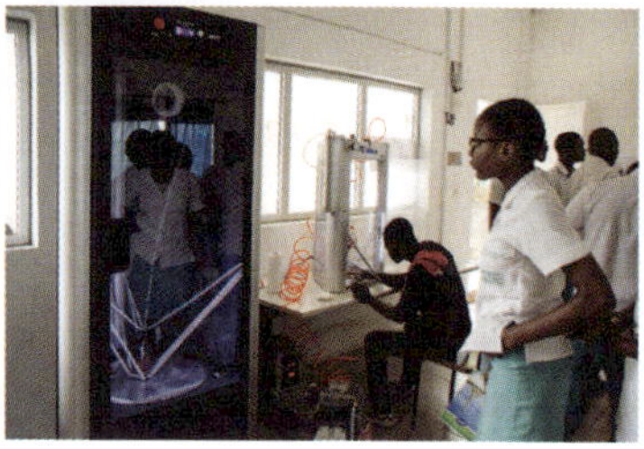

TITLE
Micro architectural fabrication

OUTPUT
Micro-architectures for the neighbourhood

METHODOLOGY
Community oriented design,collaborative fabrication

STUDENTS
Ndasse Michel Thresor,
Balla Awoumau
Landry Guy,
Siezau Youmbi
Francois Joel,
Domwa Christelle,
Danielle Kengne,
Ongong Atouba Joseph

Experimenting local material and digital manufacturing

In order to feed this common ground between spheres of knowledge, we gradually introduced some basic open classes on digital manufacturing into our sessions. Since our first site visit, we understood the potential of experimenting with additive and subtractive fabrication processes using the materials available on-site: clay and timber. I still remember the first day when the CNC machine and the 3D printers arrived in a container at the port in Douala, and the local artisans all provided their support to transport and install them in the laboratory. The curiosity and enthusiasm around having this kind of technology available for the first time in Cameroon made us feel even more responsible for making it useful to produce new knowledge and expand opportunities. Therefore, the first thing we did, after guaranteeing a more stable energy supply to the machinery, was to involve local experts to prepare a material library to test for both 3D printing and milling processes. For the first ever 3D-printing session in Cameroon, we involved, through an open call, a mix of very experienced ceramists from the CFA and a group of young designers who wanted to learn about the mechanics, the settings, and the software on the delta model, as well as the use of digital modelling software.

For these particular aspects, we began investigating with our students the possibility of extruding vernacular patterns inspired by the earth architecture of the Musgum, an ethnic group in the far north province of Cameroon. Their houses made entirely of adobe are called *cases obus*, and they are well known for the use of structural geometric patterns to improve the stability of the dome tectonic system. Environmentally speaking, to respond to the extreme climatic conditions, local craftsmen make the external walls of the houses thicker at the base than at the summit, with the aim of improving the thermal performances of the building. The volumetric patterns generate shade on the external surface, and the veins contribute to the drainage of rain. The decorative surface also allows for further refinement and customisation. In experimenting with such a synthetic vernacular approach, the knowledge of the ceramists was crucial to understand how to transform different qualities of local clay into extrudable materials, as well as to find the right drying and firing procedures for such extreme climatic conditions.

At the same time, we began discuss the limits of these technologies, the possibility of mixing digital and traditional techniques, as well as the kind of possible productions to implement. This topic is probably the most relevant when working in these kinds of contexts. You need to fine-tune the affordability, the timing, and the human labour of the whole production chain. For this reason, after some benchmark analysis we oriented our further investigations towards the field of building components, transforming local clay into performative ceramic tiles to generate both waterproof lattices and passive ventilation systems for façades.

After the first training sessions, we proposed setting up a complete ceramic manufacturing chain in the hub, hosting the CFA ceramist atelier just in front our lab. The aim was to boost new collaborative projects and keep sharing the tools and the pottery kilns. In parallel with the additive sessions, we joined with a group of local ebonists to investigate on the possibility of transforming local timber using CNC milling machines, mainly for architectural components. Although Cameroon's timber is widely known, unfortunately it is not transformed on site and the materials available on the local market are mainly unseasoned. Our sponsors in this very complex research helped us set the CNC machine according to the different timber characteristics, and we visited many suppliers around Douala to get the right quality and the thickness of padauk that was weathered enough to avoid compromising the tools with its fibres.

At the same time, we began using digital manufacturing to develop a series of micro-architectural devices for the community in order to test the opportunity of making tailor-made components for the public spaces in the surrounding area. We began developing surgical interventions, such as repairing the existing benches in the public space in front of the only public fountain. The idea was to allow the people of the neighbourhood to have a seat while waiting their turn to collect drinking water. Meanwhile, according to our research on spontaneous urban timber structures, we started to investigate on the logic behind the perforated panels of the small street shops. This kind of informal *mashrabiya,* although often realised with precarious tectonics, works very well as a sunshade to protect users from sunlight and dust, creating a feeling of intimacy. We began developing an archive of perforated panels informed by certain environmental parameters and inspired by traditional patterns in order to test them in different architectural applications.

The results of these eco-digital fabrication sessions were not just a series of technical courses or useless prototypes but manufacturing protocols to allow our students to become autonomous in the use of the machines and in using proper material systems to develop their own projects. At the same time, we helped them develop a critical understanding of the use of such technologies to optimise resources, mitigating the environmental aspects affecting informal architectures, as well as repairing and upgrading existing domestic furniture. This new vernacular approach was the common ground for the next steps in our architectural investigations at a bigger scale.

TITLE
The African Fabbers House I

OUTPUT
House unit concept design and prototype

METHODOLOGY
Environmental design, prototyping and testing

STUDENTS
Thrésor Michel Ndasse, Danielle Kengne, Benoit Joseph, Balla Owona, Julien Mbida, Zanga, Dieudonné Ambang, Jean Ernest Kenmogne, Claire Laure Dongmo, Charlie, Landry Tamba Sohmbe, Christelle Domwa, Benoit Valery Kamdoum, François Joël Siazeu Youmbi, Cédric Ongong Atouba, Francis Tiemeni Ongong

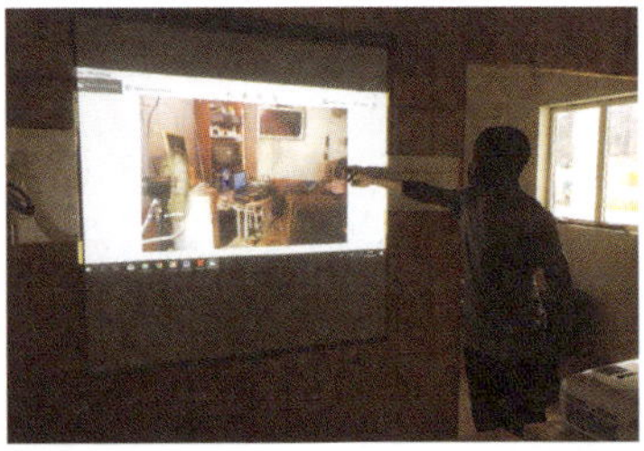

TITLE
The African Fabbers House II

OUTPUT
Self-construction of African Fabbers House

METHODOLOGY
Eco-digital fabrication, collective self-construction

STUDENTS
Thrésor Michel Ndasse, Danielle Kengne, Benoit Joseph, Balla Owona, Julien Mbida, Zanga, Dieudonné Ambang, Jean Ernest Kenmogne, Claire Laure Dongmo, Charlie, Landry Tamba Sohmbe, Christelle Domwa, Benoit Valery Kamdoum, François Joël Siazeu Youmbi, Cédric Ongong Atouba, Francis Tiemeni Ongong

1

The African Fabbers House

Once we have, with a very motivated group of students and artisans, experimented different material systems and design to manufacturing techniques we strategically decided with the team to apply such experience into a scale one to one house prototype. This with the aim to develop affordable solutions for the people of the Logbaba neighbourhood living in precarious conditions. Such paradigmatic project confronted us to the Cameroon housing scenario informal. Therefore, we have started to interview different type of households in the neighbourhood analysing their homes to better understand the kind of critical and potential issues as well as the spatial and environmental aspects to improve.

Such initial workshop gave us a sort of benchmark to ideal with in order to upgrade the informal housing performances using the material library and the building components archive developed in the previous session. At the same time, we have started to discuss with the team about the Tropical House experiments of Jean Prouvé, the failure of his imported prefabricated system but also the potential of developing a local industry approach to replicate the mass customisation construction logic and the bioclimatic solutions. According to the on-site research we set the first performative criteria focusing on a self-sufficient house unit, an environmental device able to respond to flooding dynamics providing its own energy and water due the unreliable infrastructural systems.

From the spatial and ergonomic point of view we considered the prototype as an incremental structure that could accommodate mix-used spaces where small shops and manufacturing activities could generate micro-economies. Therefore, from an initial genotype we have started to develop an initial catalogue of digital and small physical housing prototypes in order to test and compare the different configuration according to the performative criteria. The prototypes were presented to the public involving the local community into the selection of the most interesting configuration to develop at the scale one to one. The real scale project proposes local timber as an affordable material system to be used in 80% of the primary structure. Starting from wooden interlocked primary structure the house is conceived to be detached from the ground in order to avoid the risk of flooding improving ventilation performances. According to environmental analysis, the design strategy responds to the Douala condition, which has one of the most humid climates of the region. This environmental strategy shapes also the roof conceived for collecting the rain water and to generate renewable energy solar applying photovoltaic panels. The façade system is designed as an ecological skin made out timber, bamboo and ceramics digitally and manually prefabricated panels provide passive cooling ventilation for such hot and humid climate.

The whole design to build process aims at generating construction kits based on customised modular components bridging traditional and informal local techniques with a digital prefabrication approaches stimulating the creation of local industries. This The project was conceived also as a sort of training programme where a multidisciplinary group of students and carpenters could work together with local community generating a sort of social entrepreneurship activity. Therefore, the AF house was completely realized with local material systems easy to assembly, customise and replicate at different scales. The whole construction process was organised in order to test the reliability of suppliers, the level of productivity of the fabrication laboratory. Once the prototype was successfully built, we have strategically started to valorise the whole project in order to empower a network of local and international industries able to design and make high and low-tech for sub-Saharan Africa context. As a matter of facts a few months later we started to discuss with Vincent Kitio from UN Habitat and with other stakeholders' further developments of such experiments using this real life project to implement new applied reaches for upgrading slums housing conditions.

FORSUN
S1325S

CULTURAL HUB — CAMEROON 2019–2020

SITE
Douala,
4°03′N 9°42′E

CLIMATE REGION
Tropical monsoon

CLIENT
COE ngo

PROGRAMME
Cultural hub

TEAM
Paolo Cascone and Maddalena Laddaga (architect)

ENVIRONMENTAL DESIGN TEAM
Elena Ciancio, Federico Forestiero

STRUCTURAL CONSULTANT
prof. Luciano Nunziante

COLLABORATIVE DESIGN WORKSHOP STUDENTS TEAM
Thrésor Michel Ndasse, Danielle Kengne, Benoit Joseph, Balla Owona, Julien Mbida, Zanga, Charlie, Landry Tamba Sohmbe, François Joël Siazeu Youmbi, Guylandry Awoumou Balla, Cédric Ongong Atouba, Francis Tiemeni Ongong

LOCAL CONSTRUCTOR
Azate Construction construction site manager
Domenico Pernici

PARTNERS
Laba Douala

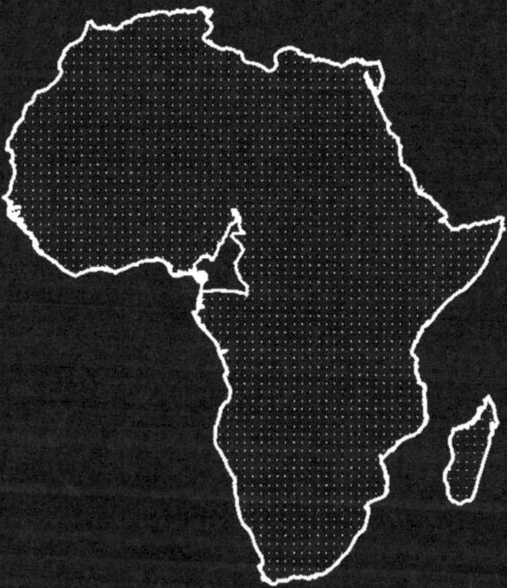

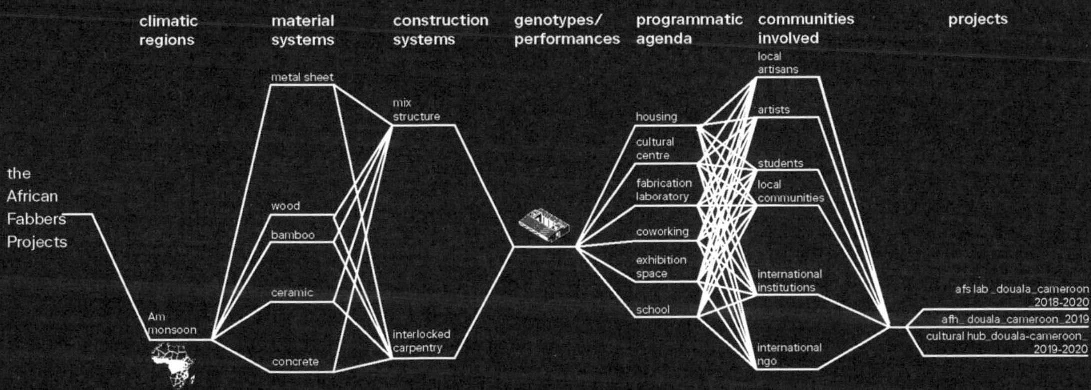

The construction of the Cultural Hub

After almost two years of activity at the African Fabbers School in Douala, the core group of students was consolidated, and the local consensus was growing, in addition to the number of people participating in our activities. For this reason, we accepted the proposal from the COE ngo (which has been involved in social initiatives in Africa for almost 50 years) to design and build the Cultural Hub in Douala. At the time, we were already collaborating with them in our African Fabbers School sessions, implementing a self-construction and digital manufacturing laboratory for community-oriented projects within the framework of the Cam'on project supported by the Italian Agency for Cooperation and Development (AICS). Their proposal represented a tremendous opportunity to connect and test the different applied research and projects we had completed in Africa over more than 10 years.

The project centred on accessibility to education and the development of creative practices to improve the quality of life in communities from both the social and the environmental points of view. With this premise, as designers, educators, and activists, we conceived the architectural project as a creative open platform, an urban infrastructure to provide production spaces for both educational activities and community-oriented projects. As directors of the African Fabbers School, we decided strategically from the very beginning to develop the project through a collaborative process involving a group of local students and artisans. The continuous dialogue that was established with the local community and with our client generated a very challenging and articulated design brief that bridges the new building with the structure of an existing refurbished one. The aim was to generate a system of ventilated and diversified courtyards, connecting a series of spaces open to the neighbourhood, including the digital manufacturing labs, an exhibition gallery, a co-working area, and a cafeteria. The hub is also home to a school of fine arts (LABA-Douala) and a guest-house, while the outdoor area is organised as a relational space with playgrounds and productive gardens.

The programmatic and architectural agenda of this project makes the building unique in Africa and beyond. The design strategy for the building was informed by a series of environmental analyses and simulations in order to respond to the very extreme climatic conditions (hot-humid) in Douala. The goal was to reduce the energy consumption while providing thermal comfort to both the outdoor and indoor spaces and maximising the passive cooling ventilation. Taking inspiration from the local informal and vernacular architectures, the central courtyard is conceived as a shaded, open-air room, reducing the surfaces exposed to direct sunlight during the hottest hours of the day. The issues of affordability and circular economy drove our strategy in terms of materials and construction systems, connecting the concrete primary structure with the local wood secondary structures. The wooden ventilated façade, made from local padauk, was realised with our local students, who experimented with new digital manufacturing protocols using the natural materials available onsite. At the same time, the roof took its inspiration from the informal metal sheet dwellings with the aim of improving the environmental performance in terms of cross-ventilation and rainwater collection. As we consider the question of self-sufficiency in architecture to be crucial, especially in Africa, we also integrated a photovoltaic system into the roof in order to reduce dependency on the unreliable energy grid. The final result of the whole design-to-build process is an open work that could be potentially evolved and upgraded directly by the users who collaborated during the construction process. Beyond any humanitarian rhetoric, we strongly believe that a decolonisation of architectural knowledge is necessary to reconsider the social role of designers towards climate sensitive and community-oriented architectures. This project was exhibited at the Venice Biennale of Architecture in the year 2021 in the African Fabbers School installation, within the framework of the Italian Pavilion, and discussions are currently underway with many local institutions to replicate the experience in other contexts.

Bilbliography

Cascone, Paolo and Laddaga, Maddalena. "Notes for a responsible architecture." *IQD* N64 (2021): 116–119.

Cinquaibre, Olivier. *Jean Prouve: The Tropical House.* Paris: Centre Georges Pomidou, 2009.

Filosa, Francesca. "Douala Cultural hub." *Platform* n° 33. (2022): 24–19.

Melis, Alessandro. Resilient Communities. Catalogue Italian Pavilion, Venice Biennale of Architecture 2021. Rome: D Editore, 2021

Myers, Lynne. Designboom. "Codesignlab builds a low-cost and off-grid housing prototype in Cameroon." 2019, https://www.designboom.com/architecture/codesignlab-african-fabbershouse-cameroon10-21-2019/

Peluso, Salvatore. Domusweb "African Fabber House is born in response to the mistakes of colonialist architecture." 2019. Accessed January 12, https://www.domusweb.it/en/architecture/2019/10/22/african-fabber-house-is-born-in-response-to-the-mistakes-of-colonialistarchitecture.html

Pensa, Iolanda. *Public Art in Africa: Art et Transformations Urbaines a Douala.* Geneva: METIS, 2017.

Poppe, Esther. "Bandjoun Art Station: The Importance of a Peripheral Institution in Cameroon". Accessed January 12, 2024. https://contemporaryand.com/magazines/bandjoun-art-stationthe-importance-of-a-peripheral-institution-in-cameroon/

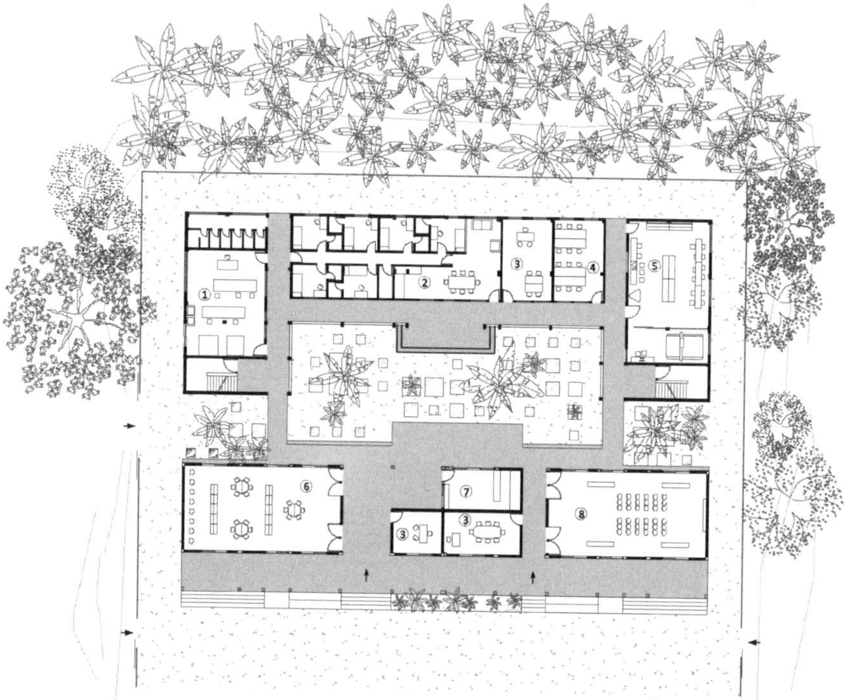

ground floor plan

1. Ceramic lab
2. Residences
3. Office
4. Co-working
5. African Fabbers school Lab
6. Media library co-working
7. Café
8. Exhibition- conference

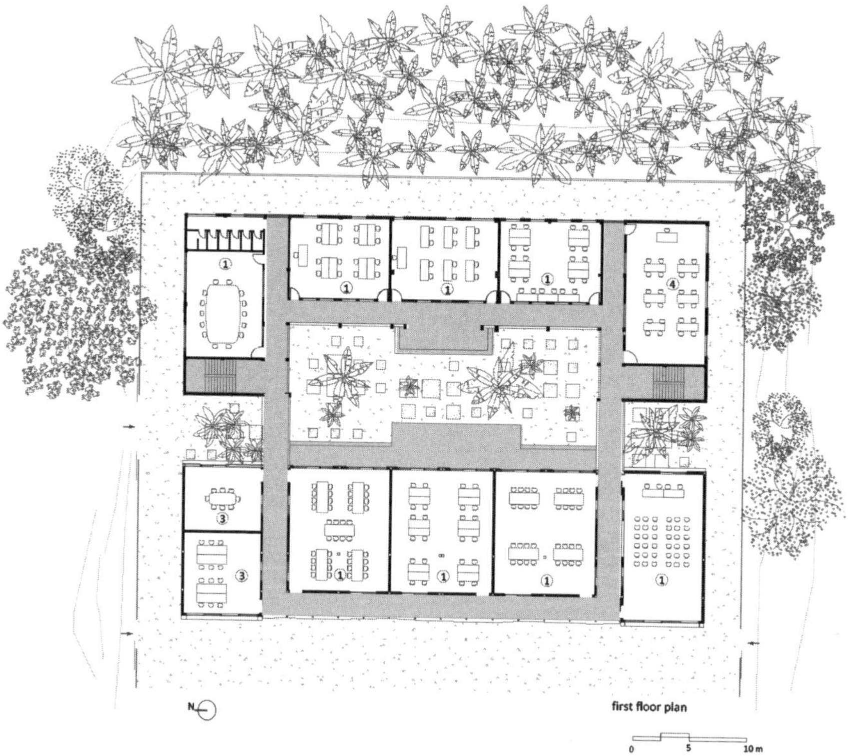

first floor plan

1. Classroom
2. Meeting room
3. Office
4. Fashion lab

Physical study model

Drone top view of construction site

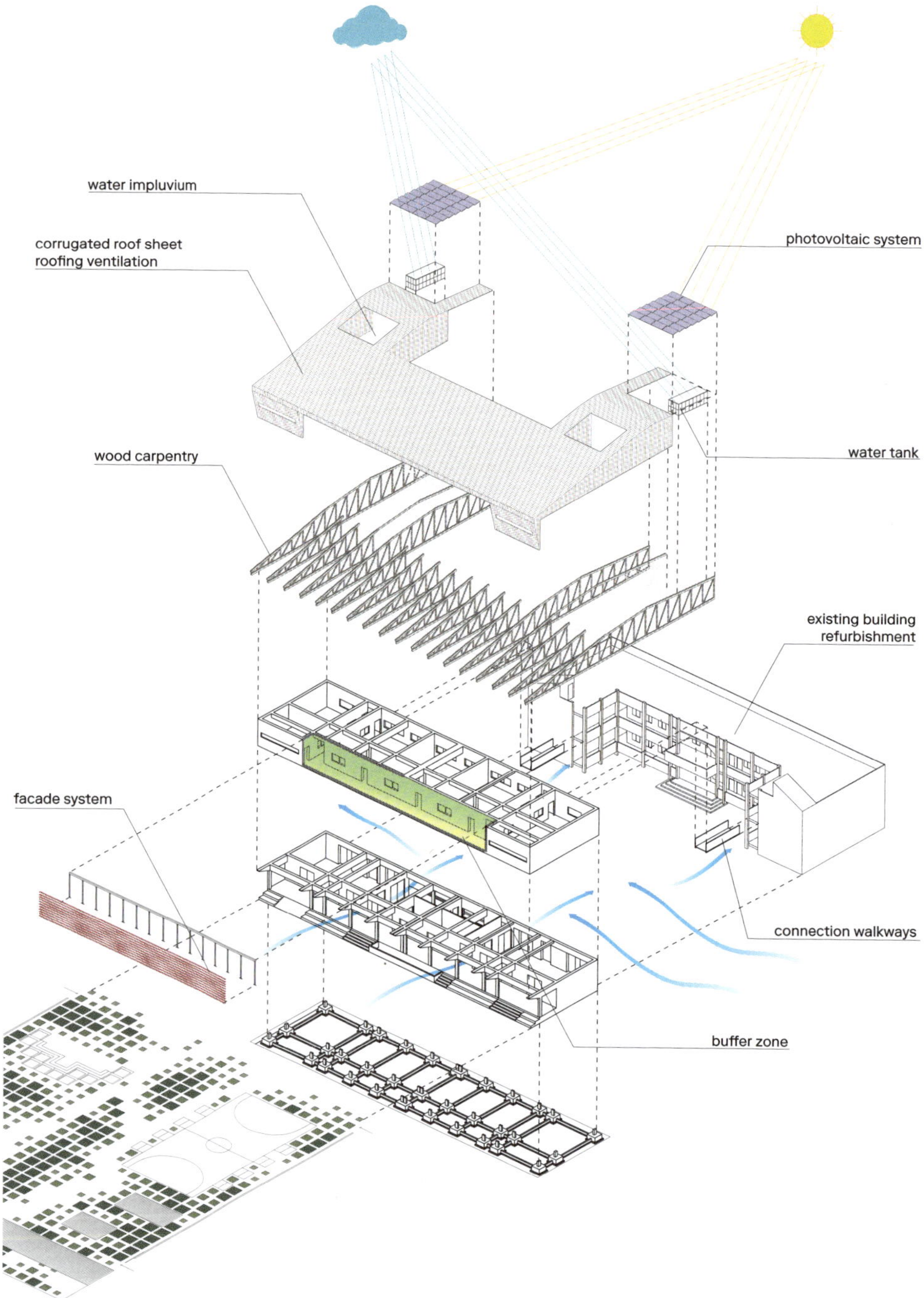
water impluvium
corrugated roof sheet
roofing ventilation
photovoltaic system
water tank
wood carpentry
existing building
refurbishment
facade system
connection walkways
buffer zone

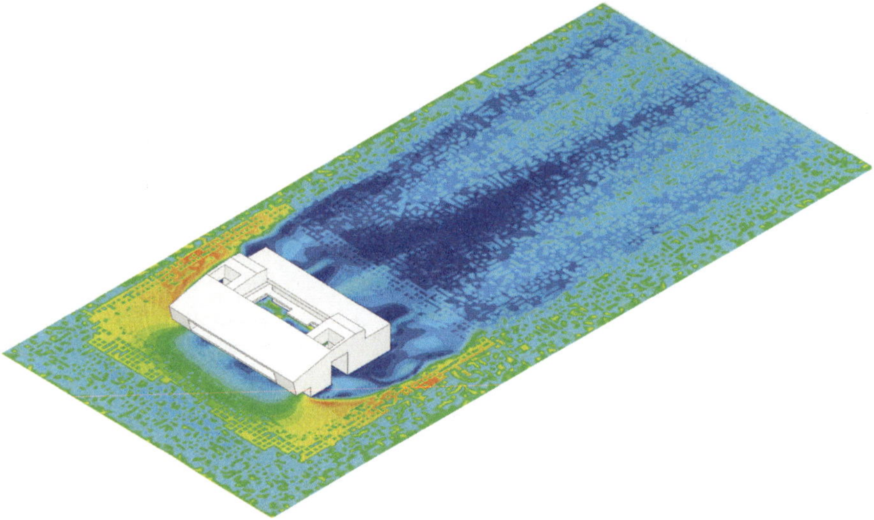

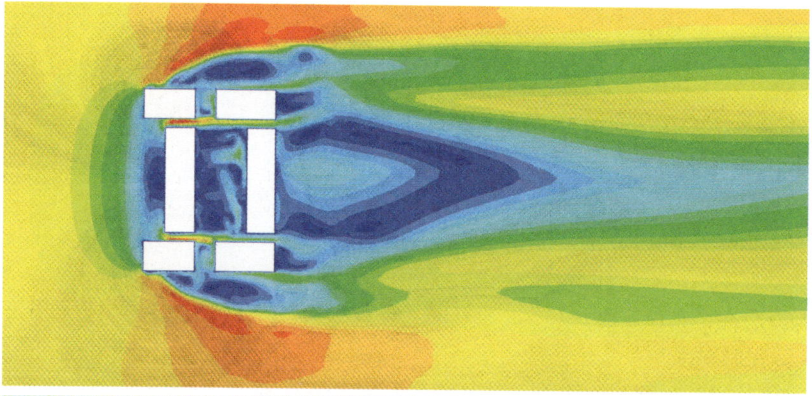

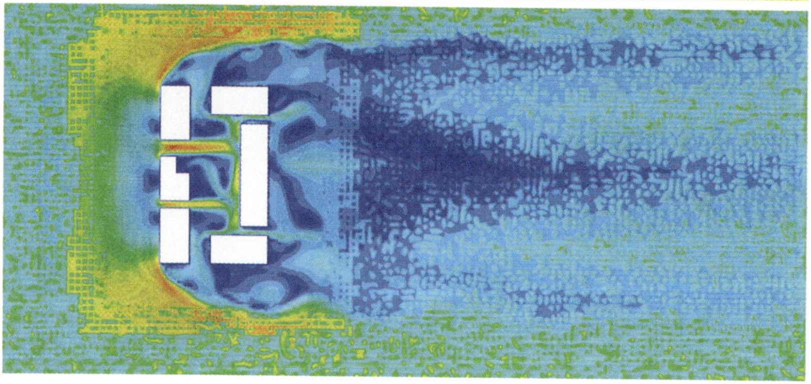

1

Nocturnal view of the hub

View of the interior courtyard

View of the interior courtyard

External views of the main façade

TITLE

HUB Wood façade

OUTPUT

Scale 1 to 1
wood façade

METHODOLOGY

Eco-digital
fabrication,
collective
self-construction

STUDENTS

Thrésor Michel Ndasse,
Danielle Kengne,
Benoit Joseph,
Balla Owona,
Julien Mbida,
Zanga, Charlie,
Landry Tamba Sohmbe,
François Joël Siazeu
Youmbi, Guylandry
Awoumou Balla,
Cédric Ongong Atouba,
Francis Tiemeni
Ongong

Views of the timber façade system

V
African Off-grid Housing

text by Paolo Cascone *and* Maddalena Laddaga

5.1 On Precarious Habitat in Sub-Saharan Africa

While the climate change is seriously affecting the continent, as recently reported by the World Bank and UN Habitat, Africa is urbanizing more rapidly than any other part of the planet.

In year 2050 the continent will double its 1.1 billion citizens and 80% of such increase will take place mostly in the slums of the cities. As analysts have predicted that Lagos – already Africa's largest city – will expand 77 people every hour between now and 2030 it is really hard to understand how this rapid growth will affects the continent.

At the same time according to a recent research from McKinsey there will be 100 African cities by year 2025 with more than one million inhabitants which is almost twice as many as in Latin America. Is Africa prepared to face such scenario?

Unfortunately, it looks like the reasons that are keeping African cities back are not just related to an urban infrastructural gap but more on a lack of planning depending on regulatory blockages and vested interests. For this reason, according to the World Bank, African cities are still very expensive to live in. As a matter of facts these are overall than non-African cities with similar income levels. At the same time locals pay a whopping 100% more for transport, 55% more for housing, 42% more for transport and 35% more for food.

On the other hand, such complex scenario has generated over the last decades a series of hyper-informal cities were spontaneous architecture and informal economies are the only way to survive. The continuous increase of informal cities and precarious neighbourhood in Sub-Saharan Africa could be mainly associated to the fact that the urbanization is not accompanied by the level of per-capita economic growth or housing investment that is observed elsewhere in global trends. In addition to this the migration from rural to urban areas driven by "push" factors such as poor yields from agriculture (Barrios et al. 2006). As the quality housing is produced and financed by the formal channels a large share of urban households doesn't have access to such market because of its major constraints. At the same time recent analysis (Dasgupta et al. 2014) have reported that formal housing investment lags behind urbanization by nine years in Africa.

In addition to this, the typical scenario is that only after housing has already been built, often in informal settlements, the capital investment in infrastructure needed to handle rapid urbanization. Due the lack of reliable data, however, is extremely difficult to identify and evaluate the quality or quantity of housing deficits (formal and informal) and a conceptual clarity is needed to evaluate existing stock, household dimensions and occupancy.

If we consider the definitions and methodologies used by governments to estimate housing deficits that generally we could calculate housing shortfalls on the basis of three different aspects:

- the numerical shortfall in dwellings (deficit);
- the qualitative shortfall in physical conditions (obsolescence or substandard construction with non-durable building materials);
- the spatial shortfall within dwellings (overcrowding).

This analysis relies on estimates of new household formation and an ideal occupancy ratio per dwelling unit, which may not reflect typical conditions. They also consider how much of the existing housing stock can be improved or eventually replaced.

Further, the UN estimates that more than 200 million people in the region will live in slums by 2020 (UN-Habitat 2014). The slum population is growing at 4.5 percent annually, a rate which will result in doubling the slum population in 15 years (Marx et al. 2013). After this period, the majority of the world's slum dwellers will live in African cities; currently all other regions are experiencing a rapid decline in the prevalence of slums.

As a matter of facts housing produced through formal channels is still far too expensive for most people. In the contrary, informal channels have become the dominant housing delivery system across the region, known to contribute around three quarters of the total housing stock (although data on the informal housing sector in Africa is scarce).

At the same time people living in slums could not have access to any kind of support simply because they do not respond to the typical criteria related to housing 'formality':

- ▸ they have a valid legal title;
- ▸ their dwelling complies with the local planning standards and building code;
- ▸ their dwelling can be pledged as collateral for a long-term mortgage loan.

If formal housing units with such qualifications are the product of coordination between public and private sector activities and benefit to housing finance the slums are still considered temporary and precarious neighbourhood without any right to be improved. Some of the mains characteristics that informal housing in Sub-Saharan Africa shares are:

- ▶ Located on the urban periphery or within the interstices of the formal city (e.g., non-buildable or risk areas).
- ▶ Self-designed and self-built using local materials.
- ▶ Does not fully comply with building and land-use standards.
- ▶ Poorly serviced by infrastructure networks and public services.
- ▶ Financed out of family/group savings and/or loans from informal lenders.
- ▶ Incrementally improved by the occupant over a long period of time.
- ▶ Lacks a legal title and is often subject to insecurity of tenure.

Nevertheless, as described by Marie Huchzermeyer in her book – Cities with 'Slums': from informal settlement eradication to a right to the city in Africa – it is clear that despite the problems that this slum community faces, residents still appreciate the unique social networks they create within the area. The lack of space and over-crowding creates a communal identity because no one has real privacy, which promotes social interaction and networking. Therefore, residents' identities are 'place-based' and communal. At the same time the fact that many of the slums' residents are from rural regions promotes the sense of community within their urban neighbourhoods. In fact, many of slum dwellers migrate to the city to work but continue to keep their connections and homes in their rural villages. Migrants bring social and cultural affiliations, traditions, cultural identities, and family ties to that of their rural villages. This creates a strong connection between the urban and rural parts of these countries because somehow slum dwellers continue their rural lifestyles among urban settlers with the same kind of resiliency and solidarity. For the above-mentioned reasons, the question of upgrading such informal settlements has to be driven by a participative approach starting from a user-centric perspective allowing slum inhabitants to have a legal title in order to have access to micro-credit policies.

Given such complex scenario a shift of paradigm is needed, such as:

- ▶ recognising the social values of slums in order to improve the life quality of such large communities avoiding any kind of eradication and involving them directly in developing affordable housing solutions. Only surpassing this dichotomy between formality and informality it will possible to create innovative and hybrid systems able to upgrade these slums with a bottom up approach.
- ▶ Substantial inequality exists between slum and non-slum households in access to water and sanitation facilities. The wealthier often enjoy high levels of service at low cost, whereas the poor pay a much higher price for a service of similar or lesser quality. The lack of water management infrastructure (economic water scarcity), in terms of both storage and supply delivery, as well as for improved drinking water and sanitation services, plays a direct role in the persistence of poverty in Sub-Saharan Africa. About 10% of the population still drank untreated surface water, and many poor people in rural areas, particularly women and girls, spent a considerable amount of time collecting water.

At the same time an innovative way of developing a local industry with a circular economy approach is needed in order to empower the African job market transforming resources on-site. Due the lack of basic infrastructures (water, electricity etc.) local industries should invest on off-grid and km0 affordable solutions in the field of construction taking advantage of the on-site resources.

African Taxonomies

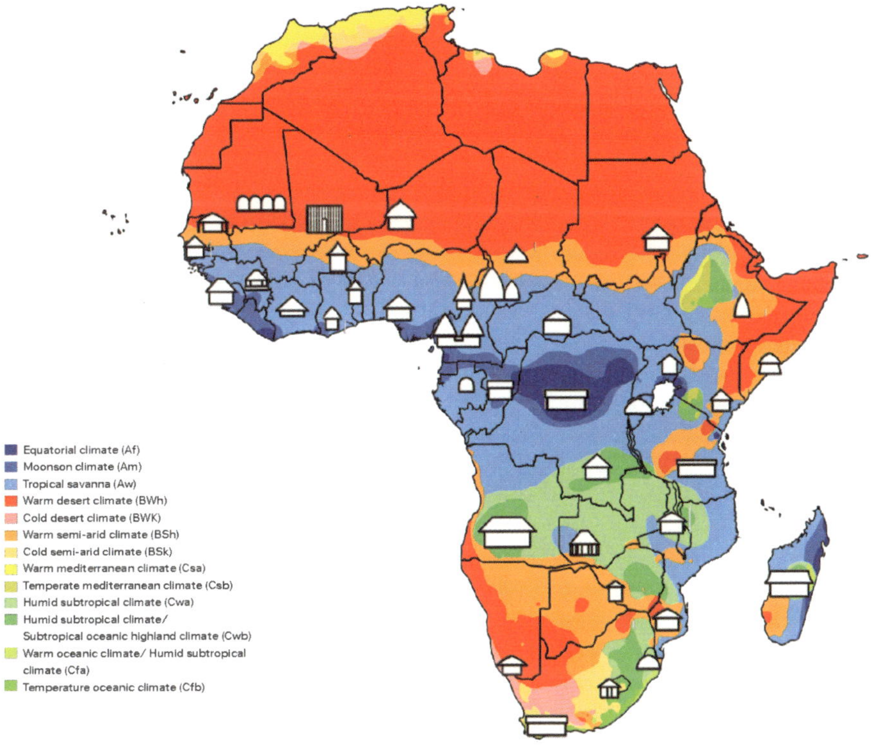

5.2 The African Off-grid Housing research project

Introduction

"Today, 600 million people in Africa do not have access to electricity and 900 million lack access to clean cooking facilities" (IEA, 2019).

With this premise, the research agenda of the African Off-grid Housing project focus on how to design and build off-grid and affordable housing solutions for Sub-Saharan Africa. This project is linked to the previous experience of the African Fabbers project and has being developed at the School of Architecture and Cities of the University of Westminster with the support of the Global Challenge Research Fund from the UKRI.

The research agenda is based on the idea of producing innovative knowledge able to bridge traditional and advanced design strategies as well as construction technologies in response to the urgent need of sustainable and performative housing in Sub-Saharan Africa. The purpose is to define innovative ideas to shape a design to manufacturing methodology for affordable and self-sufficient housing in Africa. Such methodology is informed by the interrelations between a critical understanding on how climatic and social dynamics are affecting African vernacular housing and other performative criteria related to self-sufficient housing precedents in contemporary architecture. The AOH project intends to contribute to the cultural debate on architectural research and sustainable design practices along with ecological manufacturing for local communities in the Global South and in relation to UN-HABITAT and other international institutional initiatives on the topic. In that sense, the research by design approach aims to define innovative policies for effective actions in African countries, which could eventually be adapted to suit other specific contexts. For the above-mentioned reasons, this research proposes a set of considerations to inform the design methodology.

As reported by the UNECA, Africa's population has nearly tripled from its estimated 478 million in 1980 to the current estimate of close to 1.2 billion, and it is projected to increase to 1.5 billion by 2025 and 2.4 billion by 2050. (UNECA, Demographic Profile of African Countries, 2016). Furthermore, one of the key aspects of such a scenario is the unaffordability of formal housing in African cities if we consider that 60% of the people living in urban areas of the continent are living in slums. In addition to this, we need to take in account that only 16% of urban households in Africa have a permanent roof condition – and access is even lower in rural areas. As a matter of fact, housing produced through formal channels is still far too expensive for most people. Such an informal scenario provides the majority of the housing solutions across the region, contributing around three-quarters of the total housing stock (although data on the informal housing sector in Africa is scarce). This is one of the reasons why between 70% (in the largest cities) and 98% (in rural areas) of all Africans lack access to electricity, a toilet or running water. At the same time, as recently reported by the International Energy Agency (IEA, 2019), Africa has plentiful renewable energy resources, and its economic potential is substantially larger than the current and projected power consumption of the continent. In fact, Africa is rich in minerals essential to the energy industry: for example, the Democratic Republic of Congo accounts for almost two-thirds of global cobalt production (a vital element in batteries), and South Africa produces 70% of the world's platinum, which is used in hydrogen fuel cells. On the other hand, it is crucial to highlight some interesting paradoxes about the potentiality of the African economy related to the extraction of key minerals, such as chromium (wind turbines) and manganese (batteries), and their major role in powering the global energy transition. Unfortunately, none of these resources are transformed on site and applied to the local context. Despite the evidence that Africa has the richest solar resources on the planet, so far only 5 gigawatts of solar photovoltaic (PV) have been installed, which is less than 1% of the global capacity (IEA 2019). In addition to this, we have to consider that the African energy demand is only 6% of global needs, while the electricity demand is little more than 3%. If we consider the huge availability of resources on site, the situation becomes critical: in 2019, over 65% of goods exported to the EU from Africa were primary goods (food and drink, raw materials and energy), and almost 70 % of goods exported from the EU to Africa were manufactured goods.

Another relevant paradox more related to the climate crisis in Africa is that the continent has produced only around 2% of the world's energy-related CO2 emissions so far. However, its ecosystems have already suffered disproportionately from the effects of climate change and global warming. As a matter of fact, 2019 was among the top three warmest on record for Africa since 1950, as reported by the World Meteorological Organization (WMO, 2020).This complex scenario suggests the need to develop a sustainable local industry approach for affordable and performative housing solutions in Africa. Such an approach would require the development of an information-based knowledge with the aim of evolving indigenous techniques and self-sufficient housing typologies.

Evolving vernacular taxonomies and self-sufficient housing precedents.

The AOH research by design methodology is based on an evolutionary design approach starting from the analytical study of pre-colonial African dwellings. In particular, we have started to associate a series of vernacular examples (geometry, material systems etc.) with their climatic regions using the Köppen climate classification map as a driver. A shortlist of such precedents was selected and analyzed for their capability of responding to the environmental contexts using the natural material systems available on site. Such a climate-sensitive approach is based on the passive strategies of natural ventilation and thermal mass related to the different climatic regions using indigenous construction techniques. Since Cameroon is the only nation in Africa that has five climatic regions from the equatorial (Af) to the warm desert (Bwh), we have started to analyze its vernacular architecture. Such a comparative approach on Cameroonian pre-colonial dwellings is based on the very interesting classification developed in 1950 in 'L'habitat du Cameroun' (Béguin, 1952). As we can notice from this very rich and diversified architectural taxonomy, the warm desert (Bwh) dwellings are made of clay and stones, generating a thermal mass strategy to mitigate the high temperatures. On the other hand, the equatorial (Af) examples are made out of natural fibers and tropical woods, generating some interesting porous paneling systems to dehumidify indoor spaces.

Among these extreme climatic contexts, a gradient of hybrid solutions is opening up to possible performative criteria for contemporary solutions based on a km0 approach. Therefore, the cause-effect relationship between climate and materiality of Cameroonian vernacular architecture has been considered an architectural paradigm to be adapted and modified according to different contexts with similar climatic conditions. The relationship between the process of integration of the existing technological and material heritage with the innovative systems is based on combining a naturally ventilated system made out of natural fibers for the external skin and a thermal mass skin in terracotta for the internal skin of the core. The digital innovative technologies are contributing by using environmental simulations for testing and regulating the whole system. The primary structure is conceived as a modular frame made out local timber carpentry digitally pre-fabricated. Such CAM approach and semi-industrialized approach could generate many geometrical and spatial variations. For the external skin, we have developed a multi-layered system inspired by the local pitched roof, integrating natural fibers to mitigate solar heating and corrugated metal sheets to guarantee a water proof performance. In this case, the digital innovative systems are contributing to evolve and adapt the initial shape in response to different conditions in terms of orientation (solar radiation, wind exposure), with the aim of protecting and cooling the core of the house.

The catalogue of solutions generates diversified timber joints realized within an industrial approach integrating digital fabrication technologies: for the internal core, the starting point is the use of local clay according to the local adobe heritage. In this case, the digital innovative systems are contributing to transforming this semi-fluid material into a semi-industrial porous brick through the use of 3D printing technologies. The porosity and thickness of such a construction component is informed by local data on solar analysis. In particular, we have selected the equatorial and monsoon traditional dwelling for its flexibility and environmental strategy as a possible genotype to evolve into a catalogue of contemporary off-grid houses. At the same time, we have integrated other performative criteria related to the study of more recent self-sufficient precedents realized mainly in the Global South, such as energy, water, sanitation, health strategy, modularity, etc. The negotiation between the vernacular initial bioclimatic layout and the strategies emerging from contemporary precedents is generating a sort of parametric form-finding protocol. Such a form-finding protocol is initially applied to the equatorial climatic region of Douala in Cameroon, one of the hottest and most humid cities in Africa.

Environmental parametric design process

The information-based design methodology is developed parametrically, mainly using two plugins of the Rhinoceros software: Grasshopper and Ladybug. The interaction between the two plugins is informed by the negotiation between the user's needs and the site-specific climatic conditions. Such "contextual algorithms" are shaping the geometry of both the internal and external skin according to their site-specific conditions and orientation. The result of this contextual parametric design process is a catalogue of architectural variations of the initial genotype, providing possible tailor-made solutions to be integrated into informal neighborhoods and slums. For the above-mentioned reasons, the AOH tool could be applied to different site-specific scenarios by modifying the following parameters: site weather file (relative humidity, outdoor temperature, prevailing winds, etc.), building orientation and number of users. As a matter of fact, the tool is developing a sequence of architectural operations regulated by the following parametric aspects:

— the available plot (square meters) of the existing neighborhoods informs the number of users who are informing the energy and water needs;
— the global shape of the house is informed by the solar and overshadowing analysis with the aim of protecting and naturally ventilating the internal core of the house;

— the rainwater collection system informs the roof slopes, while the solar radiation analysis localizes the areas for optimizing the distribution of PV panels.

Spatial and ergonomic strategy

The drivers of the spatial strategy are related to the most recent statistics on the trends of household size and composition in sub-Saharan Africa (United Nations, Population Division, Department of Economic and Social Affairs, 2017). Based on these data, we have decided to develop three types of house unit:

— 2 persons: young couple
— 4 persons: young couple with 2 children
— 6 persons: standard family

At the same time, the modular system is functional to an incremental approach for possible future horizontal and vertical extensions. Such possible house extensions would be related to the growth of the family and the integration of small businesses (shop, workshop, etc.). For the house's core floor plan, we have considered a minimum ratio of $20m^2$ per person. Considering the veranda/buffer zone space, this ratio is close to $40m^2$ per person. This ratio is comparable to nationally described space standards in the UK for the minimum size of new homes: "The space standard begins at $37m^2$ of floorspace for a new one bed flat with a shower room ($39m^2$ with a bathroom), ensuring proper living space for a single occupier" (UK Ministry of Housing, Communities & Local Government, 2020).

AOH bioclimatic strategy

The bioclimatic strategy is conceived as a passive way to minimize energy and water consumption. Therefore, the bioclimatic section of the AOH genotype is inspired by the vernacular double layer dwelling where the external skin protects the core of the house, generating a sort of a spatial and environmental buffer zone. The parametric modelling development of such a strategy regulates both the roof span and the porosity of the first skin according to the sunlight analysis and the overshadowing. This is made out of local natural fibers components and generates overshadowed and optimized solutions according to different possible orientations of the house. A set of different qualitative simulations on passive ventilation were also developed in order to verify the fluid dynamic performance of the envelope geometry. At the same time, in order to dehumidify the air of the house's internal core, we have developed a terracotta brick façade system realized through a mix of traditional and 3D printing techniques using natural and local materials. The internal structural pattern of the terracotta bricks is diversified in order to generate a catalogue of possible configurations providing different thermal performances according to the solar exposure of the façade. On the other hand, some of the terracotta bricks can be rotated along their Z-axis in order to generate a different degree of porosity, with the aim of accelerating the air to provide a passive cooling ventilation.

Cameroon as a paradigm

Capital: Yaoundé

Total area: 475,442 km2

Total population: 26.545.863 (2020)

Population density: 55,83 ab./km²

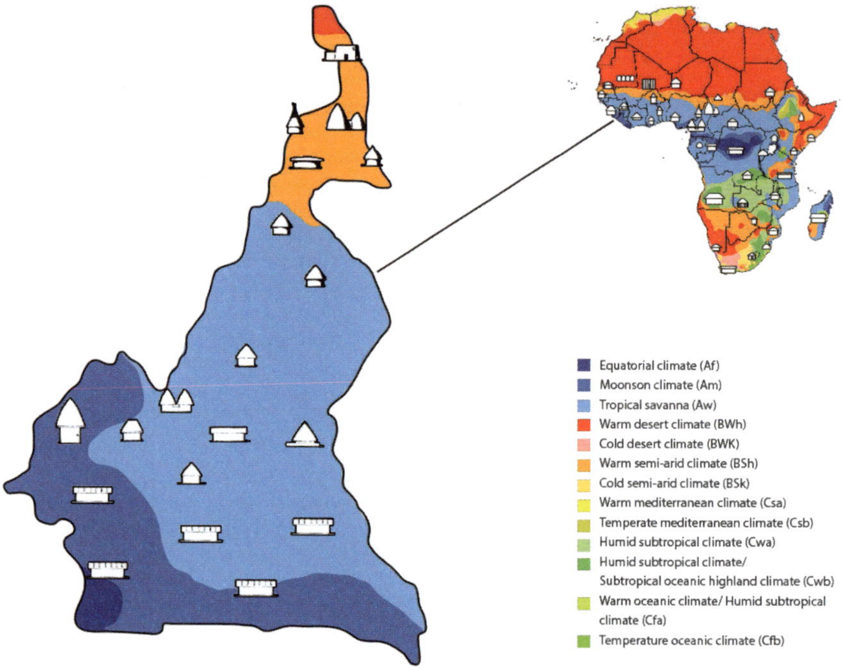

ssive strategy - overshadowing

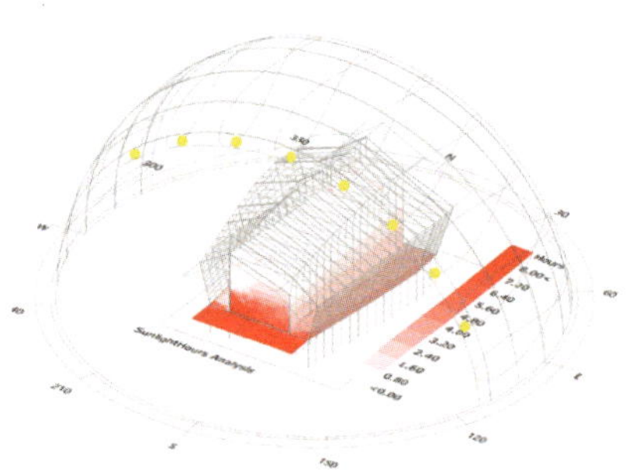

Passive strategy – roof / skin

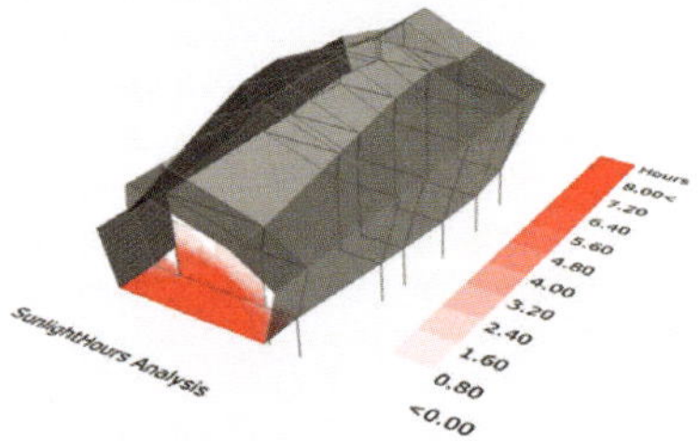

Global shape catalogue of unit configurations

Passive strategy - overshadowing

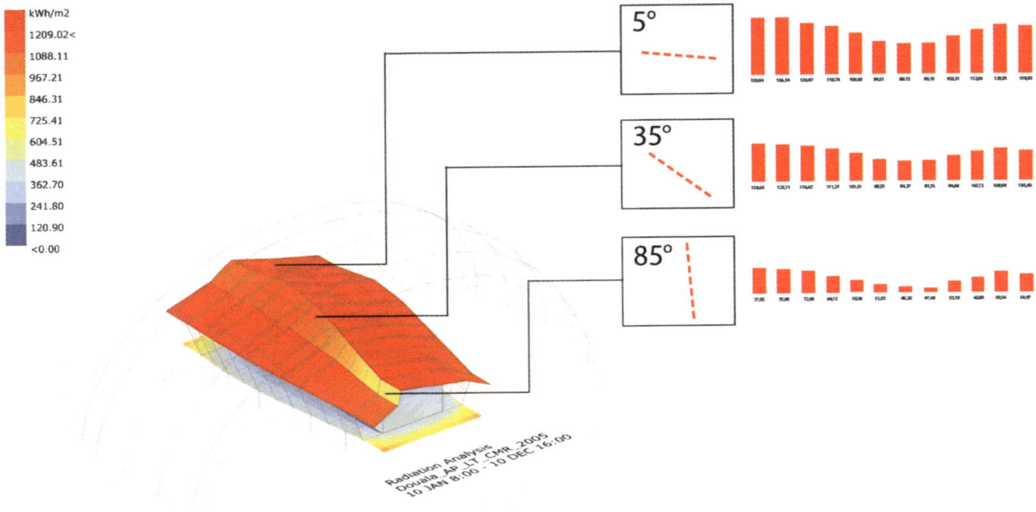

Active strategy – water collecting and stocking

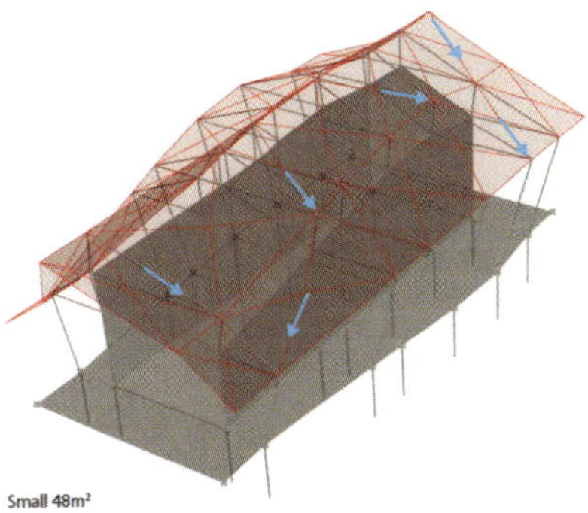

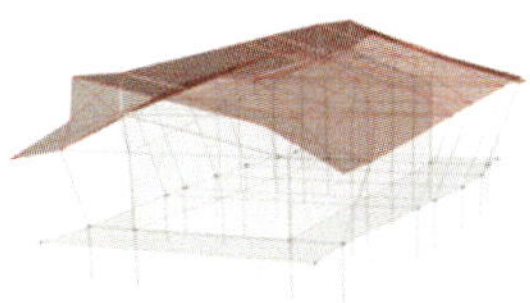

Small 48m²
2 persons
Daily water use per person 30L
drink, hygiene, cooking (filtered water)
Daily water use per person 20L
Cleaning, irrigation, toilet
Rainwater tank 100L capacity

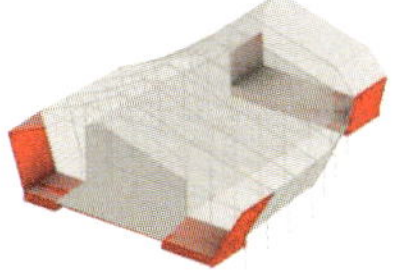

Medium 62m²
4 persons
Daily water use per person 30L
drink, hygiene, cooking (filtered water)
Daily water use per person 20L
Cleaning, irrigation, toilet
Rainwater tank 200L capacity

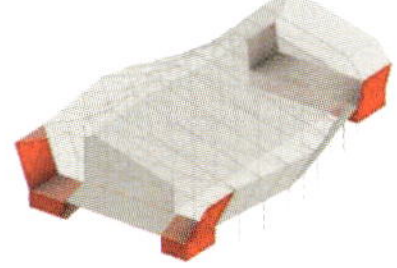

Large 75m²
6 persons
Daily water use per person 30L
drink, hygiene, cooking (filtered water)
Daily water use per person 20L
Cleaning, irrigation, toilet
Rainwater tank 300L capacity

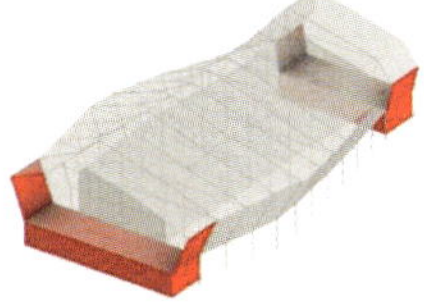

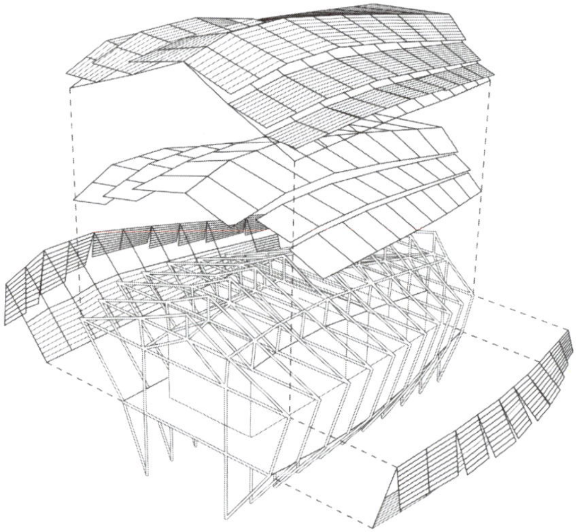

Pattern variation

material density ratio

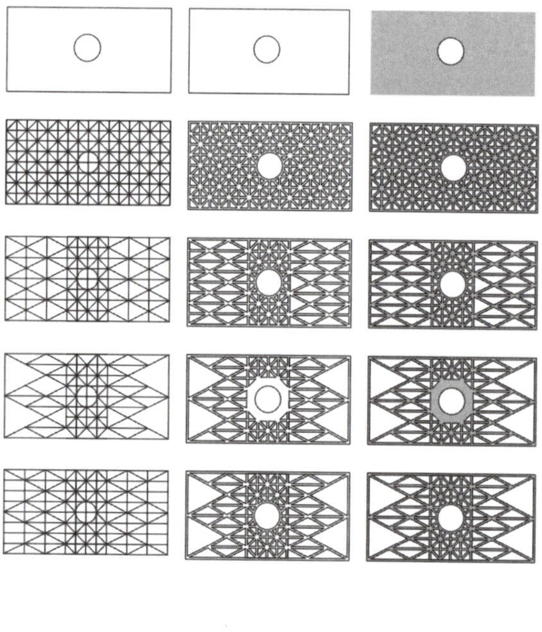

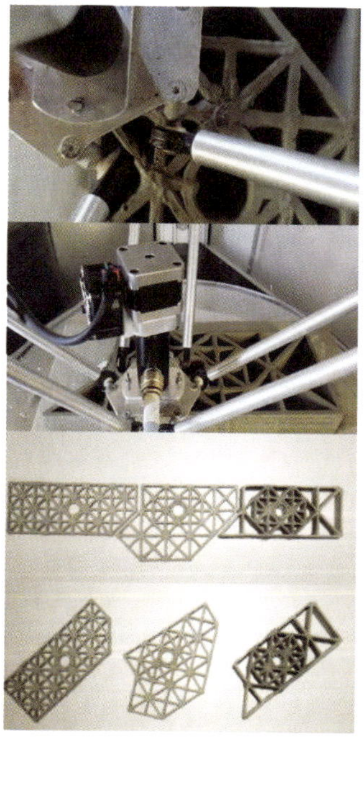

AOH energy and water strategy

The energy strategy is based on the idea of both minimizing the consumption of electricity (for air conditioning, etc.) and providing renewable energy according to the user's needs. According to the IEA report (IEA, 2019), we have considered a daily domestic energy (lighting, cooking, fridge, etc.) requirement of 1.5 kwh / per person. At the same time, we have suggested the use of a standard PV panel (dimension 1x1.7m for 300 Wp) easily available on site. With this premise, we have structured our energy parametric modelling based on the site-specific solar radiation analysis on the roof of the house prototype. This is in order to estimate the number of PV panels and localize their best position in order to achieve such performances. At the same time, we have developed this tool to provide the requested energy according to different possible house orientations for the three different household sizes. Considering the statistics on the heavy precipitation in Douala and the lack of accessibility to clean water, the form-finding drivers related to water are based on 2 main aspects: detaching the house from the ground in order to avoid flooding risk and shaping the roof in order to collect and purify the water for domestic uses. The question of detaching the house is also functional to improving the natural ventilation performances, generating spatial opportunities for storage and small businesses. At the same time, according to the UN report on African households' water use per person, we have considered the following criteria (UNFPA 2002):

- — 30L daily water use per person for drinking, hygiene, cooking (filtered water)
- — 20L daily water use per person for cleaning, irrigation, toilet.

Therefore, we have integrated a system of rainwater tanks underneath the house. The dimension and the capacity of the tanks are based on the different sizes and number of users: 2 persons / 100L, 4 persons / 200L, 6 persons / 300L (Fig. 7). The relationship between water and health is also important. Waterborne diseases are prevalent in most developing regions and the WHO estimates higher mortality rates annually from diarrheal diseases alone (WHO, 2017).

Another major cause of deaths in the region is malaria. Therefore, we have also developed another architectural low-tech strategy in order to minimize the risk of infection by integrating a layer of mosquito in the external skin of the house.

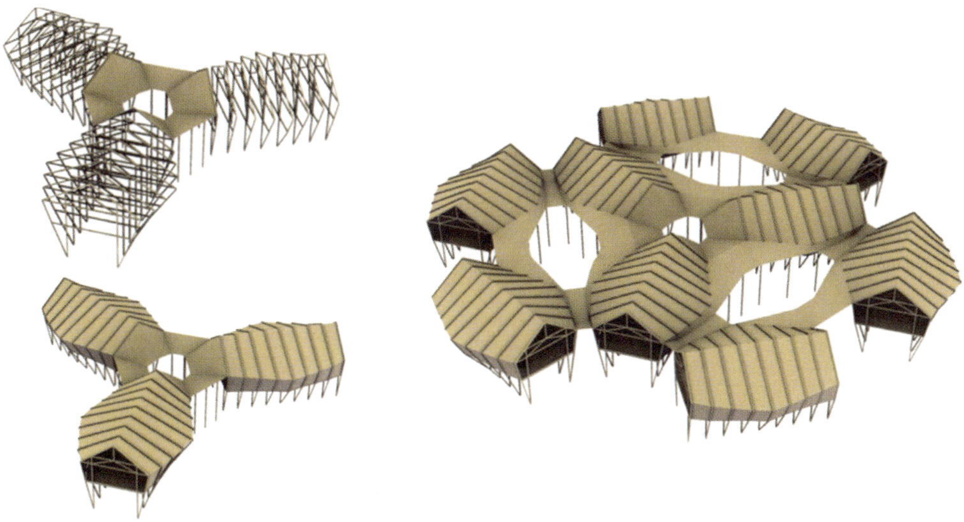

07

Small 48m^2
2 persons
Daily water use per person 30L
drink, hygiene, cooking (filtered water)
Daily water use per person 20L
Cleaning, irrigation, toilet
Rainwater tank 100L capacity

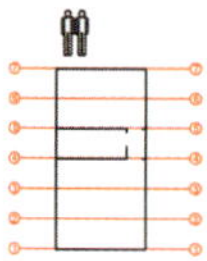

12 persons
Floor area= 185 m2
Plot area= 991.2 m2
Water needs: 600 L
Energy needs: 18 kwh/day
36 Pv panels=18 kwh/day

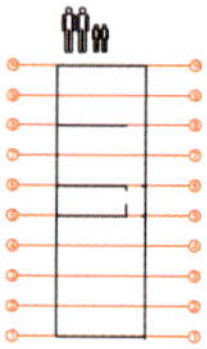

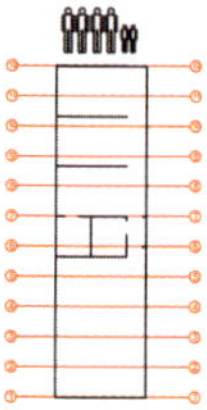

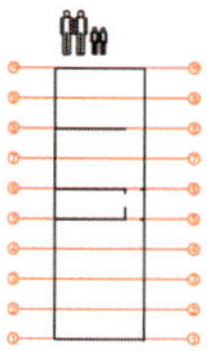

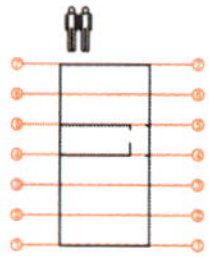

Medium 62m^2
4 persons
Daily water use per person 30L
drink, hygiene, cooking (filtered water)
Daily water use per person 20L
Cleaning, irrigation, toilet
Rainwater tank 200L capacity

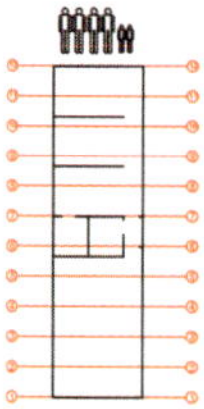

Large 75m^2
6 persons
Daily water use per person 30L
drink, hygiene, cooking (filtered water)
Daily water use per person 20L
Cleaning, irrigation, toilet
Rainwater tank 300L capacity

Overshadowing
Analysis

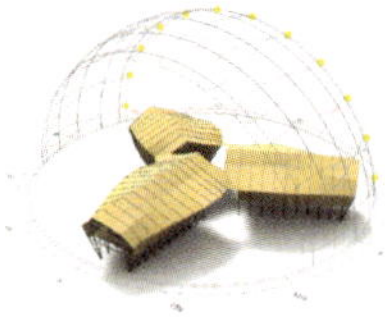

Sunlight
Analysis

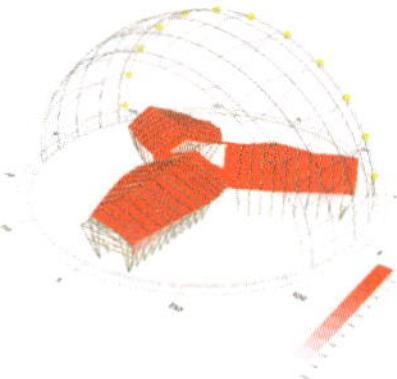

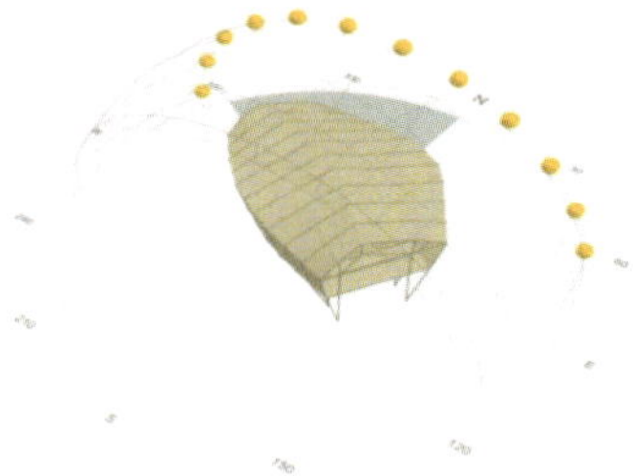

Solar radiation
analysis

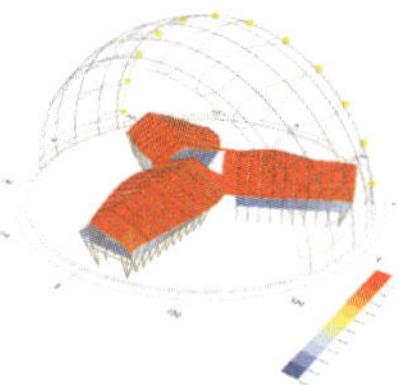

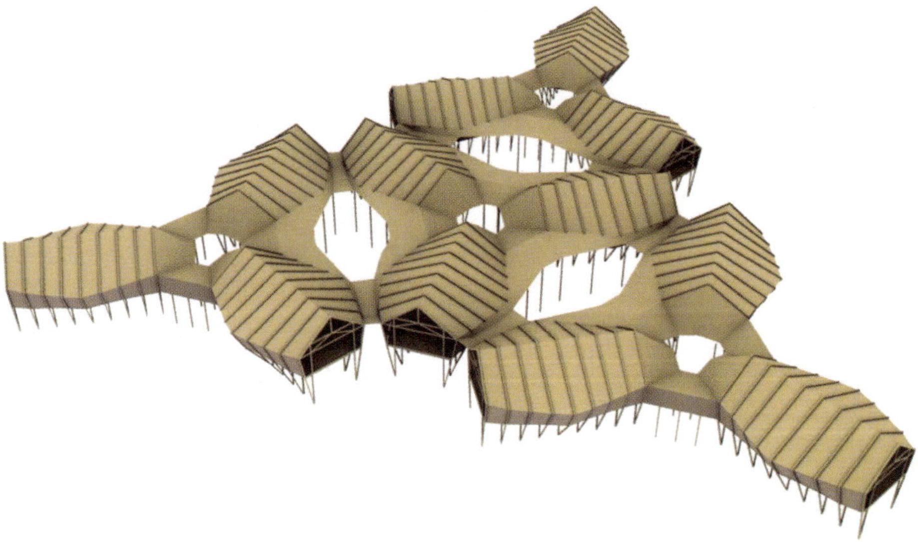

Incrementality and scalability strategies

The bottom-up approach developed in the digital form finding process aimed at generating a catalogue of different kind of incrementality strategies to leave the possibility to the local community to customize over time their own units. This strategy inspired by the Elemental's experience leaded by Alejandro Aravena is functional to the idea of recognizing a possible hybridation of the housing typologies based on the specific spatial needs of future households. The cluster is conceived also to share, especially at the roof and the ground levels, different devices to produce, store and distribute both water and energy. This idea of developing micro-grids systems is based on optimizing and sharing technological devices with the aim to organize the community in small self-sufficient groups where households could benefit to different facilities in a sustainable way. The same logic was followed to assemble more units together as architectural clusters based on sharing some communal central courtyards inspired by local vernacular typologies. This scalability approach was developed for slum of Douala (Cameroon) as a paradigm to test possible strategies able to upgrade African slums avoiding eradication dynamics. Therefore, the logic behind the scalability approach generates network of diversified and hierarchized open public spaces adapting their morphologies according to the informal urban fabric's available slots. The clusters are generating different vertical developments, conceived as growing inhabited infrastructures, in response to different degree of urban density also with the aim to augment green spaces in the neighborhoods. Such design to build process has been developed as a digital parametric tool to generate a catalogue of possible housing site specific variations to upgrade different kind of informal settlements in sub-Saharan Africa. For these reasons, we are also discussing possible synergies with different kind of public and private stakeholders as well as UN-Habitat and other possible African partners to build and test a case study.

Research Team: Dr. Paolo Cascone (Principal Investigator) - Maddalena Laddaga (Research Associate) **Advisory team:** Dr. Maria Christina Georgiadou - Benson Lau - Dr. Rosa Schiano-Phan.

Acknowledgements

The research team would like to express its gratitude to Prof. Harry Char- rington, former head of the School of Architecture and Cities of the University of Westminster, and the whole Research Office for supporting our proposal for the Global Challenges Research Fund (GCRF) powered by the UKRI. We would also like to thank Alvise Simondetti and Conor Black from Arup and Vincent Kitio from UN-Habitat who helped us a lot with their very useful advices despite their busy schedules.

Bibliography

IEA, "Africa energy outlook 2019". IEA - International Energy Agency, Paris, France, 2020. last modified November, 2019,https://www.iea.org/reports/africa-energy-outlook-2019

Huchzermeyer, Marie. Cities with 'Slums' : From Informal Settlement Eradication to a Right to the City in Africa. Claremont, South Africa: UCT Press, 2011.

J.P. Beguin, M. Kalt, J.L. Leroy, D. Louis, J. Macary, P., Pelloux, H.N. Peronne," L'habitat du Cameroun", Paris, France: publication de l'office de la recherche Scientifique Outre-Mer; Edition De L'union Francaise, 1952.

BIOGRAPHY

Author **Paolo Cascone**

born in Naples and grew-up between Italy, West-Indies and East-Africa is an AA-trained architect specialised in environmental design and sustainable constructions for climate sensitive architectures. He has started his research on the interaction between eco-digital technologies and performative architectures during his Master at the Architectural Association (London-UK) in Sustainable Design and continued it while accomplishing a PhD in environmental engineering at the CIRPS-University of La Sapienza (Rome-Italy). After several collaborations with international firms, he founded his practice CODESIGNLAB in Paris (2007), where he also started to teach as associate professor in ecological architecture at the ENSAPM and the ESA. Paolo has also collaborated with several European universities leading design studios and applied researches and he has been Scientific Director of the Open Design School for the Matera 2019 - European Capital of Culture.

More recently he has been Scientific Director of the "Digital Construction " research project financed by the Ance, the Italian National Association of Building Contractors. Paolo has founded of the African Fabbers [AF] project more than 10 years ago, the first community-oriented research and educational platform on ecological architecture and digital fabrication in Africa.

The [AF] project, after the participation at the Biennale of Marrakech and Dakar, has obtained a grant from the Italian Ministry of Foreign Affairs for implementing the African Fabbers School in Cameroon. The School has developed applied researches in the field of social design bridging advanced technologies with vernacular culture realizing scale 1 to 1 prototypes for housing solutions and urban micro infrastructures for the local community.

This work has been selected and displayed at the Venice Biennale of Architecture in the frame of the Italian Pavilion (2021).

Paolo is currently Senior Lecturer and Course Leader of the Master of Architecture and Environmental Design at the University of Westminster (London, UK) where is also principal investigator of the AOH research project on climate change and off-grid housing solutions funded by the UKRI-GCRF (Global Challenge Research Fund). On the above-mentioned topics collaborates as visiting researcher with the Milan Polytechnic.

Contributor **Maddalena Laddaga**

architect and researcher who graduated from the Bari Polytechnic University, Maddalena has developed research projects in India and collaborated with architectural firms between Rome and Berlin. More recently, she has developed applied research in the field of digital fabrication related to sustainable architecture. Maddalena has been co-director of CODESIGNLAB and the African Fabbers project since the year 2020. She has been an associate researcher at the University of Westminster on the African Off-grid Housing UKRI funded project. She has been an Associate Lecturer at Central Saint Martins, UAL in London and at the Oxford Brookes University School of Architecture as a design tutor. She is currently a PhD candidate at the DAStU in Milan Polytechnic.

ACKNOWLEDGMENTS

I cannot begin by saying that the African Fabbers as an independent project couldn't have been developed without the tremendous engagement of hundreds of people from different backgrounds mentioned in the book. As a matter of fact, this publication is also my way of expressing my gratitude to all of them. At the same time, the whole project started from a personal and cultural path that has its deep roots in the history of my family and its African connection. For this reason, it is important to start from the origins of my journey and my interests in informal cultures in Africa beyond architecture. This cultural path started with a life-long conversation with my grandmother Carmelita, who fascinated me with her stories and photographs of her childhood in Tripoli.

Therefore, I have to express my gratitude to her for sharing with me her critical understanding of colonialism issues and her genuine interest in the Arab culture, feeding my curiosity and inspiration for multiculturalism. Such growing interest continued during my first travel to Africa in 1984 thanks to my uncles Rossella and Matteo, who invited my mum and me to visit them in Addis Ababa, traveling to Asmara and Massawa and introducing me to some of the most interesting and rich African cultures. At the same time, my interest wouldn't have developed further without a continuous dialogue with my father, Giovanni, who started to work on health projects in Eastern Africa in 1985. This allowed me to experience the insights of different African contexts, both rural and urban, shifting from Mbabane to Kampala, from Nairobi to Arusha, from Cairo to Rabat, etc. Such real-life experiences were fundamental to understand the contradictions of Western development projects and the potentialities of informal and pre-colonial cultures and their capability to respond to extreme conditions. The African friends and people I met in such a childhood journey were crucial to my cultural education, and even when I had to go back to school in Naples, my hometown, my dream was to work and live in Africa.

This is why I have to thank my family for the encouragement to look for diversity, without which most of the projects published in this book wouldn't have seen the light. With this premise, I have started my personal path as an architect and researcher, for which my gratitude goes to Fabrizio Carola for his generosity in sharing his knowledge and his tremendous experience in Mali, introducing me to his local team and many principles of sustainable construction. As an educator, I would need to thank, first of all, my former student and assistant, Stephane Tapsoba, for his incredible talent and engagement in organising the first design studio in Burkina Faso. My gratitude also goes to my African and European students at ESA for their work on a synthetic vernacular architecture developed between Paris and Sourgoubila. This was the first step of a series of incredible experiences continued with another group of former Italian and African students led by Emma Polito, Andrea Giglio, Giuliano Galluccio, and Flavio Galdi, coordinated by the great Elena Ciancio. Their tremendous efforts in developing the African Fabbers sessions of Marrakech and Dakar was crucial to generate the whole project.

These sessions would not have been possible without the support of a combination of different strategic European and African partners such as the STRESS consortium, Fondazione Inarcassa, Fondazione IDIS (Italy) and the Marrakech and the Dakar Biennale, cfqmam (Marrakech) and Kier Thossane (Dakar). My gratitude also goes to the Quarter du Monde association, which was inviting me to collaborate with their members in Sale (Morocco). At the same time, I must thank Massimo Moretti and his Wasp team for their generosity in sharing their knowledge on 3d printing with natu-ral materials, which was one of the divers of many African Fabbers sessions. Such experience inspired the African Fabbers School project, for which I need to thank our partner, the COE ngo and AICS the Italian agency for international cooperation for their support, as well as the students and artisans of Douala for their tremen-dous work. At the same time, my gratitude goes to the University of Westminster for supporting the development of the African Off-grid Housing research project and to Vincent Kitio (UN Habitat) for his technical consultancy.

For the book development, I need to thank all the contributors: Christian Benimana, Cheick Diallo, Ron Eglash, Ugo La Pietra, Hanif Kara ,Vincent Kitio, Giancarlo Mazzanti, Ronald Rael, AbdouMaliq Simone, Francoise N'Thepe . For the graphic design, I must thank Mauro Bubbico for his contribution as well as his students from the ISIA. My gratitude goes also to Alessandro Melis to have invited the African Fabbers project to the Venice Biennale. At last but not at least, I must thank Maddalena Laddaga for supporting me in every way in such incredible adventure and to our son Giovanni to whom this book is dedicated.

ILLUSTRATION CREDITS

CHAPTER I

Page 8 © Paolo Cascone
Page 10 top © Figure generated using the AR6 WGI Interactive Atlas - Gutiérrez, J. M., R. G. Jones, G. T. Narisma, L. M. Alves, M. Amjad, I. V. Gorodetskaya, M. Grose, N. A. B. Klutse, S. Krakovska, J. Li, D. Martínez-Castro, L. O. Mearns, S. H. Mernild, T. Ngo-Duc, B. van den Hurk, J-H. Yoon, 2021, Atlas. In: Climate Change 2021: The Physical Science Basis. Contribution of Working Group I to the Sixth Assessment Report of the Intergovernmental Panel on Climate Change [Masson-Delmotte, V., P. Zhai, A. Pirani, S. L. Connors, C. Péan, S. Berger, N. Caud, Y. Chen, L. Goldfarb, M. I. Gomis, M. Huang, K. Leitzell, E. Lonnoy, J. B. R. Matthews, T. K. Maycock, T. Waterfield, O. Yelekçi, R. Yu and B. Zhou (eds.)]. Available from http://interactive-atlas.ipcc.ch/
bottom © Hansel ohioma, CC BY-SA 4.0, via Wikimedia Commons. https://commons.wikimedia.org/wiki/File:Flood_survival.jpg
Page 12-14 all images © Paolo Cascone/CODESIGNALB
Page 17 Reconstitution of the map Tabula Rogeriana by arab geographer Al Idrisi, by German cartographer Konrad Miller. The arabic text is transcribed in the latin alphabet.© Konrad Miller (1844–1933), Public domain, via Wikimedia Commons. https://commons.wikimedia.org/wiki/File:Tabula_Rogeriana_1929_copy_by_Konrad_Miller.jpg

CHAPTER II

Page 26 Courtesy Rael San Fratello
Page 30 Courtesy Christian Benimana
Page 34 Courtesy Cheick Diallo
Page 37 Courtesy Luanne Cadd and Ron Eglash
Page 42 Courtesy Ugo La Pietra
Page 45 Courtesy AKT II, Hanif Kara
Page 48 Courtesy Vincent Kitio
Page 51 Courtesy Giancarlo Mazzanti. Photographer Alejandro Arango
Page 55 Courtesy Rael San Fratello
Page 57 Courtesy AbdouMaliq Simone
Page 62 Courtesy Francoise N' Thépé

CHAPTER III

Page 66–70 © Paolo Cascone/CODESIGNALB
Page 71 Picture © Merril Sinéus; illustrations © Paolo Cascone/ CODESIGNALB
Page 76 top pictures © Merril Sinéus
other pictures © Paolo Cascone
Page 77–78–79–80–81–82–83© Paolo Cascone/ CODESIGNALB
Page 84–85 drawings and pictures © robotic dome team
Page 86 © Paolo Cascone/CODESIGNALB
Page 88–89–90–91–92–93 images © Paolo Cascone/ CODESIGNALB
Page 94 © Atelier Paolo Cascone – ESA
Page 95 picture © Atelier Paolo Cascone – ESA; illustrations © Paolo Cascone/ CODESIGNALB
Page 100–101–102–103 © Atelier Paolo Cascone – ESA
Page 104 © Tamara Vecchione
Page 105 pictures © Tamara Vecchione; illustrations © Paolo Cascone/ CODESIGNALB
Page 108–109 pictures © Tamara Vecchione
drawings © Paolo Cascone/CODESIGNALB
Page 110 © Tamara Vecchione
Page 111 © Paolo Cascone/CODESIGNALB
Page 112–113 © Tamara Vecchione
Page 114 © Paolo Cascone/CODESIGNALB
Page 116 top ©WASP
bottom © Paolo Cascone/CODESIGNALB
Page 117 © Paolo Cascone/ CODESIGNALB
Page 121 pictures ©Elena Bellantoni
drawing © CODESIGNLAB
Page 122–123 pictures © Massimo Moretti/WASP
drawings © Paolo Cascone/CODESIGNLAB
Page 124–125–126–127 © Paolo Cascone/CODESIGNLAB
Page 132–133–134–135–136–137© Paolo Cascone/ CODESIGNLAB
Page 138–139 © Mariana Michalcikova

CHAPTER IV

Page 140 © Prince Ngouda
Page 144 top © Edmond Fortier (1862-1928), Public domain, via Wikimedia Commons https://commons.wikimedia.org/wiki/File:Fortier_368_Timbuktu_Sankore_Mosque.jpg
bottom © Ralf Steinberger from Northern Italy and Berlin, CC BY 2.0 via Wikimedia Commons https://commons.wikimedia.org/wiki/File:Annual_repair_of_the_world%27s_largest_mud_brick_building_the_Great_Mosque_of_Djenn%C3%A9_in_Mali._(32088227574).jpg
Page 151–152–154 ©Paolo Cascone/ CODESIGNLAB
Page 159–160–161–162–163–164–166–167 ©Paolo Cascone/CODESIGNLAB
Page 170–171 © Paolo Cascone/CODESIGNLAB
Page 173–174–175 © Paolo Cascone/CODESIGNLAB
Page 176 © Francis Tiemeni Ongong
Page 177 top © Francis Tiemeni Ongong
bottom © Paolo Cascone/CODESIGNLAB
Page 178–179–182 © Paolo Cascone/CODESIGNLAB
Page 183 top © Paolo Cascone/ CODESIGNLAB
bottom © Prince Ngouda
Page 184 © Paolo Cascone/ CODESIGNLAB
Page 185 © Francis Tiemeni Ongong
Page 186 © Paolo Cascone/CODESIGNLAB
Page 187 © Francis Tiemeni Ongong
Page 188 © Paolo Cascone/CODESIGNLAB
Page 189–190–191–193 ©Dione Roach
Page 192 © Paolo Cascone/CODESIGNLAB

CHAPTER V

Page 194 © Paolo Cascone/CODESIGNLAB
Page 199 top pictures: left picture picture © Bundesarchiv, Bild 105-DOA0036 / Walther Dobbertin / CC-BY-SA 3.0, CC BY-SA 3.0 DE, via Wikimedia Commons, https://commons.wikimedia.org/wiki/File:Bundesarchiv_Bild_105-DOA0036,_Deutsch-Ostafrika,_Eingeborene_vor_ihrer_H%C3%BCtte.jpg
middel picture © Hermannkass, CC BY-SA 4.0, via Wikimedia Commons,https://commons.wikimedia.org/wiki/File:Maison_traditionnelle_%C3%A0_Alabad%C3%A8_07.jpg
right picture © H. Grobe, CC BY-SA 3.0, via Wikimedia Commons, https://commons.wikimedia.org/wiki/File:Mali1974-042_hg.jpg
second line pictures: left picture © Léo Tarpin, CC BY-SA 4.0, via Wikimedia Commons, https://commons.wikimedia.org/wiki/File:Maison_perdue_dans_la_savane.jpg
middle picture © SebEsteban, CC BY-SA 4.0, via Wikimedia Commons, https://commons.wikimedia.org/wiki/File:Cases_Moba_2_(vers_Dapaong,_r%C3%A9gion_des_savanes,_Togo).jpg
right picture © Justin Abadjaye, CC BY-SA 4.0, via Wikimedia Commons https://commons.wikimedia.org/wiki/File:Maison_%C3%A0_grenier.jpg
bottom pictures: left picture © SebEsteban, CC BY-SA 4.0 , via Wikimedia Commons, https://commons.wikimedia.org/wiki/File:Cases_Moba_(vers_Dapaong,_R%C3%A9gion_des_savanes,_Togo)_(2).jpg
middle picture © Jacques Taberlet, CC BY 3.0 via Wikimedia Commons. https://commons.wikimedia.org/wiki/File:Koussoukoingou2.jpg
right picture © Colibryus (Bruno Trédez), CC BY-SA 4.0 >, via Wikimedia Commons. https://commons.wikimedia.org/wiki/File:Koussoukoingou2.jpg
drawings © Paolo Cascone
Page 204-205-206-207-208 © Paolo Cascone